The Future of Archives and Recordkeeping

A reader

The Future of Archives and Recordkeeping
A reader

Edited by
Jennie Hill

facet publishing

Published by Facet Publishing,
7 Ridgmount Street, London WC1E 7AE
www.facetpublishing.co.uk

Facet Publishing is wholly owned by CILIP: the Chartered Institute of Library
and Information Professionals.

British Library Cataloguing in Publication Data
A catalogue record for this book is available from the British Library.

ISBN 978-1-85604-666-4

First published 2011

Text printed on FSC accredited material.

Typeset from editor's files by Facet Publishing Production in
11.5/14 pt Garamond and Frutiger.
Printed and made in Great Britain by CPI Group (UK), Croydon, CR0 4YY.

For John Symington (1974–2006)

He wore his learning lightly

Contents

Acknowledgements ix
Contributors xi
Introduction: seeing the future of archives and recordkeeping......xvii

Part 1 Defining archives..1
1 Where do we come from? What are we? Where are we going?
Situating the archive and archivists
Victoria Lane and Jennie Hill 3

2 Encounters with the self: archives and research
Sue Breakell..23

3 Strangely unfamiliar: ideas of the archive from outside the
discipline
Alexandrina Buchanan 37

Part 2 Shaping a discipline 63
4 Structural and formal analysis: the contribution of diplomatics
to archival appraisal in the digital environment
Luciana Duranti 65

5 Archivistics: science or art?
Eric Ketelaar 89

Part 3 Archive 2.0: archives in society 101
6 Archons, aliens and angels: power and politics in the archive
Verne Harris...103

7   Interactivity, flexibility and transparency: social media
    and Archives 2.0
    Kate Theimer 123

8   The impact of independent and community archives on
    professional archival thinking and practice
    Andrew Flinn 145

**Part 4 Archives in the information age: is there still a
         role for the archivist?..171**
9   The postcustodial archive
    Adrian Cunningham 173

10 Information management, records management, knowledge
    management: the place of archives in a digital age
    Nicole Convery 191

11 Appraisal and the future of archives in the digital era
    Richard J. Cox..211

Index **237**

Acknowledgements

There are many people who have contributed to the development of this book that I wish to thank. First, I wish to thank the contributors and editorial team at Facet Publishing, without whose contribution and patience the project would never have come to fruition. I'd also like to extend my thanks to colleagues and students at Aberystwyth University for the exchange of ideas and their unfailing support. Finally, I'd like to offer my heartfelt thanks to Will and Tony for helping me realize the most important lessons of my life.

Contributors

Sue Breakell

Sue Breakell is Archivist and Research Fellow at the University of Brighton Design Archives. The focus of the Archives is British design in the 20th century, although there is also much of international significance. Prior to joining the Design Archives in 2009, Sue worked mostly in national museum and gallery archives. Between two posts at Tate Archive, she was Company Archivist at Marks & Spencer, and War Artists Archivist at the Imperial War Museum (IWM), where she subsequently became the IWM's first Museum Archivist. Returning as head of Tate Archive in 2004, she was responsible for the Archive of British Art Since 1900, as well as for Tate's own institutional records during the implementation of the Freedom of Information Act (2005). She co-organized the event 'The Archival Impulse: artists and archives' at Tate Britain in November 2007, and has written in this area. She is particularly interested in multidisciplinary perspectives on archives, especially arts archives, and the intersection of custodial, critical, research and creative practices.

Alexandrina Buchanan

Alexandrina Buchanan is Lecturer in Archival Studies at the University of Liverpool, having previously worked as Archivist to The Clothworkers' Company and Assistant Archivist at Lambeth Palace Library. With a background in architectural history, she is particularly interested in the materiality of archives and their use both as historical evidence and within the creative process. She is currently writing a biography of Robert Willis

(1800–75), the first scholar to combine documentary and archaeological evidence to create 'architectural history'.

Nicole Convery

Nicole Convery has been a part-time Teaching Fellow at Aberystwyth University for the information studies and records management programmes since 2008. After graduating with an MScEcon in Records Management from Aberystwyth University in 2005, Nicole briefly worked as an Assistant Records Manager at the House of Lords, followed by a role as Records Manager for Guardian News and Media in 2006. There she was responsible for the company's corporate records and for setting up a records management programme. Nicole is currently working on her PhD proposal in records management and social media. Her research interests include records management theory, cloud computing, social media and collaborative working environments, and information security.

Richard J. Cox

Richard J. Cox is a Professor in Library and Information Science at the University of Pittsburgh School of Information Sciences where he is responsible for the archives and records management concentration in the Master of Library and Information Science (MLIS) degree. Prior to his current position he worked at the New York State Archives and Records Administration, Alabama Department of Archives and History, the City of Baltimore, and the Maryland Historical Society. He chaired the Society of American Archivists (SAA) committee that drafted new graduate archival education guidelines adopted by its council in 1988, served for four years as a member of that association's Committee on Education and Professional Development, and was a member of the Society's governing council from 1986 through 1989. Richard served as Editor of the *American Archivist* from 1991 through 1995, and is currently Editor of *Records and Information Management Report: issues in information technology,* published by M. E. Sharpe, and Publications Editor for the Society of American Archivists. He has written extensively on archival and records management professional issues.

Adrian Cunningham

Adrian Cunningham has worked at the National Archives of Australia (NAA) since 1998, where he is currently Director, Strategic Relations and Personal Records. In this capacity he has oversight of the NAA's collaborations with government, industry, professional, academic and international partners – most particularly on matters associated with digital recordkeeping and other modern recordkeeping initiatives. Adrian was Secretary of the International Council on Archives (ICA) Committee on Descriptive Standards (2002–4), and is Treasurer of the Pacific Regional Branch of the ICA, Convenor of the Australian Society of Archivists Descriptive Standards Committee and a member of Standards Australia's Committee IT/21, Records Management. Before joining the staff of the National Archives of Australia he worked at the Office for Government Information Technology and for many years as a private records Archivist/Librarian at the National Library of Australia, the Pacific Manuscripts Bureau and the State Library of New South Wales. Adrian was President of the Australian Society of Archivists, 1998–2000 and was inducted as a Fellow of that Society in 2007.

Luciana Duranti

Luciana Duranti is Chair of the archival masters and doctoral programmes at the University of British Columbia, Vancouver, Canada, and a Professor of archival appraisal and acquisition, diplomatics, and the management of digital records. She is Director of the InterPARES and the Digital Records Forensics and co-director of the Universities Institutional Repositories: copyright and long-term preservation research projects. She is active nationally and internationally in several archival associations and in boards and committees, such as the Italy's National Commission for Archives (2007–2011) and the UNESCO International Advisory Committee of the Memory of the World Program (2007–14), and has been the President of the Society of American Archivists (1998–9), of which she is a Fellow. She publishes widely on archival theory, records management and diplomatics.

Andrew Flinn

Andrew Flinn is a Senior Lecturer and Director of the Archives and

Records Management MA programme in the Department of Information Studies at University College London (UCL) and the current Chair of the UK Forum for Archives and Records Management Education and Research (FARMER). He was the lead researcher on the Arts and Humanities Research Council (AHRC) funded Community archives and identities project (2008–9) which examined community archive and heritage initiatives of Black, Asian and Minority Ethnic groups in the UK. He is presently supervising an AHRC Collaborative Doctoral Award looking at user-generated content and archival description and working more generally on bringing together professional and non-professional knowledge and approaches. Amongst other professional positions, Andrew was previously archivist of the Labour and Communist Party archives at the National Museum of Labour History in Manchester, England. Recent publications include (with Harriet Jones) *Freedom of Information: open access, empty archives?* (2009); 'Whose Memories, whose Archives? Independent community archives, autonomy and the mainstream', *Archival Science*, **9** (2009); and 'Independent Community Archives and Community-Generated Content: writing and saving our histories', *Convergence: The International Journal of Research into New Media Technologies*, **16** (2010).

Verne Harris

Verne Harris is a Programme Manager for the Nelson Mandela Centre of Memory and Dialogue at the Nelson Mandela Foundation, and an honorary research associate with the University of the Witwatersrand. He participated in a range of structures which transformed South Africa's apartheid archival landscape – amongst others, the African National Congress's Archives Committee, the Arts and Culture Task Group, the Consultative Forum which drafted the National Archives of South Africa Act, the Truth and Reconciliation Commission, and the South African History Archive. Widely published, he is best known for the books *Exploring Archives: an introduction to archival ideas and practice in South Africa* (1997 and 2000), *Refiguring the Archive* (2002), *A Prisoner in the Garden: opening Nelson Mandela's prison archive* (2005), *Archives and Justice* (2007) and *Nelson Mandela: the authorised comic book* (2008). He is also the author of two novels, both of which were short-listed for South Africa's M-Net Book Prize.

Jennie Hill

Jennie Hill lectures in archives and local studies at Aberystwyth University. Prior to this she worked for a variety of institutions, including the Royal Commission on the Ancient and Historical Monuments of Wales and The Waterways Trust. She has published work in the field of literary archives and co-organized the successful conference 'Archive Fervour/Archive Further: literature, archives and literary archives', at Aberystwyth University in 2008. Current research interests include representations of archives, literature and archives, interdisciplinary engagement with archives and the history of collecting. She is currently pursuing PhD research into the history of collecting across libraries, archives and museums.

Eric Ketelaar

Eric Ketelaar is Professor Emeritus at the University of Amsterdam. From 1997 to 2009 he was Professor of Archivistics in the Department of Media Studies at the University of Amsterdam. As an honorary fellow of his former department he continues his research which is concerned mainly with the social and cultural contexts of records creation and use. He was General State Archivist (National Archivist) of The Netherlands from 1989–97 and held the archivistics chair in the Department of History, University of Leiden, 1992–2002. In 2000–1 he was The Netherlands Visiting Professor at the University of Michigan (School of Information). In 2003–8 he was Honorary Professor at Monash University, Melbourne, where he continues to be involved as an Adjunct Senior Research Fellow. He served the International Council on Archives in different capacities, and in 2000 was elected Honorary President. He has written over 350 articles in different languages, and several books, including two general introductions on archival research and a handbook on Dutch archives and records management law. He is one of the three editors-in-chief of *Archival Science*.

Victoria Lane

Victoria Lane is an archivist, writer and curator who has worked in art archives including Tate, Henry Moore Institute and currently at the Paul Mellon Centre for Studies in British Art. She has also worked on the personal archives of the artists Richard Deacon and Barry Flanagan and is an interviewer for the Artists' Lives Project at the National Sound Archive, British Library.

Kate Theimer

Kate Theimer is the author of the popular blog, ArchivesNext. Launched in March 2007, ArchivesNext is one of the leading sources for information on the use of Web 2.0 tools by archives, and in August 2009 she launched the Archives 2.0 wiki which serves as an online directory of Web 2.0 implementations in archives. She is the author of *Web 2.0 Tools and Strategies for Archives and Local History Collections* (Neal-Schuman/Facet Publishing, 2010) and the editor of the forthcoming *A Different Kind of Web: new connections between archives and our users with Web 2.0* to be published by the Society of American Archivists in 2011. She has worked for the National Archives and Records Administration and the Smithsonian Institution, developing policies regarding archival processes and the description of archival and museum collections. She holds a MIS degree from the University of Michigan, an MA in Art History from the University of Maryland, and a BA from Wesleyan University.

Introduction: seeing the future of archives and recordkeeping

There has never been a more interesting time to be an archivist. That is something of a grand claim and one which this book hopes to reflect. Archives are moving from a profession predicated on the unquestioning repetition of routine towards a more self-aware, self-reflexive professional outlook, which can only be of benefit to the archival profession.

In the last 50 years there have been a number of changes, both inside and outside of the profession, which have impacted upon the way that archivists work and the way in which we conceive of ourselves, and these themes are echoed in this book. Chief among these themes are the impact of postmodernism on the discipline; the rapid rise of technology and the challenges that this poses for us; the increasing interest in archives outside of the profession and the resulting democratization of archives; and the place of archives within related fields, such as records and information management. It is imperative that archivists engage with these challenges if we are to remain professionally relevant in the 21st century. Each of the contributions to this book engages with one or more of these themes to explore how archivists can respond to these challenges and as a result strengthen the discipline and emerge as a renewed force.

This book is designed as a reader in archives. It is primarily aimed at those studying towards a postgraduate qualification in the subject, but will also be of interest to practitioners and those outside the discipline who wish to gain a deeper understanding of how archival theory and practice has been evolving. It is not intended as a practical guide to professional practice, but rather as a reader around the concepts and themes highlighted above. Each of the chapters question the changes that have taken place in archives since its early theoretical foundations, and how these have occasioned rethinking and revisioning of the archival mission. Although grouped around four core themes, outlined below, there is no expectation that readers will need to follow the specified order. Each chapter represents a defined argument in its own right to enable readers to dip in and out of the collection as they wish. The structure is there to guide readers as to the content of the collection and to highlight chapters that share a common theme.

The role of the archivist is a privileged one, often misunderstood by those outside of our discipline, and occasionally much maligned. Archives, or the archive, have never been as popular as they are currently. Jacques Derrida's *Archive Fever: a Freudian impression*, whether we like it or not (or indeed, whether we have even read it or not) has done much to promote the notion of archives in disciplines such as literature, philosophy and psychology. After many years in the wilderness, discussed only amongst archivists and a handful of historians, archives are finally on the larger agenda and it is imperative that the archival community engage with these debates and discussions if we wish to ensure that our discipline is heard.

Defining archives

How we view the nature of archives, the role of the archivist, and our users has changed significantly in the last 20 years or so. The notion of the archives as the static, impartial, carriers of truth has been challenged; the role of the archivist as a neutral guardian of records has been questioned; the way in which users approach archives, and their engagement with them, has been re-thought. The chapters in this section examine the reasons behind, and the effect of, these challenges. Lane and Hill's chapter (Chapter 1) explores the move away from Jenkinson's positivistic vision and explores the impact and possibilities afforded by a postmodern outlook on the nature of archives. In contrast, Breakell (Chapter 2) explores the changing nature of the user within this framework and challenges archivists to understand how the needs and expectations of users has developed as archives have become more prominent in popular culture. In addition, just as the archive is becoming more prevalent in popular culture, so too has it become an important aspect of multiple academic discourses.

Finally, this section, through Buchanan's chapter (Chapter 3), examines the rise of 'the archive' outside of our discipline.

Shaping a discipline

The chapters in this section examine the supposed conflict between tradition and new ways of thinking. Have we completely re-thought archival theory and practice? Duranti (Chapter 4) explores how diplomatics, the traditional study of the form of documents, has gathered new meaning in the digital age. Ketelaar (Chapter 5) examines the dichotomy between archive administration, or archives as an 'art', and archives as a 'science'.

Archives 2.0: archives in society

In recent years those inside and outside of the profession have had cause to question the role that archives play in our society. Is the archive a site of democracy, or of state-imposed memory? Should the role of the archivist in the selection and processing of archives be minimized? How can society take greater control over its own written memory? Harris's chapter (Chapter 6) on power structures within archives explores how democratization of the archive can only come from full participation in archives from all sections of society. Tracing developments from early web-based projects, Theimer (Chapter 7) explores how interactivity between archives, archivists and users can be exploited more fully through the technological possibilities of Web 2.0. Flinn (Chapter 8) considers the development in community archives and how active participation in such archives does not so much undermine traditional archive thinking, but rather, highlight the fact that notions of stability and neutrality were always a myth.

Archives in the information age: is there still a role for the archivist?

Where do we go from here? How are we to grasp the current wave of enthusiasm for the archive and push our way forward? The need to adapt to the changing world around us is not new – as early as the 1980s Gerald Ham was arguing that the profession needed to change and adapt, if it was to remain a relevant cultural force in an increasingly automated world. The notion of the archive as a physical space necessary for the accessing and contemplating of archives is challenged by the rise of electronic records. Cunningham's chapter (Chapter 9) asks us to consider the issue of postcustodialism and whether, in the electronic age, archives need to adapt to the notion of having to provide access to records outside of their physical custody. In Convery's chapter (Chapter 10), it is contended that archivists have a cultural mission that is often ignored or overlooked in our rush to justify our importance as 'recordkeepers' – that is, as guardians of 'evidence' and the 'authentic'. It is this cultural mission that Cox picks up on in the final chapter (Chapter 11) of this collection, on archival appraisal. This is the vital mission of the archivist, asserts Cox, it is what marks us out as a distinct category of information professionals. It is this role which will give us authority in the coming years.

So how much has changed since the first attempts to capture our profession in the 19th and early 20th centuries. Is the archival landscape today one which Muller, Feith and Fruin, Jenkinson, and Schellenberg would recognize and embrace, or has the landscape changed irrevocably? That the landscape is shifting, terraforming, before our eyes is indisputable, but that is not a bad thing. As I said at the outset, there has never been a more exciting time to be an archivist. We are living in Terry Cook's 'paradigm shift'.

How then are we to understand this paradigm shift that Cook speaks of? In much the same way that we understand much to do with archives – we are slow to change and adapt, reluctant to let go of past principles that do not always hold, whilst the world moves on around us. And yet still we stand on the cusp of something great – a rethinking, a re-appraisal if you will – of our profession and our role within society, and this collection aims to get to the heart of those issues. We cannot see the future precisely because we are not repeating those same gestures uncritically; we are witnessing the real birth of our discipline. Yes, indeed, there has never been a more exciting time to be an archivist.

Part 1
Defining archives

1

Where do we come from? What are we? Where are we going? Situating the archive and archivists

Victoria Lane and Jennie Hill

Introduction

This chapter examines archives and archivists in the context of past, present and future. It foreshadows many of the themes discussed elsewhere in this book – the growing influence of postmodernism on the profession pervades many of the chapters here, the interconnectedness of creator, user and archivist (see, for example, Breakell [Chapter 2], Theimer [Chapter 7] and Flinn [Chapter 8]), as well as the need to balance the 'traditional' skills with recent developments in digital technology and the place of the archivist within these changes (see, for example, Duranti [Chapter 4], Ketelaar [Chapter 5], Cunningham [Chapter 9], Convery [Chapter 10] and Cox [Chapter 11]) and the growing interest in the notion of archives from outside the discipline (Buchanan [Chapter 3]). It explores the broad movement within archives from the positivist outlook, which highlighted the impartiality and transparency of the archivist, through more recent reactions to the postmodern turn in archives which has enabled us to challenge this positivist ideology and question the role of archives, archivists, users and creators in new ways, and concludes by looking at the future challenges and directions for archivists.

In the shadow of Jenkinson

Recently the subject of the archive has moved from obscurity to prominence in both the academy and society at large. This interest has not come from inside the discipline but rather from outside. Tom Nesmith has characterized this as bringing archivists 'to a major turning point in the intellectual history of their profession' (2005, 260) and indeed archivists in Canada, Australia, South Africa and latterly America have taken up the challenge of the fundamental reconstruction of both the archive and the archivist's identity. Within the profession in the UK there are certain noises in this direction but these are deafened by the resistance to what is seen as a dangerous threat to the sanctity of the epistemological bedrocks of our archival practice and the traditions that were inscribed by Hilary Jenkinson (1965) in his 1922 *A Manual of Archive Administration*.

Hilary Jenkinson's ideology fixed the archivist's 'career as one of service . . . . His Creed, the Sanctity of Evidence . . . . The good Archivist is perhaps the most selfless devotee of Truth the modern world produces' (quoted in Cook, 1997, 23) and contended that archives 'themselves state no opinion, voice no conjecture; they are simply written memorials, authenticated by the fact of their official preservation, of events which actually occurred and of which they themselves formed a part . . . [which provide] an exact statement of the facts' (Jenkinson, 1965, 4). If we isolate the terminology of this ideology we can reconstruct the persona of the Jenkinsonian archivist (and his supporters) as follows: unobtrusive, passive, invisible, disinterested, neutral, tacit, objective and innocent, and his or her role as servant, guardian and custodian. These are the necessary preconditions of the person who will provide the physical and moral defence of the archive in order to maintain its impartiality, authenticity, immutability, reliability, evidentiality, integrity, truth, authority, accuracy, order, uniqueness and trustworthiness.

Jenkinson presents a methodology where selection is made by creators and archivists are relegated to voiceless custodians. The archive is presented as a naturally occurring phenomenon that archivists inherit. They do not provide interpretation or interfere with its original order or provenance as this would lead to contamination of its integrity. Kaplan (2002, 215) has remarked that 'this is positivism in a singularly unreflective cast' and Terry Cook (2008) has demonstrated how the contextual influences of Darwinian evolutionary theory and positivist historiography were instrumental in formulating Jenkinson's position. This positivistic outlook, with its emphasis on logic and scientific rationalism, is problematic for archives because its universalizing and 'natural laws' have led to the assumption that 'the meaning of the word "archives" is simple, stable, and uncontested . . . [and that] archives reflect reality' (Harris, 1997, 133). This notion of archives as a stable, fixed, uncontested *reality* is the one area above all others that postmodernism has forced the profession to confront.

Elisabeth Kaplan (2002, 210), in response to such issues, questions why the profession is so intellectually isolated and in doing so highlights one of the most important features of where we have come from. In essence, her analysis points to Jenkinson's regressive positioning of the archivist as someone who would perform a passive role 'without external interests'. Kaplan demonstrates Jenkinson's reactionary position by placing him against his contemporary equivalent in the field of archaeology, Bronislaw Malinowski, who published his *Argonauts of the Pacific* also in 1922. In contrast to Jenkinson, this proposed a progressive approach in which the archaeologist would become an active 'participant observer'. This shift in focus is essential to an understanding of where the field of archival theory has been heading for the past 20 years. We have witnessed a shift away from the view of the archivist as a passive observer and neutral custodian, to a position where we recognize that the archivist shapes the archive every bit as much as the creator, for example, in our collecting policies, appraisal actions and the language of our finding aids.

Jenkinson's shadow has purveyed the whole field of archival education and practice in the UK for nearly a century. His positivist ideology has been naturalized and given rise to its mistaken identity as the traditions of practice. As Nesmith (2002, 27) has argued, it is 'so deeply ingrained that it has been treated by some archivists as if it were part of the natural order of human recording and communication'. It is at this juncture that a seeming polarization emerges in the profession between those who engage with theoretical concerns presented by postmodernism and those who see those concerns as irrelevant to the day-to-day practice of archives and nothing more than 'much ado about shelving' (Roberts, 1997). Similarly, in a short piece on archival education that appeared in *ARC Magazine*, the Society of Archivists publication, Richard Hunt (2009, 10), then a student on a UK archive course, described the 'descent of spirits at the impenetrable mass of writing by postmodernists on recordkeeping, all of which seemed to proclaim the end of a career which for us hadn't even begun' and later the revival of spirits after being 'reassured' by several Society of Archivists (now Archives and Records Society) members '(who should probably remain anonymous) that they never paid any attention to postmodernist theory or the continuum at any point during their careers'.

This polarity is in fact illusory, and even Jenkinson saw the necessity for a theory which informed practice, and many of those in the profession who have engaged with postmodernism stress that: 'theory and practice are not opposites . . . but integrated aspects of the archivist's role and responsibility' (Cook and Schwartz, 2002, 171).

Jenkinson's paradigm persists and has enjoyed a resurgence in what has been termed a neo-Jenkinsonian approach. Luciana Duranti (1994, 343), one of its most important advocates, speaks of a betrayal of responsibility if the archivist does not act with 'impartiality . . . and as objectively . . . as possible'. She has identified four characteristics of archives as: impartiality (inherent truth); authenticity, through unbroken custody; naturalness; and interrelationship. These reveal the nature of archives as evidence in a fiscal and legal sense. This position is echoed by other theorists who have reinscribed the values that Jenkinson espoused as a touchstone. Michael Moss (2008, 81), for example, suggests that it is an archivist's obligation to maintain objectivity and voices his desire that 'I want the truth to be knowable.' This notion of what truth and whose truth is explored more fully in the following section.

If archivists are to have a role in Nesmith's intellectual changing point in the profession we have to regard Jenkinson as an important pioneer who shaped our thinking but need to discard the straightjacket of his positivist framework. His work should be seen in the context of the time – the first part of the 20th century – when it was written. Rather than cling onto its empiricist agenda and attempt to mutate its relevance to our present situation we should allow ourselves to be open to new conceptualizations of the archive. In the UK we are already very late on the uptake. Postmodernism is nothing new, and in fact some would argue that it is already over (see for example Alan Kirby (2009)), but its impact on the traditions and fundamentals of the archive profession are still to be explored. It is no accident that postmodernist theory, and particularly the rise of the different concepts of what an archive can be, developed at the same time as electronic technology. The latter is an area keenly recognized as requiring a response from archivists but this is usually dealt with more in terms of business management than for any philosophical implications it might have. A memory crisis prompted by the anxiety of digital amnesia is precisely the place where philosophical concepts of the archive have been harnessed and contested. Our voice needs to be added to the discourses that are defining our discipline's ontological status, such as history and literary and cultural theory, otherwise we risk becoming an irrelevant voice on the periphery of a much wider debate. The remainder of this chapter explores recent challenges to this positivistic outlook.

Challenging the positivist framework: the development of postmodernism in archives

Postmodern influences

There are many ways in which the revision of old paradigms has been suggested from inside the profession. The tenor of these represents archives through postmodern discourses and this has had an important impact on both theory and practice. However, before proceeding it is necessary to examine here the reason for the shift from Jenkinson's positivist view of archives to more recent debates about the nature of archives, and the archivist, in the light of postmodern questioning. How and when does the shift take place from an overly determined view of archives to one which opens up the archives to questions of truth, fragmentation and instability?

Defining postmodernism is not easy. Even Charles Jencks, widely considered the 'founder' of the term (although, in true postmodern style, even this is debated), described postmodernism as 'a sinuous, even tortuous path. Twisting to the left and then to the right, branching down the middle, it resembles the natural form of a spreading root, or a meandering river that divides, changes course, doubles back on itself and takes off in a new direction' (1986, 2). Almost all definitions of postmodernism accept that it is a slippery concept and one that is not easy to pin down. Indeed, the fundamentals of postmodernism change according to disciplinary boundaries, concerns and conventions. At its heart, however, postmodernism can be said to represent a shift away from the Enlightenment ideal of human progress. It rejects the notion of a unified view of society progressing towards one all-encompassing end. This is why postmodern perspectives of archives conflict with Jenkinson's positivist viewpoint. Seen through the lens of postmodernism, Jenkinson's 'Truth' becomes a series of contingent 'truths'. His view of archives as a place where meaning can be found, becomes a contested space where meanings are hidden, subverted, altered and absent. It takes what was once regarded as a 'fixed', stable entity, and questions its reality and even its singularity.

In terms of archives, the most useful place to start to offer any definition is with the now oft quoted Jean-François Lyotard. In his work *The Postmodern Condition: a report on knowledge*, Lyotard famously declared the postmodern to be an 'incredulity towards metanarratives' (1984 [1979], xxiv). In this statement, Lyotard asserts that postmodernism rejects a totalizing view of the world in which we can seek reassurance in the answers provided by grand over-arching concepts, such as religion, suggesting a move from the meta- to the micro-narrative, where the world is viewed as a series of contingent 'truths', rather than as an overarching 'Truth'. This concept is particularly important for archives, as explored in the section which follows, as, if archives hold no 'Truth', what exactly is their purpose and function? Surely archives, seen from a Jenkinsonian standpoint, must have a single, objective truth if we are to be able to use them as a window on the past. What postmodernism does is take that window and make it opaque rather than transparent. It is easy to see why archives have viewed postmodernism with some distrust and, possibly, some dismay.

With its emphasis upon communication in particular, it is not surprising that postmodernism has impacted on archives. Postmodernism challenges our assumptions about what we can know about our environment through our communication with it. For the postmodernist, images, texts and language are all signs to be interpreted and interrogated, none of them maintain a stable, static, meaning. This has given rise variously to notions such as the 'death of the author' (Barthes, 1967) in cultural studies, whereby authorial context is considered a limiting factor in the interpretation of the text, and Baudrillard's evocation of the hyper-real, where the artefact comes to stand for a totalizing picture of a reality that never existed (Poster, 1988). In a discipline which is predicated upon writing, this questioning of how language and writing convey meaning, and our role in it, is crucial if we are to understand the nature of archives and archiving, the place of archives in cultural theory, and the role of archives as memory spaces.

Leading on from this difficulty in communication, by far the most influential impact on archives currently in terms of postmodernist thought is the work of Jacques Derrida. Despite earlier writings on the notion of the archive, it was the deconstructionist's publication of *Archive Fever* which really caught the attention of the archive field. Derrida (1998, 17) argues that societal communications are not fixed but constantly changing processes. He refers to this as *archivization* which 'produces as much as it records events'. Nesmith (2005, 262) has demonstrated how this inflects on our understanding of the record which becomes 'an evolving mediation of understanding about some phenomenon – a mediation created by social and technical processes of inscription, transmission, contextualization, and interpretation'. The archival document is not, therefore, a static and stable construct, but rather a fluid concept which changes according to the interactions of archivists and users.

What does archivization mean for archivists? Nesmith notes in particular how postmodernism has helped us to realize the archive, not as an unmediated 'truth' space, but as a place where records are made and re-made by archivists. Citing the example of Douglas Brymner, Nesmith notes how his unimpeded arrangement and selection of material held at what is now the National Archives of Canada was seen by Brymner as having quite a minor impact; he was 'like a mere clearer of land rather than a productive farmer' (2002, 32). Nesmith goes on to note how 'This perfectly captures the tension within the central archival professional myth: enormous power and discretion over societal memory, deeply masked behind a public image of denial and self-effacement' (2002, 32). This is what Derrida unmasks through his deconstruction of the archive. The Jenkinsonian notion of the archivist as 'impartial custodian' is no longer valid; the traditional footing on which the archival profession has for so long been based is not as stable as it once was (or rather, never was anyway). It is perhaps no wonder that archive students question what they are doing on the course when postmodernism has already appeared to render their profession without foundation. The answer, of course, is that being aware of these issues, and the role that we as archivists play in the co-creation of records, through our selection and cataloguing, *strengthens* our position.

Creating order from chaos

The lights that such concepts throw on who we are as archivists dispel numerous myths suggested by positivist ideology. One of the most compelling is the role that archivists have in relation to the archives in their care. As the archive is seen as part of a process, its archivization recognizes the archivist as an active participant. There is a shift from a passive and objective status towards an acknowledgement that the subjectively motivated actions of the archivist have a critical role in the construction and creation of archives to the extent that their interpretations make them another author of the records' constantly evolving meanings. Nesmith (2002, 27) has commented that 'contrary to the conventional idea that archivists simply receive and house vast quantities of records, which merely reflect society, they actually co-create and shape the knowledge in records, and thus help form society's memory'. Cook (1997, 46) also argues that 'Archivists have become . . . very active builders of their own "houses of memory". And so, each day, they should examine their own politics of memory in the archive-creating and memory-formation process.' The archive as a site where power is 'negotiated, contested [and] confirmed' (Cook and Schwartz, 2002a) implicates the archivist in this process and holds them accountable for their participation.

The way in which the archive has moved from the passive noun to the active verb of archiving can be illustrated through some of the hidden aspects of our practice. For example, the simple act of packaging archival material in order to increase its long-term preservation shows how we dramatically transform its physical character and alter the experience of engaging with the material. When a new archive arrives it might be housed in anything from plastic bags to old suitcases. As we take the documents out of these unsuitable containers, perhaps seeing them for the first time, we might compare this to the feelings Walter Benjamin describes when he is unpacking his library:

> The books are not yet on the shelves, not yet touched by the mild boredom of order. I cannot march up and down their ranks . . . I must ask you to join me in the disorder of crates that have been wrenched open, the air saturated with the dust of wood, the floor covered with torn paper, to join me among the piles of volumes that are seeing daylight again . . . so that you may share with me a bit of the mood . . . of anticipation.
>
> (Benjamin, 1992, 61)

This is an unseen aspect which the archivist is privy to and from this disorder we construct the 'mild boredom of order'. The difference between the states gives us two startlingly contrasting images and demonstrates the way that the archivist actively shapes the archive from piles of 'stuff' to a neatly regulated order in acid free boxes and folders.

This physical control of archives is reinforced through the means by which we intellectually control them. The methods we use to, for example, describe archives are ostensibly within the bounds of objectivity and facts in which all documents are accorded equal status. Here the fixedness of language of the positivist discourse is made concrete. There must be no passion, no feeling, no hint or impartiality in our descriptive mechanisms. All the knowledge and subjective values the archivist acquires during this process are eradicated so that the documents are treated with the same enervating rhetoric which mimics the style found in the paradigm of the dictionary or encyclopedia. This objectivity persuades the user of the authority of the information it imparts and the voice of the archivist slips into the background as an anonymous interlocutor between the archive and the researcher. Duff and Harris remind us that 'Description is always story telling – intertwining facts with narratives, observations with interpretations... archivists tell stories about stories, they tell stories with stories' (2002, 276). Rendering our descriptive aids as objective can be seen as just another fictionalization which precludes potentially important information that the archivist has discovered through their cataloguing and research.

Archives and context

The nature of contextual knowledge about records has always been a feature of the profession but this has been given a new prominence in relation to postmodern insights. Context has traditionally been perceived as a fixed relationship between the creator and the records, and between the records themselves. Nesmith (2005, 260) has argued that postmodernism has 'encouraged the view that context is virtually boundless. This expansive conception of context draws heavily on cultural and societal dimensions of context . . . [and] rather than a single appropriate context, there are various contextualties which are relevant to archival work'. This challenges our describing practices and encourages us to encompass a broader view, turning away from the description of records as finite objects towards an attempt at describing the various processes of becoming that the document engenders subsequent to its initial inscription. In what could be termed a biography of the document, Nesmith (2005, 273) proposes sets of contextual essays which would 'get behind . . . the less visible and complex histories that produce and shape the evidence they may bear'. In addition, the technology of Web 2.0 provides the opportunity for finding aids to become interactive and collaborative, which provides a new realm of contextualities.

Archives in the expanded field of contextuality has had an impact on other fundamentals. Eric Ketelaar (2000, 322) notes how this affects the basis of the principle of provenance which changes it from being 'defined by stable offices and roles to one of dynamic process-bound information'. By broadening the notion of provenance so that it encompasses a societal dimension the complex identities and multifaceted interactions which go towards its formation are highlighted. In a similar way the traditional conception that archivists must preserve the original order of an archive becomes defunct. The fluid nature of *archivization* suggests that the forms of archives are constantly shifting, and rather than working on the idea that when an archive comes into a repository its order represents that of its original state 'we should speak of the received order of the records' (Nesmith, 2005, 264).

Archives and truth

If we examine the concept in which the archive is depicted as a locus of 'truth' the first thing to question is *whose* truth is being represented? Whilst archivists seem happy to accept that the content of documents do not necessarily represent 'the truth', if we go a step further and question the actual 'truth' of the artefact this offends the notions of authenticity which many archivists see as their duty to defend. If we take a wider view, out from the individual document, to its contextual *raison d'être*, this raises a whole set of questions about why such documents were made, for whom, by whom, why a particular medium was used, who kept it and for what reasons. Rather than being a conduit of 'truth' the document is inflected with a whole range of positions which situate the artefact within a socio-cultural framework, which, in turn, colours its politics. Postmodernism has exposed the power systems which sit tacitly behind such concepts (White,

1973). This is not to say there is no such thing as truth but that there are many possible truths and that these are contingent. It is through this contingency, through an archives' contextuality (which can be endless), that we should locate its meaning. As David Bearman pointed out twenty years ago:

> The truth is not an absolute, but a contextual reality. The past is not a given, but a mutable creation. There is no law in history to select the forces of causality – causality is an intellectual tool we use to make sense of too much evidence. The pasts we construct are all discussion with the present, axes in today's intellectual battles, not monuments to some fixed reality.
>
> (Bearman, 1989)

Truth has traditionally been captured by the archivist through our guiding principles of *respect des fonds*, original order, and provenance, and yet in recent years each of these has been 'unpicked' as the repercussions of postmodernism have been felt in the profession. The first, for not representing the 'whole' of a body of records at all, and the second and third for failing to maintain any meaningful link between creator and records. Cook and Schwartz (2002b, 174) note how 'from the archivist's "inside" perspective, archival records are still seen, ideally, to reflect an "original order" in order to reflect better some reality or "Truth" about the records' creator'. In practice, however, these fundamental principles remain, they continue:

> Because these routine practices have thus been valorized and interiorized through 'social magic' as badges of professional identity, the resulting archival performance 'sustains belief in its own obviousness' . . . as something natural, normal, and unquestioned (175).

The continuum

The shift in the position of where we were to where we are is most notable in the two models which have been developed to explain the temporal and spatial properties of record operations: the life cycle model and the records continuum. If we critically examine the life cycle model which incorporates three classical stages of birth, life and death, it becomes apparent that it is based on Judaeo-Christian models of the life ritual. The record is born, either analogue or digitally, has its useful life and at any point can be destroyed. If it is kept it then goes into a latent phase where it is stored and might sometimes be referred to, which might be analogous to Purgatory. Finally its historical relevance is assessed, in a day of judgement, usually by an archivist, and it is either discarded or destroyed and consigned to hell or has an after-life in the stasis of archival heaven. The life cycle model is a linear one in which records progressively work through usefulness until they degrade into uselessness and death which becomes synonymous with the archive. As such it only offers one temporal dimension of existence for the archive.

If we move to the model of the records continuum, developed in the 1990s in Australia, this proposes a system that is at once compatible with postmodernist thinking and with the iterability inherent in the digital environment. Records do not simply go through a life cycle from creation and currency through to inactivity and the archive; rather they move in and out of 'currentness', having qualities both current and historical from the moment of their creation. This allows the records to become disembedded and carried forward into new circumstances where they are re-presented and used. The records continuum model suggests a continuous time/space construct in which temporalities are not linear. Upward (1996) emphasizes the fluidity and interactions of the complex: 'No separate parts of a continuum are readily discernible, and its elements pass into each other.' The place of the document in this is based in an act and is a prosthetic representation of that act. Its form and modes of communication are established by its content, structure and context. Upward (1996) goes on to explain that 'The record is a memorialized [disembedded] form of the document usually linked with other documents. It should have additional layers of context to those present in a document, and may be a surrogate record of that document. It is this additional information about context which is the key to "disembedding" the document from its narrower contexts of creation and carrying it through time and space as a record.' This accords with the coordinates of network information architectures.

Where are we going?

The final section of this chapter explores the question 'where are we going?' We have now moved out of Jenkinson's positivistic shadow into a view of archives as a contested space where we have begun to question the fundamentals of our professional discourse. It is a space that should not be seen as daunting, or one for unravelling the work of the archivist, as Hunt feared, but rather as a space for exploring the nature of what we are and what we do. Rather than view postmodernism as a force that has unravelled the 'truths' we always accepted about archives, we should view it rather as an opportunity to celebrate, as Cook has postulated, our professional rebirth.

The aura of the archive

To examine why it is important that we find an architecture for framing archives that is commensurate with the digital environment we need to look at what makes an archive an archive starting from the concept of the uniqueness of the archival document. As long as the idea of uniqueness is embedded in the archival document it carries with it a simultaneous desire for its transformation through its reproduction. Some archives, such as photographs, have a built-in reproducibility and digital technology has increased the transmutability of the archive through copying and virtual dissemination. In the first part of the 20th century the technology of mechanical reproducibility produced a crisis in artistic practice. Walter Benjamin (1992, 215) designated an aura to an original artwork that was diluted through mechanical reproduction and caused a tremendous shattering of its context. At the time that Benjamin was developing this theory he was in correspondence with André Malraux. Malraux accepted that reproducibility eroded originality but he contended that it simultaneously constructed a 'museum without walls' that indefinitely expanded the concept, producing a virtually endless museum.

Archives have not suffered the same fetishization of the original item as artworks except in rare cases, through extreme age or the designated 'beauty' of documents that often includes art as an integral aspect of its form. Value has traditionally resided in the importance of the informational content of the item rather than its aesthetic form and as such archives have seamlessly crossed this shift into different forms, especially in the digital realm. The dissolution of the aura of the archival artefact in cyberspace (more than any mechanical reproduction which came before) marks a destruction of the contextual values of records on a potentially endless scale, which in effect produces a desire and demand for the archivist to provide a greater contextuality.

The impact of the digital age on archives has, according to Cook, provided the conditions for archives without walls. This new space remodels the archive as a hub in which digital records are left outside in their originating systems capable of being reproduced or repeated within different contexts (Cook, 1994, 314). The archive without walls is part of a wider shift in archival thinking, defined as 'postcustodialism', in which the archive of the future is not tied to the physical limits of the repository building but can exist also in the infinite iteral space of the web. Postcustodialism also encompasses a mindset which shifts 'from the physical to a conceptual framework, from a product-focussed to a process-orientated activity, from matter to mind' (Cook, 1997, 48).

As storage and the form of the records becomes an intangibility, which are characterized as existing 'within the clouds', the evanescence of the digital archive has given rise to discourses on place. Duranti has argued that the physical place of archives is an absolute necessity if archivists are to continue the tradition of recordkeeping practices and maintain the integrity of the archive. She posits an evocative image where documents only become part of an archive if they cross the 'archival threshold'. The concept of the threshold has been defined by Foucault (1972, 14) as a site of discontinuity and rupture in which boundaries are contested. When a document crosses the archival threshold it is transformed from what was possibly an ordinary entity outside of the archive to something which has essential value in the construction of collective memory that requires preservation. This rupture, Duranti contends, demands a physicality of place:

> It is essential that the archival institution establish an architecture in which the records of all creating bodies, once received, can be put into clearly defined and stable relationships, and in which their broader context can be identified and the associations among the records never broken . . . . The abandonment of the connection between archival documents and a central official place of preservation under a distinct jurisdiction would imply the impossibility of exercising precisely that guardianship so dear to Jenkinson's heart, the moral defense of archives, not only by the archivist but also by the people.
>
> (Duranti, 2007, 464–5)

What will this architecture of the future repository look like as it takes on the new possibilities offered by the digital realm? Does it have to exist within Duranti's actual building or can it operate in relation to the virtual as Cook suggests? If we go back to Malraux, and the context of the translation from his original French to the English of the 'museum without walls' we see that in the first instance Malraux defined it as *'le musée imaginaire'* and it is from here that we might take a cue. The architecture of the new archives is still to be determined and is the stuff of imagination. Perhaps we can make suggestions for this new imaginary space based on concepts, visions and fantasies. What form would it take, for example, if it was a space that embraces the multiplicity which is inherent in web-based technology? How would it look if it was reformulated not just as written records but also as live memory? This approach is one that is embedded in the model of the records continuum.

The material to the immaterial

If the site of archives as live memory, in the conceptualization of a new imaginary archive, causes uneasiness or incredulity we have only to remind ourselves of the relatively short space of time in which the written record (which is already semantically consigned to the past as a fixed entity) has enjoyed currency. M.T. Clanchy (1993, 294) has demonstrated that 'there was no straight and simple line of progress from memory to written record. People had to be persuaded – and it was difficult to do – that documentary proof was sufficient improvement' on oral testimony. Duranti (1994) disclaims that oral testimonies have any place in archives, viewing them as interpretative in that they do not exhibit the strict characteristics of archives based on the evidential authenticity she accords to written records. Culturally we have come to assume the pre-eminence and immutability of the written word. The slippage between the oral and written traditions activated the passage between nature and culture; between the real and the symbolic. However, Clanchy reminds us that the oral was supplanted by the written record and thus points to the potential impermanence of this hierarchy.

The point at which Duranti rejects oral testimony from her archival threshold proves critical in establishing the limits of her model which are ultimately confined to written records. The oral and the written are the two systems which represent the way in which society and culture has produced memory-structures through the immaterial and the material. The conventional institutional archive has privileged and been founded upon the written. Arjen Mulder and Joke Brouwer (2003, 4) have argued: 'Next to these stiff and stable archives there have always been flexible and unstable archives of what one can call "immaterial information" that followed a different rationality – the labyrinthine, fuzzy logic of oral culture, that is, a culture without written records.' It is the unstable, immaterial archives of oral culture which represent the antithesis to Duranti's classical archives and are therefore designated as non-archival and have to be resisted else they dissemble the fundamental essence of archives.

However, the digital environment is already undoing this classical notion of archives. Duranti's response to the challenge of the digital is to employ the discipline which has legitimated written records and is postulated in her book *Diplomatics: new uses for an old science* (1998). Here she determines that the electronic environment exhibits characteristics which find all their roots and equivalence in analogue records, and that through the application of diplomatics we can comprehend, order and make sense of the digital. But does it all fit that neatly? How can what is essentially an analogue artefact correspond in identical fashion to what is an expanded field of interconnectedness in the virtual realm? How does this take account of the multimedia nature of the digital in which the visual not only has parity but dominates the written? How does this account for the dynamic and fluid characteristics of electronic records rather than their stability? If we attempt to fix such modes will we not see, right that at the point of order, the archive slipping away? (Derrida, 1998)

It has been argued that technological changes are much closer in character to the oral than the written. As Mulder and Brouwer define:

> What used to be material archive-systems have become immaterial information-banks. Unlike classical archive forms, recent digital databases need not be ordered linearly – grid-like and hierarchically. They are made accessible through complex linking technologies which no longer work linearly . . . but as random and non-linear . . . . Flexibility and instability have become technical qualities instead of problems to be controlled. Digital archives are unstable, plastic, living entities, as stories and rituals were in oral cultures.
>
> (Mulder and Brouwer, 2003, 5)

The rhizomic character (where we view archives as networks, rather than as hierarchical structures) of the digital has the potential to construct new identities for archives and in order to get to these we have to introduce redefinitions that venture 'into the undefining of archives' (Hamilton, Harris and Reid, 2002, 16). This undefining requires what Ketelaar (2000, 323) has called a 'shift in focus from skills to attitudes'. This is not positing that we return solely to an oral tradition but rather that we see a system which embraces such forms of archive within it. Nor does it suggest that we abandon Duranti's insightful studies of diplomatics but that we see the written as just one textual inscription in the multimedia environment of the virtual realm. Digital culture represents the shift in which the two memory-structures intersect and requires a fresh look at the neglected qualities of the immaterial.

Conclusion

Returning to Jencks to conclude this chapter, his notion of 'double coding' is an intriguing one for archivists, both in terms of how we think of ourselves, our work, our archives and our users. Jencks proposed that postmodern architecture could be recognized by its use of what he termed 'double-coding':

> the combination of Modern techniques with something else (usually traditional
> building) in order for architecture to communicate with the public and a
> concerned minority, usually other architects. The point of this double coding was
> itself double. Modern architecture had failed to remain credible – and partly
> because it didn't make effective links with the city and history. Thus the solution I
> perceived and defined as Post-Modern: an architecture that was based on new
> techniques and old patterns. Double coding to simplify means both elite/popular
> and new/old and there are compelling reasons for these opposite pairings.
>
> (Jencks, 1986, 14)

For archives the notion of double-coding opens up new ways of thinking about what we are doing and where we are going. We see this very much in our everyday work as archivists – an ISAD(G) (General International Standard Archival Description) compliant catalogue speaks to archivists very differently to how it speaks to the users. Open that catalogue up for user-annotation via Web 2.0 technologies and the new techniques and old patterns, central to Jencks's argument for double-coding, become apparent. Additionally double-coding is a useful metaphor for developments in archive theory itself. Moving out of the shadow of Jenkinson has afforded us the opportunity to re-think much that has previously been taken as given, and yet we continue to carry that tradition with us. The conflict between new and old ways of viewing archives should not see us separate into our individual camps – that is the very nature of the postmodern archive.

References

Barthes, R. (1967) The Death of the Author, (trans. Howard, R.), *Aspen*, **5&6**, www.ubu.com/aspen/aspen5and6/threeEssays.html#barthes.

Bearman, D. (1989) *Archival Methods*, Archives and Museum Informatics Technical Report #9, Pittsburgh, Archives & Museum Informatics, www.archimuse.com/publishing/archival_methods.

Benjamin, W. (1992) *Illuminations,* Fontana Press.

Brothman, B. (2001) The Past That Archives Keep: memory, history, and the preservation of archival records, *Archivaria*, **51** (Spring), 48–80.

Clanchy, M.T. (1993) *From Memory to Written Record: England 1066–1307*, Blackwell Publishing.

Cook, T. (1994) Electronic Records, Paper Minds: the revolution in information management and archives in the post-custodial and post-modernist era, *Archives and Manuscripts*, **22** (2), 300–18.

Cook, T. (1997) What is Past is Prologue: a history of archival ideas since 1898, and the future paradigm shift, *Archivaria*, **43** (Spring), 17–63.

Cook, T. (2001) Appraisal Methodology: macro-appraisal and functional analysis, part a: concepts and theory, National Archives of Canada, www.archives.ca/06/061101_e.html.

Cook, T. (2005) Macroappraisal in Theory and Practice: origins, characteristics, and Implementation in Canada, 1950–2000, *Archival Science*, **5** (2–4), 101–61.

Cook, T. (2008) Understanding Archives from the Inside: myths, misconceptions, realities, possibilities, Keynote lecture at *Archive Fervour/Archive Further: literature, archives and literary archives conference, Aberystwyth University, 9–10 July 2008*.

Cook, T. and Schwartz, J. M. (2002a) Archives, Records, and Power: the making of modern memory, *Archival Science*, **2** (1–2), 1–19.

Cook, T. and Schwartz, J. M. (2002b) Archives, Records, and Power: from (postmodern) theory to (archival) performance, *Archival Science*, **2** (3–4), 171–85.

Deleuze, G. (1973) *Proust and Sign,* Allen Lane, The Penguin Press.

Derrida, J. (1998) *Archive Fever: a Freudian impression,* The University of Chicago Press.

Duff, W. M. and Harris, V. (2002) Stories and Names: archival description as narrating records and constructing meanings, *Archival Science*, **2** (3–4), 263–85.

Duranti, L. (1994) The Concept of Appraisal and Archival Theory, *American Archivist,* **57** (2), 328–44.

Duranti, L. (1998) *Diplomatics: new uses for an old science,* Scarecrow Press.

Duranti, L. (2007) Archives as a Place, *Archives & Social Studies: A Journal of Interdisciplinary Research,* **1** (0), 445–66, first published in *Archives & Manuscripts* **24** (2), 242–55.

Foucault, M. (1992) *The Archaeology of Knowledge*, Routledge.

Hamilton, C., Harris, V. and Reid, G. (2002) Introduction. In Hamilton, C., Harris, V. and Pickover, M. et al. (eds), *Refiguring the Archive,* Springer., 7–17.

Harris, V. (1997) Claiming Less, Delivering More: a critique of positivist formulations on archives in South Africa, *Archivaria,* **44** (Fall), 132–41.

Hunt, R. (2009) Starting Out: the thoughts of this year's students on the MARM Course, *ARC Magazine,* (233), 10.

Jencks, C. (1986) *What is Postmodernism?,* Academy Editions.

Jenkinson, H. (1965) *A Manual of Archive Administration,* reprint of 2nd edn, Percy Lund, Humphries & Co. Ltd (first published in 1922 by The Clarendon Press).

Kaplan, E. (2002) Many Paths to Partial Truths: archives, anthropology, and the power of representation, *Archival Science,* **2** (3–4), 209–20.

Ketelaar, E. (2000) Archivistics Research Saving the Profession, *The American Archivist,* **63** (Fall/Winter), 322–40.

Kirby, A. (2009) *Digimodernism: how new technologies dismantle the postmodern and reconfigure our culture*, Continuum.

Lyotard, J. (1984) *The Postmodern Condition: a report on knowledge,* (trans. Bennington G. and Massumi, B.), University of Minnesota Press.

Malkinowski, B. (1922) *Argonauts of the Pacific,* E. P. Dutton.

Moss, M. (2008) Opening Pandora's Box: what is an archive in the digital environment? In Craven, L. (ed.), *What are Archives: cultural and theoretical perspectives: a reader*, Ashgate, 71–88.

Mulder, A. and Brouwer, J. (2003) Introduction, *Information Is Alive: art and theory on archiving and retrieving data*, NAI Publishers.

Nesmith, T. (2002) Seeing Archives: postmodernism and the changing intellectual place of archives, *American Archivist*, **65** (Spring/Summer), 24–41.

Nesmith, T. (2005) Reopening Archives: bringing new contextualities into archival theory and practice, *Archivaria*, **60** (Fall), 259–74.

Poster, M. (ed.) (1988) *Jean Baudrillard: selected writings*, Stanford University Press.

Roberts, J. W. (1997) Archival Theory: much ado about shelving, *American Archivist*, **50** (Winter), 66–74.

Upward, F. (1996) Structuring the Records Continuum – Part One: postcustodial principles and properties, *Archives and Manuscripts,* **24** (2), http://infotech.monash.edu/research/groups/rcrg/ publications/recordscontinuum-fupp1.html.

White, H. (1973) *Metahistory: the historical imagination in nineteenth-century Europe*, The Johns Hopkins University Press.

2

Encounters with the self: archives and research

Sue Breakell

Introduction

Over the past few years two diverging tendencies have characterized perceptions of archives from popular and academic perspectives. First, a varied discourse has considered the archive as a sphere of critical debate, in the context of, for example, postmodernism, postcolonialism and museology. Meanwhile to the general public the notion of the archive has become at once more familiar and less fixed, with the term perhaps becoming a kind of stand-in for history or notions of historicity. Both these tendencies have given little attention to the work of the archivist.[1] Tom Nesmith (2002, 28) has discussed the 'self effacement' of the archivist, which links to the putative invisibility of the archivist's encounter with the material in their care. But where does this omission from discussions leave archivists? Some have engaged with critical debates, sometimes in response to the new challenges of the digital environment, others through encountering interdisciplinary notions of archives which may be vastly different from their own experience or frame of reference.[2]

The rise of archives in popular culture

This is an interesting time to be an archivist, with archives becoming not only embedded in people's daily lives but also emblematic in political and social culture. In the popular imagination, archives seem to be associated with control, order and stasis; or imagined as dusty basements, treasure troves of dramatic stories and truths untold. Given that archivists are often part of these scenarios, it is important, first, to be aware of how archives are seen by others, and thus what they imagine archives to be, and, second, to consider what archivists would like to be known and understood about their professional work. Although archivists strive for objectivity in their own engagement with the archives for the purposes of cataloguing, many have commented on the invisible impact of the archivist, shaping the archive as it is experienced by the user (see for example Nesmith, 2002, 28). The history of archival theory has tended to focus on the custodial and administrative histories of archives; the Jenkinsonian authority of the text; or Schellenberg's functional appraisal. But if, as has been argued in contemporary archival debate, the archivist's function now is to serve not those in authority but 'the people' (Ketelaar, 2003, 18), this shifts the emphasis from the material's previous life to its future, and archivists must understand what 'the people' want from them, incorporating this into their own sense of purpose and the principles that underpin their work. Archivists need to be considering what the possible future lives of the archives might be – not simply in anticipating research subject trends, but also in considering research methods and mechanics.

Over the past 15 years or so there has been a marked shift in the public profile of archives. This is in part due to the appropriation of the term by information technology (and a consequent notion of *archiving* appearing to offer permanence in an impermanent digital world), but there has also been a repositioning of history and historical sources as a reference point for popular culture.[3] Since the early 1990s, the industry of family history research has grown exponentially, driven by the combination of technological developments and the online access to catalogues and digital surrogates that this has facilitated. Jerome de Groot has written of the 'purported enfranchisement of the historical consumer' (2009, 59) and the 'emancipation of the historical subject' (2009, 61), implying not only that present-day researchers have been enabled to carry out their own historical research, but also that in doing so they are able to free up the individual stories of their forebears, thus 'bringing history to life' for themselves and, in a politically expedient concept, understanding something new about their own identity as a result. The less visible aspect of this enfranchisement (and the implication of de Groot's use of the word 'purported') is the fact that the growth of archival research as a popular leisure pursuit is also reflective of the commodification of history and consequently of archives as the currency by which history can be consumed; de Groot talks of 'an economy in which the consumption of such goods is driven by a desire to understand the self and make complete' (2009, 75).

The past (or, more specifically, life in the past) has also become fertile territory for television programme makers, and a kind of creative playground for reality television, a phenomenon which perhaps began with *Time Team* (focusing on an archaeological dig), via fictive realities such as *The History House* format (beginning with *The 1900 House* and moving through various other time periods and locations), to current manifestations such as *Who Do You Think You Are?* (hereafter *WDYTYA?*), now on primetime BBC 1 after starting in a niche slot on BBC 2, and its daytime cousin *Heir Hunters*, both of which focus on genealogical detective work carried out in archives. A recent posting on the *WDYTYA?* website even calls for families to take part in a family history related TV quiz – surely unimaginable ten years ago. That such programming strands have moved from niche to primetime is indicative of a cultural trend which television first reflects (discovering that it taps into a wider public interest than anticipated) and then facilitates (encouraging via associated websites, network resources and blogs[4]). Such popular history networks are described by de Groot (2009, 74–5) as a 'collaborative trajectory', helping to erode notions of archivists as gatekeepers who control access, and 'creating a virtual information economy in which the individual user is the driving force'.

Louise Craven has written about how and why individuals find meaning in archives. Citing recent research into identity in the museum context, she argues that archives similarly 'facilitat[e] identity construction' (Craven, 2008, 11). This identity is both on an individual level, based on the user's own background and experiences, and at a community or cultural level – so we might say that it is about the self and the context of the self. In this model of use, Craven argues, the user may well have no interest in the context of a document except as it relates to the subject of their own research, their focus being simply the meaning which it has for them in relation to other sources they have found. A family history researcher might place a copy of a relevant document among their own research papers gathered from a variety of sources around that focus – and so, as Craven (2008, 20) points out, 'the content has become the context'. This reflects a demand in the digital environment for user-driven content, which in the archive sphere has meant that users want to be able to compile and curate their own selections of content, through the agency of the archive's website, but centred on their own interests, perhaps creating their own entry points in the form of tags. So even as archivists pursue the goal of standardization of description and entry points, the pull of the general user is in the opposite direction entirely, towards creating customized structures and meanings, through which archives are continually becoming different things to different people.

It might be said that family history allows people to make sense of their own place in the world, to see their own reflection in a culture/society which continually encourages the individual to look outside him/herself for affirmation and meaning, a never-ending and self-perpetuating process. The celebrity in *WDYTYA?* is presented as a representative of the ordinary viewer, as each projects contemporary and personal pre-occupations onto the actions of their equally ordinary forebears, ascribing feelings and motives with which they can empathize, regardless of whether there is evidence of such between the lines of the recorded information. Another facet of the phenomenon is that in a time of networks of communication which bring together common interest users in a way never previously possible, there is perhaps some kind of reassurance in documentation; a sense that a life is only truly lived if it has left certain traces, symptomatic of an industrialized society which has tended to privilege the written over the spoken.[5]

In his popular book *The File: a personal history* (2009), Timothy Garton Ash describes how, after the fall of Communism, he gains access to the file kept about him by the Stasi while he lived in East and West Germany in the late 1970s and early 1980s. The file records what agents and informers discovered and observed about him, and considers this 'evidence' as one account of this period in his life, an encounter with his younger self, which he compares with his own diary notes and memories from the time.

> Now the galling thing is to discover how much I myself have forgotten of my own life. Even today, when I have this minute documentary record – the file, the diary, the letters – I can still only grope towards an imaginative reconstruction of that past me. For each individual self is built, like Renan's nations, through this continuous remixing of memory and forgetting
>
> (Ash, 2009, 221)

Of course, as this book demonstrates, no number of sources can ever capture or recreate an actual event or experience; there are only perspectives, and the context which informs those perspectives, and already we are skewed by only being able to start from the archive. Where, Garton Ash muses, does the truth lie, between his memory, his diary, the Stasi files, and the wider political environment from which the files (and the informants who contributed to them) drew their justification and function?

The File highlights the difference between experienced reality and the record. But in many popular uses of the word *archive* there has been a blurring of boundaries to the point that archives have become at times a stand-in for, or a physical representation of, history or the accumulation of past events. There is now an expectation that documentation will exist. Most archivists will have experienced a researcher who cannot believe that the material or information they seek is not there. We are all aware of the pitfall of believing that things only happened/exist if they are documented: thus making the archive not only a 'prosthetic memory' (Landsberg, 2004) (by its nature an imperfect or incomplete substitute), but memory itself. We rely on the internet and recording media not only to keep our memories but to *be* our memories. For example, the BBC has not always kept its past programming, but it is now one of the foremost producers and consumers of archive footage, re-presenting and re-contextualizing its own content. Because of the facility of this activity, there is now an expectation of total recall of past events in this way, and that any discussion of recent history can be accompanied by documentary footage. In this sense, through the increasing momentum of this re-presentation, the past is catching up with itself as it becomes part of our present experience and is absorbed within it, and time and memory are loosed from their locational tethers.

The act of looking to the past for some kind of answer to questions in the present, highlights an essential quality of the archive and what we find in it. Archives can be seen to exist in contrast or opposition to something – a way of trying to see ourselves by our reflection in, or by comparison with, the source we are looking at. There is a sense of perspective in looking at the past, which becomes harder to achieve or claim if the past we are looking at is too close. The present is by its very nature unfixed and always moving – it might be described as a state of being, not a place – whereas the past gives an illusion of being fixed, resolved. This is just one of many contrasts which come into play when looking at the past (as found in the archive) from the notional position of the present, through which the present may seem better or worse by comparison, depending on the context of the encounter. Written documentation as opposed to thought or speech; outdated/cutting edge (the implication being that we are wiser now); concrete/nebulous; innocence/experience; the record of an event/the experience itself; time/space; permanent/ephemeral – we might go on. Moving into the sphere of critical theory, such contrasts can be related to the poststructuralist concept of binary opposition.

Archives as texts

Binary opposition suggests that there is dependence between two objects, of which one is powerful in comparison with the other, a power that depends on the subjugation of that other. The hub of such binary oppositions is, in this case, the reader of the document. While not the most cutting-edge literary theory, reception theory or reader response theory can offer another approach for further consideration here. This theory posited that the key process in the experience of reading is not the authorial creation, but the interaction between the reader and the text, as the reader brings to the work his or her unique combination of both personal and conditioned responses. Thus there is not one authoritative reading of any text, but, once created, the text has an infinite number of potential manifestations. A key source for this theory is Roland Barthes' 1967 essay 'The Death of the Author', which describes the conventional structuralist reading of a literary text thus:

> The explanation of a work is always sought in the man [sic] who has produced it, as if, through the more or less transparent allegory of the fiction, it was always finally the voice of one and the same, the author, which delivered his 'confidence'.

> (Barthes, 1967)

For present purposes we might rephrase this quotation to describe the activity of using archives, thus:

> The explanation of an *archival document* is always sought in the *activity* which has

produced it, as if, through the more or less transparent allegory of the *function,* it was always the voice of one and the same, the *authority,* which delivered their '*account*'.

By shifting the direction of interaction with the text from the creator to the reader, Barthes (1967) argues, 'the unity of a text is not in its origin, it is in its destination'.

If we apply this principle to archives, it helps to highlight a clear distinction between the original activity or impulse which created the record, and to which it alludes (for it can never fully *record* in the sense of fully capturing or replicating, and there remains the vast and impenetrable body of both the unrecorded and unrecord*able* past), and the infinite potential future lives of archives when they are used and reanimated in new ways by users of all kinds, who, as we have seen, bring their own individual and collective identities into play. Archival theory and discussion has tended traditionally to focus on the former process, the context of creation. Indeed it is right to perpetuate the importance of this principle, as it is potentially the most in danger of loss in the digital environment, where documents are loosed from their contexts, and the processes of cultural memory may not privilege the questioning of the origins of the information appearing in response to a search.

Furthermore the notion of intertextuality argues that in the creation of any text, there is not so much creative originality as a re-presenting of ideas and influences from other texts and cultural sources. Julia Kristeva (1980, 69) has written that 'meaning is not transferred directly from writer to reader but instead is mediated through, or filtered by, "codes" imparted to the writer and reader by other texts'. In other words, the way we approach a text is influenced not only by our existing expectations about that text (based on what we already know of it or of the form it takes, or, in an archival sense, what the catalogue may tell us) but by all the other texts we have read before, and how they were received and incorporated into our body of experience. Such ideas might usefully be compared with aspects of archive theory, notably diplomatics, and our expectations of the structure of a document, its form and content, and the layers of codes these impart.

We can also consider here Jacques Derrida's (1982) notion of *différance,* which holds that, because of the limitations of language, and the subjective nature of our understanding of what any word means, writing can never give precise expression to what the writer is attempting to convey, and can only convey what it does by virtue of the reader's understanding of the difference between that word and a similar one. Thus in such communication the meaning is perpetually deferred and always changing, and can never be fixed. This idea can also be related to the notion of multiple and unfixed meanings of the archive.

Archives and research

Such ideas from critical theory, then, in considering the engagement between a reader and a text, can also be applied to the process of using archival documents – in other words, the activity of research. Thus the reader is the centre around whom the binary oppositions are set, moving through their own self-curated selection of documents and sources, based on the individual experiences, cultural reference points and framings peculiar to that researcher. While the academic researcher may not be following so overtly the 'personal' as the genealogist, there can be argued to still be an essence of the self which is the driving force behind the research. Carolyn Steedman has written powerfully about the subjective aspects of archival research:

> The past is searched for something . . . that confirms the searcher in his or her sense of self, confirms them as they want to be, and feel in some measure that we already are . . . [but] the object has been altered by the very search for it . . . what has actually been lost can never be found. This is not to say that *nothing* is found, but that thing is always something else.
>
> (Steedman, 2001, 77)

A number of recent publications, perhaps inspired by Steedman's descriptions of her physical encounters with archives, have explored the role of the individual or the self in the process of research. In the field of history in particular, these have tended to combine this 'subjective turn' with the postcolonial historical perspective.[6] Much of this writing is by historians; occasionally an archivist writes an introduction, including a defence of archive theory and practice, before leaving centre stage in the unfolding drama.[7] Otherwise archivists appear only as players in the story, often as two-dimensional ciphers who hinder or help the historian on their quest to rescue archives (from gatekeepers) and history (from colonial or other exclusive perspectives). In the index of one publication by Burton, for example, under the heading 'Archivists' are the sub-headings 'as enablers of research', 'family as', 'as gatekeepers', 'professionalisation of', 'women as' and 'working conditions of', which sounds more like an anthropological or sociological study than a view of archivists as partners in the study of history (Burton, 2006, 386). Clearly in some cultures archivists may be subject, personally and professionally, to constraints which place them in difficult positions between employer and user; and even where there are professional freedoms, an archivist may be more or less open to critical thinking beyond the walls of the archive. Nevertheless, in the subjective turn which focuses on the historian's (or other's) encounter with the archive, the simplistic trope of the monolithic authoritarian archive's servants remains all too seductive.[8] One exception is the volume *Refiguring the Archive* (2002), which places the perspective of the archivist alongside those of other disciplines as a critically engaged participant with something particular to contribute, rather than as an unquestioning agent of governance or prejudice (Hamilton et al., 2002).

Archivists and researchers as collectors

In a parallel which draws the researcher onto the other side of the institutional divide, Celeste Olalquiaga compares the activities of the researcher with those of the collector:

> researchers and collectors deploy similar strategies: they compile and compose, each new element reconfiguring the whole in such a way that this process could be carried on indefinitely and still would make sense . . . . Research is taking stock of cultural merchandise, as well as of the personal baggage often tagged onto it, and attempting to re-establish its value anew . . . it is a way of 'finding' ourselves, quite literally, through an activity where subject and object are interwoven enough to become indistinguishable.
>
> (Olalquiaga, 2008, 43)

Regardless of whether we concur with this view of research, there is recognition here of a personal element of engagement with archive material. Yet if an archivist described their work thus then they would be deeply implicated in the shaping of the collection they offered to the user. It is interesting to note that the activities for which archivists are most vulnerable to criticism (collection, selection, interpretation and overall interference with archives) are also activities which draw in many academic archive users to their own encounter. Like these users, archivists too have awareness of both the subjective and objective facets of their engagement with the archive.

When archival theory is considered in the context of this focus on the activities of the researcher, the archivist's aim might be said to be to ensure that all researchers using an archive have the same experience of encounter with the original material, rather than it bearing traces of other researchers' activities or footprints – for example, a well meaning researcher reordering a collection around the focus of their own interests, their own research the organizing principle, and the centre, of their path. Such a process can be compared to the way that hypertext works in the digital environment: by continually following the links of their own research journey, the user brings together material which has no other link than this research. Thus the 'academic' researcher's work operates in a similar way to that of the leisure researcher as we saw earlier.

> As readers move through a web or network of texts, they continually shift the center – and hence the focus or organizing principle – of their investigation and experience. Hypertext, in other words, provides an infinitely re-centreable system whose provisional point of focus depends upon the reader . . . anyone who uses hypertext makes his or her own interests the de facto organizing principle (or center) for the investigation at the moment. One experiences hypertext as an infinitely de-centreable and re-centreable system.
>
> (Landow, n.d.)

One might also comment here that a peril of hypertext is that, like Hansel and Gretel, one can become lost: not being able to return easily to an earlier path from which an intriguing link led us away. This neatly illustrates that this method of working limits the traditional pre-eminence of context and original (or suitably imposed) order is limited and in fact may be of less interest to many users of archives. The archivist's insistence on this pre-eminence may make their practices subject to justifiable scepticism and criticism. To give a practical example, we may wish to explore a collaboration with a partner organization as a means of securing funds for cataloguing, yet the partner's interest in creative re-presentations of archival material may bear little relation to the shape or structure of the catalogued archive, or the processes that produce it; although from the archivist's point of view it is essential to have cataloguing completed before such creative re-presentations can take place. Our own version of the archives in our care is but one of many, and so our work is more about capturing an archive at this particular point in its life – a moment of transfer, transition, transformation even – in order to enable its potential future lives. This process might be comparable with, for example, capturing a website or a database at a given moment, before allowing it to carry on reshaping itself. Such an approach – that of capturing original context in order to liberate the content – presented to non-archivist users and potential partners, demonstrates an open mind to other perspectives on the archives we steward.

Art archives offer relevant context here. Artists have manipulated archival forms for much of the 20th century,[9] seeing in the discontinuities and ambiguities of the archive a fertile territory for creative practice, which Hal Foster (2004, 5) has described as turning 'sites of creation . . . into sites of construction'. The French artist Christian Boltanski, a pioneer in what has since become a well trodden field, is often described as an archival artist, because of his use of archival forms such as photographs (his own and other people's) and the museum's spaces and modes of representation. He has been particularly interested in the quality of what he has described as 'small memory': 'Large memory is recorded in books and small memory is all about the little things' (Boltanski cited in Semin, Garb and Cuspit, 1997, 19). In one typical early piece he considered an anonymous collection of family photographs and attempted to construct a family history based simply on interpretations of the photographs. From this, he said he discovered that his own conclusions were based on the viewer rather than the viewed: 'I realized that these images were only witnesses to a collective ritual. They didn't teach us anything about the Family D . . . but only sent us back to our own past.'[10] Many of his later, larger scale installation works have used the presence of the viewer to fulfil the work, bringing their own 'small memories' to interact with the repurposed archival forms.

> An artwork is open – it is the spectators looking at the work who make the piece, using their own background . . . a lamp in my work might make you think of a police interrogation, but it's also religious, like a candle . . . there are many

> ways of looking at the work. It has to be 'unfocussed' somehow so that
> everyone can recognize something of their own self when viewing it.
>
> (Boltanski cited in Semin, Garb and Cuspit, 1997, 24)

As we have seen, it is these qualities of the archive which repeatedly and continuously attract users of archives. It is this that we as archivists should nurture, even while meeting our own imperatives as archive practitioners – so that through our own performance on the archive, we open it up for others to find their own reflections.

Conclusion

The archivist's function is at once more important than ever and more devolved, with users wanting their own control and ownership of their personalized research resources. Archival perspectives and expertise deserve to be better represented in critical debates about the archive and the various manifestations of history in contemporary culture. The better the archivist can understand the context of the user's interaction with archives, as well as the context of the archives they want to see, the better we can both engage with discussion and accommodate the changing needs of our audiences.

References

Ash, T. G. (2009) *The File: a personal history*, Atlantic Books.

Barthes, R. (1967) The Death of the Author, (trans. Howard, R.), *Aspen*, **5&6**.

Burton, A. (ed.) (2006) *Archive Stories: facts, fictions and the writing of history*, Duke University Press.

Cook, T. (2001) Archival Science and Postmodernism: new formulations for old concepts, *Archival Science*, **1** (1), 3–24.

Craven, L. ed. (2008) *What are Archives? Cultural and theoretical perspectives: a reader*, Ashgate.

de Groot, J. (2009) *Consuming History: historians and heritage in contemporary popular culture*, Routledge.

Derrida, J. (1982) Difference. In *Margins of Philosophy*, (trans. Bass, A.), University of Chicago Press. Also available at http://hydra.humanities.uci.edu/derrida/diff.html).

Foster, H. (2004) An Archival Impulse, *October*, Fall.

Hamilton, C., Harris, V., Pickover, M. and Reid, G. (eds) (2002) *Refiguring the Archive*, Springer.

Ketelaar, E. (2003) Being Digital in People's Archives, *Archives and Manuscripts*, **31** (2), 8–22.

Kristeva, J. (1980) *Desire in Language: a Semiotic approach to literature and art*, Blackwell.

Landow, G. P. (n.d.) Hypertext and de-centering, www.cyberartsweb.org/cpace/ht/jhup/decenter.html.

Landsberg, A. (2004) *Prosthetic Memory: the transformation of American remembrance in the age of mass culture*, Columbia University Press.

Nesmith, T. (2002) Seeing Archives: postmodernism and the changing intellectual place of archives, *American Archivist*, **65** (Spring/Summer), 24–41.

Olalquiaga, C. (2008) The Researcher as Collector of Failed Goods. In Holly, M. and Smith, M. (eds), *What is Research in the Visual Arts? Obsession, archive, encounter*, Sterling and Francine Clark Institute/Yale University Press.

Semin, D., Garb, T. and Cuspit, D. (1997) *Christian Boltanski*, Phaidon.

Steedman, C. (2001) *Dust*, Manchester University Press.

Notes

1   For example, Charles Merewether (ed.) (2006) *The Archive* (Whitechapel/Massachusetts Institute of Technology), part of the series Documents in Contemporary Art, does not include writing by archivists but focuses on artists and critical theorists. One exception is Sven Spieker's (2008) book *The Big Archive: art from bureaucracy* (Massachusetts Institute of Technology) in which discussion includes some archival theory, primarily from the American and German traditions.

2   See, for example, Cook, T. (2008) 'Archival Science and Postmodernism: new formulations for old concepts', www.mybestdocs.com/cook-t-postmod-p1-00.htm (accessed 24 February 2008), an article which originally appeared (2001) in *Archival Science*, **1** (1), 3–24. The British archives community has been slower to engage with such debates, prompting the Canadian theorist Terry Cook to praise a recent British publication as 'at last bring[ing] British thinking about archives onto the world stage' (cited on the back cover of Craven, L. [ed.] [2008] *What are Archives? Cultural and theoretical perspectives: a reader*, Ashgate).

3   Writers such as Raphael Samuels, David Lowenthal and David Cannadine have

discussed the rise of popular history and its commodification in a media age. See Lowenthal's *The Heritage Crusade and the Spoils of History* (Cambridge University Press, 1998) and Cannadine's *History and the Media* (Palgrave Macmillan, 2004)

4   See, for example, the *Who Do You Think You Are?* online magazine, www.bbcwhodoyouthinkyouaremagazine.com (accessed 28 September 2009) which as well as discussing the programme itself, acts as a portal and forum for genealogical research.

5   Two opposing sides of the debate about the benefits of the vast quantities of online information can be found in, for example, Anderson, C. (2007) *The Long Tail: how endless choice is creating unlimited demand,* Random House and Keen, A. (2007) *The Cult of the Amateur: how today's internet is killing our culture and assaulting our economy,* Nicholas Brealey.

6   See, for example, Burton, A. (ed.) (2006) *Archive Stories: facts, fictions and the writing of history,* Duke University Press, Kirsch, G. E. and Rohan, L. (eds) (2008) *Beyond the Archives: research as a lived process,* Southern Illinois University Press, Stoler, A. L. (2009) *Along the Archival Grain: epistemic anxieties and colonial common sense,* Princeton University Press.

7   As in Lucille M. Schulz's foreword to Kirsch, G. E. and Rohan, L. (2008) *Beyond the Archives: research as a lived process,* Southern Illinois University Press.

8   See, for example, van Alphen, E. (2008) Archival obsessions and obsessive archives, in Holly, M. and Smith, M. (eds), *What is Research in the Visual Arts? Obsession, archive, encounter,* Sterling and Francine Clark Institute/Yale University Press.

9   For discussion of this phenomenon, see Sven Spieker, or Enwezor, O. and Hartshorn, W. E. (eds) (2008) *Archive Fever: uses of the document in contemporary art,* Steidl.

10   Christian Boltanski discussing his work 'Album de Photos de la Famille D, 1939–1964' (1971), quoted in Gumpert, L. (1999) *Christian Boltanski,* Flammarion.

3

Strangely unfamiliar: ideas of the archive from outside the discipline

Alexandrina Buchanan

Introduction

The archive has become contested territory. In an age identified as postepistemological (Cheetham et al., 1998, 2), there has been encroachment in the field of archives from a number of disciplines whose scholars were previously accustomed to viewing the archive as a common resource, but who seem now to have settled within its boundaries and claimed ownership. Perhaps mindful of Derrida's (1996, 90) warning 'Nothing is less reliable, nothing is less clear today than the word "archive"', few have attempted definitions but many have claimed the right to identify what is archival, to categorize archival characteristics and alternately to castigate or celebrate the archive's power. In the process, the idea of the archive with which the professional archivist is familiar has become overlaid and blended, even diluted or adulterated, with concepts drawn from the newly engaged disciplines: the text, the oeuvre, the corpus, the canon and the repertoire. In associated literature the archive has also become almost indistinguishable from other types of resource: the library, the museum and the archaeological site. Indeed, as a cultural keyword (Williams, 1976), it has come to stand for all these concepts (Chabin, 1996, 2002 and 2005). The archive thus identified, however, may seem strangely unfamiliar, even threatening, to those who have by tradition acquired, preserved and made archives accessible.

The aim of this chapter is to explore the understanding of the archive in other disciplines, especially those of history, art and literary studies, from the perspective of the archivist. It will therefore be discussing issues in which this author is neither a participant, nor from which time has provided sufficient distance for critical overview and assessment. It cannot claim to represent the practitioners whose productions are discussed, nor do they all contribute to a single, cohesive project. Every example cited has its counter-example: an alternative and contradictory appraisal could readily be composed. All this chapter aims to do, therefore, is share an understanding of the current situation and identify possible points of contact and potentials for productive dialogue. Although as archivists we may feel estranged by some definitions of 'the archive' found in other disciplines, nevertheless it is hoped that readers may also see parallels. Such interdisciplinary encounters can provide occasions for reflection, just as Stephen Greenblatt (1997, 14), a literary historian, found that the ideas of Clifford Geertz, an anthropologist, 'made sense of something I was already doing, returning my own professional skills to me as more important, more vital and illuminating than I had myself grasped'.

Interdisciplinarity

The title of this chapter refers to 'ideas of the archive from outside the discipline'. A discussion of 'discipline' may therefore be necessary. History as an academic discipline and the archive as an institution have an interdependent history. From Leopold von Ranke (1795–1886) onwards, academic history has been defined by its use of archives, an approach which was first codified in the 1897 *Introduction aux Etudes Historiques* by Charles-Victor Langlois and Charles Seignobos (1932). When the role of the archivist was first identified, it was one of the first means of gaining paid employment as a historian. Historians and archivists were virtually indistinguishable as 'historical workers' (Levine, 1986, 122–34; Procter, 2006). Tensions, however, were soon apparent. Traditionally, archives have been identified with 'facts' and therefore with 'truth': for Hilary Jenkinson (the first to codify archival practice for an Anglophone audience) only archives could be guaranteed always to tell the truth (Jenkinson, 1966, 12), making the archivist 'the most selfless devotee of Truth the modern world produces' (Jenkinson, 1947, 259). Truth, however, was not always the concomitant of archival use and thus became (for archivists) a distinction between themselves and historians. His American counterpart, T.R. Schellenberg, went even further than Jenkinson: despite being merely the 'hewers of wood and drawers of water' (Joshua 9:23) for scholars

(Schellenberg, 1956, 236; Lamb, 1963, 385), archivists were nevertheless 'the guardians of the truth, or, at least, of the evidence on the basis of which truth can be established' (Schellenberg, 1956, 236). This was in contrast to historians, whom he argued could easily lose their balance and objectivity. He described them, in biblical terms, as 'clouds that are carried by the tempest', and his Mennonite education would doubtless have supplied to his mind the rest of the quotation: 'These are wells without water, clouds that are carried with a tempest; to whom the mist of darkness is reserved for ever. For when they speak great swelling words of vanity, they allure through the lusts of the flesh, through much wantonness, those that were clean escaped from them who live in error' (2 Peter 2, 17–18, King James version). Nor was criticism one-way: historians in the 1960s and 70s became less willing to accept archival absences and silences as a fact of life – for those working on formerly marginalized subjects, they were to be investigated and if possible supplemented by the creation or collection of additional sources, through oral history (Thompson, 1978) and 'activist' archival practices (Zinn, 1971; Taylor, 1997; Johnson, 2008).

Meanwhile, archivists began to reject the role which relegated them to support staff in the historiographical process. From the 1970s, archival educators and research-active archivists struggled to define archive administration as a distinctive profession, with numerous statements made in the 1970s and early 1980s which sought to distinguish archives from history, in particular, although the literature tends to be more representative of the opposing position (Taylor, 1977; Cook, 1977–8; Hull, 1980; Nesmith, 1982; Russell, 1983; Bolotenko, 1983; Spencer, 1983–4; Vaisey, 1983–4; Taylor, 1984; Cox, 1984–5; Spandoni, 1984–5). Ongoing debates over professional education asked whether archives (including recordkeeping) could be a discipline in its own right and the establishment of the journal *Archival Science* in 2001 became a milestone in this identification of archives and recordkeeping as a distinct area for academic research. It could be argued, therefore, that what has become known as 'archival science' (see Chapter 5) is too new to engage in interdisciplinary endeavours: interdisciplinarity is certainly a problematic concept in an area which is not universally accepted as a discipline. Disciplinary boundaries are not an inevitable development, and/or necessary for knowledge creation. Since disciplines are themselves an artificial construction, such borrowings are nothing new; however, academic fashion, institutional rationalizations and recent funding streams have encouraged and institutionalized such developments, especially since the 1980s. Borrowings, identified as 'turns', represent an inter- or cross-disciplinary trend as scholars look outside the discipline with which they normally identify, to adopt techniques or approaches from another. Given its history, however, this is not a disciplinary pattern matched by archival science. Although archivists have been exposed to the 'visual turn' (Schwartz, 2004), and the 1990s' interest in codes of ethics could be identified as participation in the 'ethical turn', it has been claimed that archives have never passed through the 'linguistic turn' (Brothman, 1999) and it seems that conscious participation in the 'cultural turn' (Chaney, 1994) also passed us by.

A number of disciplines have recently experienced what have been identified as an 'archival turn', a 'historical turn' or an 'archival impulse' (McDonald, 1996; Comay, 2002; Manoff, 2004; Foster, 2004), first apparent in history in the late 1980s (e.g. Farge, 1989). To some extent, the developments in the separate disciplines are connected, as the practitioners involved are aware of and inspired by one another's methods. Nor can the increased visibility of archives in contemporary culture be ignored: in particular the fall of the Berlin Wall which brought into stark significance the future role of secret police files; issues of data protection and freedom of information are also common cultural currency. The monetary value of the personal archives of writers and artists acquired by universities and art galleries has been the subject of media debate and the collections thus formed have provided resources for study and intensified interest in writers' and artists' documentary practices. There are thus commonalities to be explored. There are, however, important distinctions to be made between approaches, which can be related to disciplinary differences.

The attack on the archive

Although the chronology is by no means clear-cut, this chapter argues that the 'archival turn' represents a reassessment of the positive value of archives, in the wake of the criticism they have received. The 'truth-claims' of archives have been subjected to attack from both outside and within the profession – indeed, this is one of the themes on which archival writings have been most frequently quoted by 'outsiders' (e.g. Booth, 2006). Archival theory has become familiar with (and often insufficiently critical of) the charge that the archive is an agent of oppression – this view is associated most closely with Foucault and Derrida but prefiguring their accusations lie the thoughts of Walter Benjamin. In another famous quotation, he noted:

> There is no document of civilization which is not at the same time a document of barbarism. And just as such a document is not free of barbarism, barbarism taints also the manner in which it was transmitted from one owner to another. A historical materialist therefore dissociates himself [sic] from it as far as possible. He regards it as his task to brush history against the grain.
>
> (Benjamin, 1989, 257)

With such exhortations ringing in their ears, it is easy to see how critical theorists can seem hostile to the archive. It is yet another institution to be subjected to critique. Acceptance of and working with the historical contingencies of historical records is not the aim of most 'archival turn' scholars. Traditional archives (the 'organic', institutional, or bureaucratic archives upheld by Jenkinson as the pinnacle of documentary objectivity) in particular, have been censured for their exclusions, their silencings and their active involvement in oppression. For example, in a recent Canadian conference entitled 'Unforgiving Memory', it was reported that 'the National Archives of Canada were singled out as harbingers of brutal Anglo-colonialism' (Kabatoff, 2001).

The violence in such comments is notable. Whether this results from disillusionment that a resource once believed to be authoritative has been revealed to have feet of clay, from avant-gardist or iconoclastic desire, or merely ignorance of methodological commonplaces may be debated (Johnes, 2007); it cannot, however, be denied that exploration of the fictive nature of archival material has had a wide response, from scholars in numerous disciplines, to artists, such as Jamie Shovlin, whose 'Naomi V. Jelish' (2001–4, Saatchi Collection) is an entirely fictive, or forged, archive (Shovlin, 2004). This work exhibited the drawings said to be by a disappeared schoolgirl, whose disappearance was attested by newspaper cuttings and diaries, which were displayed alongside documents associated with John Ivesmail, the schoolteacher said to have found her drawings.

Documents become clues and evidence of a life never-lived and a lost innocence that never was. As deconstructions of the archive, artistic works are often conceptually derivative with little original to say, other than to those who have not previously recognized the fragility of archival truth-claims (Baron, 2007; Godfrey, 2007). As artistic strategies and aesthetic objects, however, they offer possibilities not available to those working in a textual medium. In particular, they allow the investigation of archives to be represented by non-narrative, even non-textual, means. This means, however, that verbal discussion of these works inevitably simplifies them, for it is where language fails that they offer the most rewarding experiences. Archival artworks can provide opportunities for reflection on the material and experiential qualities of the archive, aspects which the information science or content-driven aspects of archival science tend to overlook, particularly in the drive to digitization and mass consumption of archives (Yee, 2007).

Within archival literature, critique of archival construction is carried out primarily in relation to issues of appraisal and acquisition. Outside our domain, equal attention is given to the internal dimension of archival systems and structures, in particular the question of classification. It is commonly assumed that classification (the deliberate structuring of information or objects according to a taxonomy which is logically separable from the material being classified) is a basic principle of archiving. As an example of this assumption, we read: 'The Nazis were master archivists. This becomes clear when we realize that the most notorious concentration camp, Auschwitz, the name of which has become synonymous with the Holocaust, was modeled on archival principles' (Alphen, 2008, 67). The 'archival principles' are defined as 'fanatical' list-making, transformation from individual, known by name, to object within a larger collective, known by number and sorting into groups on the basis of a fixed set of categories. Each of these activities is likened to processes within both archives and museums, but are described as 'archival' rather than 'museological'. Classification is another theme which has captured the imagination of artists interested in interrogating the archive: from Christian Boltanski's projects from 1988 onwards (Hobbs, 1998; Alphen, 2009) to Ydessa Hendeles's 2002 work *Partners (The Teddy Bear Project)*, both of which make specific reference to the Holocaust (Alphen, 2009).

As archivists, we are very alert to the differences between archives, museums and libraries. Archives are ordered according to principles of *fonds*, provenance and original order: these may be (relatively) fixed principles but their details cannot be known without reference to the specifics of individual archives. Unlike a library or museum, where the classification scheme can exist entirely independently of the collections, archivists do not normally create taxonomies into which archival *fonds* (records defined as a unit by virtue of the circumstances of their creation: ISAD(G), 10 (International Council on Archives, 2000), or their contents, are slotted. It is a basic tenet of archival science that individual items within an archive take their meaning in part from their relationship with the other items within that archive and that that relationship is defined by the original creators and by the users of the records, not the archivist. The physical sorting of Jews from non-Jews, men from women, potential workers from the infirm which took place at Auschwitz destroyed existing relationships and is thus in direct contravention of professional archival principles. For archivists, the use of such classification schemes generally reflects a failure in recordkeeping earlier in the life cycle, such that the creator(s)' intended order is unidentifiable. The other role of taxonomies lies in the use of thesauri for indexing. Undoubtedly an index is yet another system which both permits and limits different possibilities of access (the gendered nature of many thesauri is often cited, e.g. Burton, 2004, 283–4), however the primary purpose of indexing is not to control the inherent chaos of the archive or to silence subversive aspects, but rather to assist the user by allowing the archive to be accessed according to a variety of orders, without making any permanent change to its original structure.

The notion of the 'archive' as both a totality of knowledge and as an actively constructed collection has been promulgated in particular by Richards (1993), a key text for postcolonial and literary studies. Richards correlated Britain's creation of an empire with the collection and organization of knowledge about that empire, the one being impossible without the other. The 'archive' thus becomes an agent of imperialism, fundamental to maintaining the fiction of identity and control which an empire requires (see Anderson, 1983). Richards openly referred to Foucault's use of the 'a' word but the institutions to which he made most frequent reference are museums: the British Museum, with its universal collecting policy, and the Lahore Museum of Kipling's *Kim*. There is, however, no evidence that the institutions and practices described were ever defined by their contemporaries as 'archival': the ahistorical nature of archival identifications is a problem in much 'archival turn' scholarship (e.g. Spieker, 2008). The extension of the 'a' word's remit to cover literary *corpora* (Derrida, 1996, 3) and canons also refers to the interpretation of the archive as an active construction, which excludes as well as includes and which is always open to new exclusions/additions (in contrast to the traditional archival *fonds*). Nevertheless, as archivists, we are not entirely innocent of such expansionist tendencies, for much archival literature shows similar trends, especially our interest in 'documentation strategies' and 'total archives' which include materials ranging far beyond institutional, or bureaucratic, archives.

Recognition of the limitations of institutional archives has encouraged 'archival turn' scholars to look elsewhere for their source material: to museums, libraries, oral history, etc. Again, none of this is new, but the indiscriminate labelling of these resources as 'archival' *is* a more modern phenomenon and surely relates to the identification of archival research as a fundamental characteristic of the disciplines involved. The definition of all the traces of the past (or pasts) as 'archival' has been supported by Foucault's identification of the 'archive' with the 'episteme', a metaphysical system which determines what can, and what cannot, be conceptualized and spoken at any given point in time. This metaphorical usage may be disconcerting to some archivists (e.g. Marquis, 2006, 36), but to others it may chime with the records continuum notion of the archive as a system into which individual records are captured but which is not identical to the totality of all the records it contains.

Although confusion over classification probably stems from the identification of all types of informational resource as 'archival', nevertheless, here again there are aspects of archival theory which should give us pause for thought. For the structuring of institutional archives by their creators usually *does* involve taxonomies, subject-based classification schemes, file plans and naming conventions. Traditionally, these are systems associated with records management, rather than archiving, and their implementers are not 'archivists'. In the earlier quotation, it would be undeniable that the Nazis, in common with most totalitarian regimes, were fanatical creators of archives. But if the archive is held to pre-exist the act of consignment (the decision to preserve for posterity, the crossing of the archival threshold), as in continuum thinking, this eliminates the boundaries between records and archives and between the cultural role of the archivist and the bureaucratic role of the records manager (Greene, 2002; Moss, 2006). It therefore becomes harder to draw a clear distinction between the records' manager's construction of systems to assist the purposes of the records' creators and the archivist's maintenance of those systems as an important aspect of their context. As archivists, we need therefore to be clear that we are maintaining that framework not in order to uphold 'the continuum of historical succession' (Benjamin, 1999, 475 [N10, 3]) but to provide a context from which the individual archival object can be 'torn' by the user (Benjamin, 1999, 476 [N11, 3]). Carolyn Steedman has described this relationship: 'The Archive then is something that, through the cultural activity of History, can become Memory's potential space, one of the few realms of the modern imagination where hard-won and carefully constructed place can return to boundless, limitless space' (Steedman, 1998, 83). Whether History is the only activity that can exploit archives' potential should be questioned but her recognition that archival power may be unleashed in countless directions, but that it only represents potential until used, should be welcomed. The archivist's role is to maintain the archive in a state of readiness for such use – and this chapter will now consider in more detail the role of archives within the practices of the three disciplines, and how these relate to the practices of the archivist.

The archive and the anecdote

In his essay on the craft of the historian, unfinished at his death by Nazi firing squad in 1944, Marc Bloch reflected both on the nature of the archive and the way in which historians should make their methods visible. His words are prescient:

> Despite what the beginners sometimes seem to imagine, documents do not suddenly materialize, in one place or another, as if by some mysterious decree of the gods. Their presence or absence in the depths of this archive or library are due to human causes which by no means elude analysis. The problems posed by their transmission, far from having importance only for the technical experts, are most intimately connected with the life of the past, for what is here at stake is nothing less than the passing down of memory from one generation to another.
>
> (Bloch, 1953, 71)

He went on to suggest that the normal practice of listing the archival files consulted is insufficient – the historian should instead include a series of paragraphs at relevant points entitled 'How can I know what I am about to say?', telling the story of the investigation, with its successes and reverses.

This approach did not become normal practice: indeed the *annaliste* tradition which Bloch helped found focused less on archives than on long durational trends. For Fernand Braudel, another pioneering *Annaliste*, the pleasures of the archive were dangerous distractions. As he recalled in 1972: 'I remember my delight in discovering the marvellous registers of Ragusa at Dubrovnik in 1934: at last, here were ships, bills of lading, trade goods, insurance rates, business deals. For the first time I saw the Mediterranean of the sixteenth century' (Braudel, 1972b, 452). Archives were filled with 'that miscellany of trivia and daily happenings which rises like a cloud of dust from any living civilization' (Braudel, 1972a, II, 758). Such sources are 'the most exciting of all, the richest in human interest, and also the most dangerous. We must learn to distrust this history with its still burning passions, as it was felt, described, and lived by contemporaries whose lives were as short and as short-sighted as ours' (Braudel, 1972a, I, 12).

In Braudel's image (surely a reference to its use by the 19th-century French historian Jules Michelet) 'dust' is not literal: it refers instead to the anecdotes, or 'historemes', which have often been the building blocks of historiography (Fineman, 1989, 57). The 'archival turn' was preceded and to a certain extent prefigured by the importance of 'microhistory' and 'New Historicism' (in literary studies), which relied on archival anecdotes for both strategic and narrative purposes. Partly as a reaction against the *longue durée* approach of the mid-century *Annalistes*, with its deliberate rejection of human content, historians like Carlo Ginzburg, Robert Darnton and Natalie Zemon Davis focused on minute incidents or single individuals, discovered through archival research, as entry points into contemporary world views. Through their work, the reader is introduced to Mennocchio, the cosmologically minded miller of Friuli (Ginzburg, 1980), a massacre of cats in 18th-century Paris (Darnton, 1984) and the is-he or isn't he? figure of Martin Guerre, later made into a film (Davis, 1983). Emphasis on the specific (termed by Clifford Geertz 'thick description'), rather than the contextual, forms a powerful narrative device which has also been used by New Historicists. Each of the chapters of

Greenblatt (1988), opens with a story, rarely uncovered by Greenblatt himself, but redolent of archival discovery and again, used to construct a context for the Shakespearean text. However, the effect here is self-consciously literary, delighting in the juxtaposition of seemingly unrelated events and asserting the aesthetic within literary studies (Laden, 2004). It should, however, be noted that other scholars have criticized each of these works for over- or mis-interpretation of their archival sources (Evans, 1997, 245–8): a work may both foreground the archive and use other strategies of historical reconstruction at one and the same time.

Anecdotes and narratives form an important aspect of one strand of the artistic practices identified as 'archival' (Foster, 2004). Some works have involved research by the artist, for example Tacita Dean's series of works *Disappearance at Sea* (from 1996), researching, documenting and meditating upon the story, the faked logbook and the beached boat of the would-be round-the-world yachtsman Donald Crowhurst (Dean, 1999). Another approach, also employed by Dean (2001), is the use of 'found' materials (often photographs). These documents without context, whose poignancy lies in their resultant inability to communicate their intentions, are, like the historeme, available for insertion into new contexts, constructed by the artist or by the viewer. Such works play on the audience's desire to find meanings and make connections: viewers try to contextualize the images, or find in them a narrative, but the impossibility of the endeavour forces them to recognize the muteness of photographs and the loss of identity of those portrayed in them. The idea of the *objet trouvé* may have originated in art, but as a metaphor it has also resonated with historians: as Eric Hobsbawm wrote, 'If history is an imaginative art, it is one which does not invent but arranges *objets trouvés*' (Hobsbawm, 1997, 359).

'Archival turn' scholarship across the disciplines shares an awareness of the tensions between the specific, which the researcher is normally seeking, and the totality of the archive, which tends to 'slip away into the background' (Orlow, 2006a, 40). As a deliberate contrast to the normal focus on the detail (Osborne, 1999, 58), Uriel Orlow's *Housed Memory* consists of nine hours of video, with the handheld camera tracking the shelves of the Wiener Library (London), whilst voices of the library's staff and users explain what the library and its contents mean to them. The length of the piece bears witness to the sheer scale of the collection, and thus the scale of the atrocity it documents (the Holocaust). The tracking technique references Alain Resnais' film, *Toute la mémoire du monde* (1956) about the Bibliothèque Nationale and, just as pertinently, his earlier film *Nuit et Brouillard* (1955), the first documentary film to tackle the Holocaust, in which the tracking shots along the empty triple-decker bunks of the dormitory quarters of the concentration camp prefigure his use of the same technique along the library shelves. The fullness of the library forms a stark contrast with the empty bunks; equally harrowing is the 1955 film's use of archival material, including camp registers written for their captors by the prisoners themselves, exactly the type of record now held at the Wiener Library. The soundtrack of Orlow's video makes another subtle point. That archives allow the voices of the past to be heard is a common trope in historiography, from Michelet onwards. Yet in reality, archives are hushed – it is only in their users' imagination that their voices may be heard. In the film, the contents of the archive boxes are not merely silent, but also invisible; all we hear are the experiences of those in the present who have access to the pasts' soundless traces. Yet despite the melancholy of absence, the work is also evidence of a form of triumph. The Nazi burning of books has been reversed and the contents of the library have been used to call war criminals to account.

That archival anecdotes could be used to subvert, rather than to compose, the metanarratives of history is a possibility that has excited critical scholars from Walter Benjamin (1892–1940) onwards. Benjamin's historical materialist method, exemplified in his unfinished *Arcades (Das Passagen-Werk) Project* consisted of collecting a montage of quotations, assembled into subject files, interfused with commentaries. His 'constructive' approach was in deliberate contrast to the 'additive' method of conventional historiography and had emancipatory intentions. Differentiating his work from the famous goal of Leopold von Ranke, Benjamin argued 'The history that showed things "as they really were" was the strongest narcotic of the century' (Benjamin, 1999, 463 [N3, 4]). Each quotation was 'torn from its context' (Benjamin, 1999, 476 [N11, 3]) as part of a revolutionary commitment to wresting the past from the possibility of its appropriation by a present unsympathetic to its casualties. Practitioners of the New Historicism have also voiced a commitment to emancipatory political ideals, suggesting the possibility of alternative potential futures within each moment of the past, whilst Hal Foster has welcomed the 'archival impulse' as evidence of greater political commitment by artists (Foster, 2004). The ideal of salvaging the past's victims by giving voice once more to their stories was the aim of Foucault in his 'The Life of Infamous Men' (Foucault, 1979); such a project has also been described by Jacques Rancière in his *The Names of History* (1994), again taking inspiration from Michelet (and Benjamin).

The archive and research

Microhistory and New Historicism were both products of a period when poststructuralism had begun to question the preconceptions of traditional methods and objectives, and and openness was being shown to the new approach, without accepting all its claims.

Deconstructionist historians have focused on the unknowability of the past reality, rather than the knowability of its present traces. It is often contended that the identification of some 'traces of the past' as 'original sources' inevitably suggests that by using them the historian claims to have achieved 'genuine (true/deep) knowledge' (Jenkins, 1991, 47). This thus 'fetishises documents, and distorts the whole working process of making history'. Having released his readers from the idea that primary sources are the foundations of history, Keith Jenkins (perhaps the foremost proponent of deconstructionist history in the UK) has maintained that 'the debate over evidence need not detain us long' (Jenkins, 1991, 48), being merely a relic of the Carr/Elton debate of the 1960s (Carr, 1961; Elton, 1967). Neither Hayden White and Frank Ankersmit, whose emphasis on the narrativity of history did much to shape the debate, nor their other followers had much to say about archives, but the explicitly Derridean tone of Jenkins' more recent work, however, resulted in the introduction of the adjective 'archival' to qualify the past's traces (Jenkins, 2003, 39). By his use of the word 'archival', not 'historical', Jenkins intended to liberate these traces from their inevitable connection with historians: 'they can become the objects of enquiry of any number of discourses without belonging to any of them; historians have no exclusive rights to the archive' (Jenkins, 2003, 39). Because the past (the 'before now') has no meaningful existence beyond the efforts of historians (or those acting as historians) to impose a structure or form upon it, no one can have a patent on it and anyone can create it in a form suitable to her/his own purposes. 'Consequently, no historian or anyone else acting as if they were a historian returns from his or her trip to "the past" without precisely the historicisation they wanted to get; no one ever comes back surprised or empty-handed from that destination' (ibid., 11). In this respect, Jenkins's 'history' is far closer to what David Lowenthal has identified (and castigated) as 'heritage' (Lowenthal, 1985, 1996 and 2006) and what in archival literature is usually referred to as 'memory'. However, as Lawrence Stone (1992, 193–4) argued, postmodernism's denial of any reality beyond the subjective creation of the historian: 'destroys the difference between fact and fiction, and makes entirely nugatory the dirty and tedious archival work of the historian to dig "facts" out of texts'.

In the aftermath of the postmodernist attack on the positivist notion of Truth, any truth-claims made by either archivists or historians on behalf of archival information are invariably provisional and circumspect, as Stone's use of inverted commas around the word 'fact' suggests. Nevertheless, most historians have rejected the deconstructionist insistence that story-telling lies at the heart of historical practice (e.g. Evans, 1997). As suggested, the opposing view emphasizes the importance of research and hence, of archives. The 'archival turn' may thus be identified as a qualification (but not entire rejection) of poststructuralism's 'linguistic turn'. In art, too, the 'archival impulse' should be related to an emphasis (here new), on research as a defining feature of artistic practice. It is doubtless significant that a number of 'archival' artists have undertaken university-based research projects, some at MA level, some as part of practice-led PhDs (which require a textual representation of the research process) (Smith, 2008, esp. footnotes 15–21) and that their subsequent work has often been supported by artist residency or commissioned projects in collaboration with cultural institutions, including archives. To cite but a few (British) examples, the Jane and Louise Wilson's *Stasi City* (1997), made whilst on a Deutscher Akademischer Austausche Dienst scholarship in Germany and their more recent *Unfolding the Aryan Papers* (2009), based on the Kubrick archive, commissioned by Animate Projects and the British Film Institute (BFI); Ruth Maclennan's Leverhulme artist-in-residence in the London School of Economics and Political Science (LSE) Library Archives, resulting in *The Archives Project: Part 1* and *Out of the Archives* (Donelly, 2008); the Henry Moore Foundation-funded 2005 *Third Campaign* project by Neal White using the Epstein archive at the Henry Moore Institute; Rebecca Spooner's 2006 Artworks Wales-funded collaboration with Newport Museum and Art Gallery entitled 'Rough Notes' (Spooner, 2006) (see also Lewandowska and Cummings, 2000; Orlow, 2006b; Orlow and Maclennan, 2004; Pui San Lok, 2005; Smith, 2006; Lanyon and Connarty, 2006).

Nevertheless, the 'archival turn' should not be viewed as a conservative reassertion of traditional values. The self-identification of its participants as researchers has shifted the epistemological debate from 'What is history/literary studies/art?' to 'What are we doing when we do history (etc.)?' Such questions are the mark of what has been identified as the postepistemological age; they have also been defined as a 'reflexive turn'. An important aspect of the 'archival turn' has been the emergence of reflections on using archives as their own sub-genre, beginning with Farge (1989) and followed by Steedman (2001) and Burton (2005). Initially, this 'reflexive turn' seems yet another example of postmodernist interest in subjectivity, narrativity and institutional critique, especially given the focus on archival absences and censure of recordkeeping practices offered by some of Burton's contributors. However, their reflexivity about their working practices (rather than their autobiography as a whole, for which see Popkin, 2005) represents a departure from the practices of those theorists of most influence on poststructuralist historians (such as Geertz and Bourdieu) (Foley, 2002, 475–6) and, in the case of Steedman, engages critically with Derrida (see the opening quotation to this chapter). Such reflexivity also differentiates 'archival turn' scholars from both practitioners of microhistory and more traditional historical archival scholarship.

In what could perhaps be identified as another manifestation of the 'archival turn', some historians identified as practitioners of 'New History' were interviewed about their work (Pallares-Burke, 2002). Much of what they had to say involved the defence of their methods against the deconstructionist attack. As might be expected, their arguments emphasize the importance of archive study (described by Robert Darnton as 'the artisanal side of historical research' [ibid., 167]) and include personal reports of the archival encounter. These share many similarities – as they do with the tropes of archival research in fiction (Keen, 2001). A common focus is on the physical aspects of the archive (sometimes pleasurable, often uncomfortable) recognizing that these bring a peculiarly direct relationship with the past, through the continuing tangibility of its traces. As Peter Burke (ibid., 140) explains: 'Working in archives is an exciting experience, somewhat different from other kinds of research. It allows a closer relationship with the past, than is usually possible in the case of libraries – reading letters which were not meant for us, for example, with some of the sand that was used to dry the ink still remaining in the envelope after 400 years.' A similar sentiment has been expressed by Tim Hitchcock (2008, 133): 'When you unwrap the parchment document enclosing the two hundred year-old evidence given at a coroner's inquest, and the sand used to blot the ink spills into your lap, it is difficult to maintain an appropriate distance – regardless of whether that distance is post-modern, or empirical in character.' Although such experiences can be dismissed as romantic, even fetishistic (Woods, 2000), they nevertheless account for an important attraction of archival work, which archivists, for whom they may be everyday occurrences, can sometimes overlook in their enthusiasm for seeing archives primarily as information resources.

As Stone's comment, quoted earlier, suggests, the value of archival work is enhanced by emphasis on its tedious, even painful, character, a trope which Steedman satirises in the first chapter of *Dust* (2001). A typical example reads: 'The archives at Lyon, France, are housed in an old convent on a hill overlooking the city. It is reached by walking up some three hundred stone steps. For the practical realist – even one equipped with a laptop computer – the climb is worth the effort; the relativist [i.e. the post-modernist] might not bother' (Appleby, Hunt and Jacob, 1994, 251). In such narratives, the archive and the archivist rarely fare well. We are well aware that as well as being hewers of wood and drawers of water, we are gatekeepers and dragons (in cardigans); we should also recognize that our commitment to widening access may have made our searchrooms less welcoming to their traditional occupants (Mortimer, 2002). At times, accounts of archival research read as black romances: 'As we know, seduction is often necessary to soften a recalcitrant curator when pressure and menace have failed, but sadism is always present as well' (Guilbaut, 2008, 110), or as epic struggles between the stubborn record and the heroic historian: 'To get something out of archives, you better beat the world/word out of all that dust. After having traced archives for so long like a private eye, you need to force them to surrender some form of meaning, and torture might at times be necessary to achieve the connections you actually need and want' (ibid., 111). The violence of the archive (Derrida, 1996, 7) is met by the violence of the researcher: in vain the archivist might plead that torture rarely produces useful information!

Another common feature of these accounts is a moment of revelation; for example, Carlo Ginzburg recalled: 'When I discovered the document on the *benandanti*, for instance, I was more or less working at random, but when I saw it as potentially relevant, it's because I was already involved and interacting with it, so to speak. Usually my works start from a flash, from a sort of Aha! reaction, and then I have to unfold this Aha! in order to discover the question' (Pallares-Burke, 2002, 203). The moment of recognition, or 'archival jolt' (O'Driscoll and Bishop, 2004, 2) is one which many archivists will have experienced; it may even have been the lure which brought some of us into the profession. The experience has been analysed in some detail by Roland Barthes (1993, 22–30), writing of photographs, observations which seem equally applicable to other documentary forms. Barthes identified two types of relationship between the spectator and the photograph: '*studium*' and '*punctum*'. *Studium* enables the spectator to understand the information conveyed by the photograph, allowing her/him to engage with the photographer's intentions. In recordkeeping terms, this type of encounter can be facilitated by appropriate practices, providing the user with information about the document's context of creation and thus its intended meaning. Although he does not acknowledge it, Barthes's analysis of the photographs whose affect alerted him to the *studium* response, depended on their situation within a magazine, enabling him to identify their subject matter as conflict in Nicaragua and their photographer as Koen Wessing. The second reaction, the *punctum,* is entirely personal: 'it is what I add to the photograph and *what is nonetheless already there*' (ibid., 55). It leads the viewer's imagination outwards into the blind field of the photograph, the life of its subjects, external to the document (ibid., 57). This individual response can neither be predicted, nor predicated, on any deliberate action by the archivist, which surely accounts for our invisibility in descriptions of the archival encounter. We must accept that we *are* marginal to the experience. Like the civil servants on whom Jenkinson modelled his ideal archivist, we may engineer circumstances but the affect depends on a fiction of being alone with the past (Steedman, 2001, 81).

There is, however, a difference between the 'Aha!' moment experienced by the archivist and that of the historian, because each is interacting with the archive for different purposes. The *punctum* experience is always one of chance, the unexpected connection between viewer/reader, archival content and the context of its use (i.e. specifically not the context the archivist aims to preserve). Because the *punctum* experience has no direct relationship to any action taken by the archivist, s/he has no need to unfold it, to discover the question: it is merely one of the incidental joys of archival work. By contrast, for the historian, the *punctum* represents a turning point in research. Keith Thomas recalled the origin of his *Religion and the Decline of Magic* being 'a tiny scrap of paper', a note written by the Leveller, Richard Overton, to the astrologer William Lilly, pinned inside one of Lilly's casebooks. Further consideration of this miniscule item, which had nevertheless caught his attention, led to his recognition that Lilly's casebooks, the record of his consultation with around two thousand clients each year, could be a wonderful source for the hopes and fears of 17th-century people (Pallares-Burke, 2002, 97).

The 'unfolding of the Aha!' involves trying to identify the relationship between the *punctum*, the element or anecdote which has caught the historian's attention and the context s/he is investigating. On many occasions, the *punctum* is a moment when the strangeness of the past and its recognizability enter into a new relationship. Robert Darnton described the experience thus:

> The reason for [archival research] being invigorating is that you go to the archives with conceptions, patterns and hypotheses, having, so to speak, a picture of what you think the past was like. And then, you find some strange letter that doesn't correspond to the picture at all. So what is happening is a dialogue between your preconceptions and your general way of envisaging a field, on the one hand, and on the other hand, this raw material that you dig out and that often does not fit into the picture.
>
> (Darnton, 1984, 169)

A similar sentiment is voiced by Patrick Wright (2007): 'I also use archives a lot, not just as repositories of detail that can be lined up as evidence to justify preconceived conclusions, but as a way of defamiliarizing and questioning present conformities.' Here again the archive is presented as having disruptive potential: research is presented as a confrontation with otherness.

Conclusion: Beyond the 'archival turn'

Although the ideas of Foucault and Derrida have inspired and informed much of the debate associated with the 'archival turn', they should not be seen as its sole point of origin (indeed, both writers are very dismissive of the search for origins and influences). As has been shown, there are issues of disciplinary identity, contexts of funding and institutional support and wider cultural factors at work as well. Moreover, there are signs within 'archival turn' scholarship that there is a move to turn sites of excavation (the Foucauldian model) into sites of construction (the Benjaminian model), an intention that the past should no longer be viewed as holding no possibilities other than the traumatic (Foster, 2004, 22). Institutional critique is moving once more towards qualified celebration – as one archive user (Ferguson, 2008) has asked 'While taking recent critiques of archives seriously, why not facilitate those sorts of archival spaces in which we can dance?'

The new ideas of archive are ones with which the archival profession should engage, not in a defensive rearguard action, nor in a spirit of pathetic gratitude that it is our 'turn' now (especially since, after 20 years, it seems likely that the current 'archival turn' will soon have run its course). We have a role to play in these debates over the archive (more multifarious than even my lengthy bibliography); through our active participation, they can become an opportunity to expand our own discourse and celebrate our interdisciplinary status. Far from being a storehouse, plundered by other disciplines, the archive is, or could be, the shared territory in which scholars make encounters, across which bridges can be built to mutual benefit. Some important collaborative work has been done, but most of the archivists who are seeking to share and compare their understandings of the archive with those in other disciplines, seem to feel themselves to be isolated pioneers. The profession as a whole appears too willing to dismiss alternative ideas of the archive as incorrect, and therefore unhelpful, rather than different, and therefore potentially revelatory. Understandings may be extended if the encounter with alterity, both archival and disciplinary (the hallmark of true research), becomes the occasion for identifying the peculiarities and constructive possibilities of different archival formations as evidential and experiential resources. Instead of allowing all forms of evidence about the past and all types of repository to merge into a uniformly khaki 'archive', archival scholars from all disciplines can come to recognize, investigate and wonder at their diverse and distinctive hues.

References

Alphen, E. van (2008) Archival Obsessions and Obsessive Archives. In Holly, M. A. and Smith, M. (eds), *What is Research in the Visual Arts? Obsession, archive, encounter*, Clark Studies in the Visual Arts, Sterling and Francine Clark Fine Art Institute.

Alphen, E. van (2009) Visual Archives and the Holocaust: Christian Boltanski, Ydessa Hendeles and Peter Fogacs. In Van den Braembussche, A., Van, Kimmerle, H. and Note, N. (eds), *Intercultural Aesthetics: a worldview perspective*, Springer. Also available online, www.springerlink.com/content/q830968498237856/fulltext.pdf.

Anderson, B. (1983) *Imagined Communities: reflections on the origins and spread of nationalism,* Verso.

Appleby, J. O., Hunt, L. and Jacob, M. (1994) *Telling the Truth about History*, W. W. Norton.

Baron, J. (2007) Contemporary Documentary Film and 'Archive Fever': history, the fragment, the joke, *The Velvet Light Trap*, **60**, 13–24.

Barthes, R. (1993) *Camera Lucida: reflections on photography*, (trans. Howard, R.), originally pub. in French in 1980, Vintage.

Benjamin, W. (1989) Theses on the Philosophy of History. In Bronner, S. E. (ed.), *Critical Theory and Society: a reader*, Routledge.

Benjamin, W. (1999) *The Arcades Project*, (trans. Eiland, H. and McLaughlin, K.), Harvard University Press.

Bloch, M. (1953) *The Historian's Craft*, (trans. Putnam, P.), Vintage.

Bolotenko, G. (1983) Archivists and Historians: keepers of the well, *Archivaria*, **16**, 5–25.

Booth, D. (2006) Sites of Truth or Metaphors of Power? Refiguring the archive, *Sport in History*, **26** (1), 91–109.

Braudel, F. (1972a) *The Mediterranean and the Mediterranean World in the Age of Philip II*, 2nd edn, (trans. Reynolds, S.), 2 vols, Collins.

Braudel, F. (1972b) Personal Testimony, *Journal of Modern History*, **44** (4), 448–67.

Brothman, B. (1999) Declining Derrida: integrity, tensegrity, and the preservation of archives from deconstruction, *Archivaria*, **48**, 64–88.

Burton, A. (2004) Archive Stories: gender in the making of imperial and colonial histories. In Levine (ed.), *Gender and Empire*, The Oxford History of the British Empire Companion Series, Oxford University Press, 281–93.

Burton, A. (ed.) (2005) *Archive Stories: facts, fictions and the writing of history*, Duke University Press.

Carr, E.H. (1961) *What is History?*, Penguin.

Chabin, M.-A. (1996) Les Nouvelles Archives ou Conclusion d'une Revue de Presse (The New Archives or Conclusions of a Media Review), *Gazette des Archives*, **172**, 107–30.

Chabin, M.-A. (2002) Presentations at the International Conference of the Round Table on Archives 2002 (abstract in English, http://old.ica.org/new/citra.php?pcitraprogramid=12&plangue=eng.

Chabin, M.-A. (2005) Presentation at the meeting of the Association of Catalan Archivists (PowerPoint presentation, www.archive17.fr/images/pdf/barcelone_archive_chabin.pdf.

Chaney, D. C. (1994) *The Cultural Turn: scene-setting essays on contemporary cultural history*, Routledge.

Cheetham, M. E., Holly, M. A. and Moxey, K. (eds) (1998) *The Subjects of Art History: historical objects in contemporary perspectives*, Cambridge University Press.

Comay, R. (ed.) (2002) *Lost in the Archives*, Alphabet City.

Cook, T. (1977–8) Clio: The Archivist's Muse?, *Archivaria*, **5**, 198–203.

Cox, R. (1984–5) Archivists and Historians: a view from the United States, *Archivaria*, **19**, 185–90.

Darnton, R. (1984) *The Great Cat Massacre and Other Episodes in French Cultural History*, Penguin.

Davis, N. Z. (1983) *The Return of Martin Guerre*, Harvard University Press.

Dean, T. (1999) *Teignmouth Electron*, Bookworks in association with the National Maritime Museum.

Dean, T. (2001) *Floh*, Steidl.

Deleuze, G. (1999) *Foucault*, (trans. and ed. by Hand, S.), Continuum.

Derrida, J. (1996) *Archive Fever: a Freudian impression*, (trans. Prenowitz, E.), University of Chicago Press.

Donelly, S. (2008) Art in the Archives: an artist's residency in the archives of the London School of Economics, www.tate.org.uk/research/tateresearch/tatepapers/08spring/donnelly.shtm.

Elton, G.R. (1967) *The Practice of History*, Sydney University Press.

Evans, R.J. (1997) *In Defence of History*, Granta.

Farge, A. (1989) *Le Goût de l'Archive*, Le Seuil.

Ferguson, K. E. (2008) Theorizing Shiny Things: archival labors, *Theory & Event*, **11** (4), http://muse.jhu.edu/journals/theory_and_event/v011/11.4.ferguson.html.

Fineman, J. (1989) The History of the Anecdote: fiction and fiction. In Aram Veeser, H. (ed.), *The New Historicism*, Routledge.

Foley, D. E. (2002) Critical Ethnography: the reflexive turn, *Qualitative Studies in Education*, **15** (5), 469–90.

Foster, H. (2004) An Archival Impulse, *October*, **110**, 3–22.

Foucault, M. (1979) The Life of Infamous Men. In Foss, P. and Morris, M. (eds), *Power, Truth, Strategy*, Feral Press.

Ginzburg, C. (1980) *The Cheese and the Worms: the cosmos of a sixteenth-century miller*, Johns Hopkins University Press.

Godfrey, M. (2007) The Artist as Historian, *October*, **120**, 140–72.

Greenblatt, S. (1988) *Shakespearean Negotiations: the circulation of social energy in Elizabethan England*, Clarendon Press.

Greenblatt, S. (1997) The Touch of the Real, *Representations*, **59**, 14–29.

Greene, M.A. (2002) The Power of Meaning: The Archival Mission in the Postmodern Age, *The American Archivist*, **65** (1), 42–55.

Guilbaut, S. (2008) Factory of Facts: research as obsession with the scent of history. In Holly, M. A. and Smith, A. (eds), *What is Research in the Visual Arts? Obsession, archive, encounter*, Clark Studies in the Visual Arts, Sterling and Francine Clark Fine Art Institute.

Hitchcock, T. (2008) Digital Searching and the Re-formulation of Historical Knowledge. In Greengrass, M. and Hughes, L. (eds), *The Virtual Representation of the Past*, Ashgate.

Hobbs, R. (1998) Boltanski's Visual Archives, *History of the Human Sciences*, 11 **(4),** 121–40.

Hobsbawm, E. (1997) *On History*, Weidenfeld & Nicholson.

Hull, F. (1980) The Archivist should not be a Historian, *Journal of the Society of Archivists*, **6** (5) 253–9.

International Council on Archives/Conseil International des Archives (2000) *ISAD(G): General International Standard Archival Description: adopted by the Committee on Descriptive Standards, Stockholm, Sweden, 19–22 September 1999*, 2nd edn, 10, www.ica.org/sites/default/files/isad_g_2e.pdf.

Jenkins, K. (1991) *Re-thinking History*, Routledge.

Jenkins, K. (2003) *Refiguring History: new thoughts on an old discipline*, Routledge.

Jenkinson, C.H. (1947) The English Archivist: a new profession, given as the

inaugural lecture of the course on Archive Administration at University
College London in 1947. In Ellis, R.H. and Walne, P. (eds), *Selected Writings of
Sir Hilary Jenkinson*, Alan Sutton.

Jenkinson, C. H. (1966[1922]) *A Manual of Archive Administration*, 2nd edn, Lund
Humphries.

Johnes M. (2007) Archives, Truths and the Historian at Work: a reply to Douglas
Booth's refiguring the archive, *Sport in History*, **27** (1), 127–35.

Johnson, E. S. (2008) Our Archives, Our Selves: documentation strategy and the
re-appraisal of professional identity, *The American Archivist*, **71** (1), 190–202.

Kabatoff, M. (2001) Report on the conference 'Unforgiving Memory' held at the
Banff New Media Institute, 22–25 August,
www.banffcentre.ca/bnmi/programs/archives/2001/unforgiving_memory/re
ports/unforgiving_memory_report.pdf.

Keen, S. (2001) *Romances of the Archive in Contemporary British Fiction*, University of
Toronto Press.

Laden, S. (2004) Recuperating the Archive: anecdotal evidence and questions of
'Historical Realism', *Poetics Today*, **25** (1), Spring, 1–28.

Lamb, W. K. (1963) The Archivist and the Historian, *American Historical Review*, **62**
(2), 385–91.

Langlois, C. V. and Seignobos, C. (1932) *Introduction to the Study of History*, (trans.
Berry, G. G.), with preface by F. York Powell, H. Holt (originally published
1897).

Lanyon, J. and Connarty, J. (eds) (2006) *Ghosting: the role of the archive within
contemporary artists' film and video*, Picture This Moving Image.

Levine, P. (1986) *The Amateur and the Professional: antiquarians, historians and
archaeologists in Victorian England 1838–1886*, Cambridge University Press.

Lewandowska, M. and Cummings, N. (2000) *Documents*, PhotoWorks.

Lowenthal, D. (1985) *The Past is a Foreign Country*, Cambridge University Press.

Lowenthal, D. (1996) *The Heritage Crusade and the Spoils of History*, Viking.

Lowenthal, D. (2006) Archives, Heritage, and History. In Blouin jr, F.X. and
Rosenberg, W. G., *Archives, Documentation, and Institutions of Social Memory: essays
from the Sawyer Seminar*, University of Michigan Press.

Manoff, M. (2004) Theories of the Archive from Across the Disciplines, *portal:
Libraries and the Academy*, **4** (1), 9–25.

McDonald, T. J. (1996) *The Historic Turn in the Human Sciences*, University of
Michigan Press.

Marquis, K. (2006) Not Dragon at the Gate but Research Partner: the reference archivist as mediator. In Blouin jr., F. X. and Rosenberg, W. G., *Archives, Documentation, and Institutions of Social Memory: essays from the Sawyer Seminar,* University of Michigan Press.

Mortimer, I. (2002) Discriminating Between Readers: the case for a policy of flexibility, *Journal of the Society of Archivists,* **23** (1), 59–67.

Moss, M. (2006) Archivist Friend or Foe?, *Records Management Journal,* **15** (2), 104–14.

Munslow, A. (1997) *Deconstructing History,* Routledge.

Nesmith, T. (1982) Archives from the Bottom Up: social history and archival scholarship, *Archivaria,* **14,** 5–26.

O'Driscoll, M. and E. Bishop (2004) Archiving 'Archiving', *English Studies in Canada,* **30** (1), 1–16.

Orlow, U. (2006a) Latent Archive, Roving Lens. In Connarty, J. and Lanyon, J. (eds), *Ghosting: the role of the archive within contemporary artists' film and video,* Picture This Moving Image.

Orlow, U. (2006b) *Deposits,* Green Box.

Orlow, U. and R. Maclennan (2004) *Re: the archive, the image, and the very dead sheep,* School of Advanced Study and TNA.

Osborne, T. (1999) The Ordinariness of the Archive, *History of the Human Sciences,* **12** (2), 51–64.

Pallares-Burke, M.-L. (2002) *The New History: confessions and conversations,* Polity Press.

Popkin, J. D. (2005) *History, Historians, and Autobiography,* University of Chicago Press.

Procter, M. (2006) Consolidation and Separation: British archives and American historians at the turn of the twentieth century, *Archival Science,* **6** (3–4), 361–79.

Pui San Lok, S. (2005) *News,* Aldgate Press.

Rancière, J. (1994) *The Names of History: on the poetics of knowledge,* (trans. Melehy, H.), University of Minnesota Press.

Richards, T. (1993) *The Imperial Archive: knowledge and the fantasy of empire,* Verso.

Russell, M. U. (1983) The Influence of Historians on the Archival Profession in the United States, *American Archivist,* **4** (3), 277–85.

Schellenberg, T. R. (1956) *Modern Archives: principles and techniques,* F.W. Cheshire.

Schellenberg, T. R. (1969) Obituary of T. R. Schellenberg, *Mennonite Research in Progress,* www.bethelks.edu/mennonitelife/bibliographies/1969a.pdf.

Schwartz, J. M. (2004) Negotiating the Visual Turn: new perspectives on images and archives, *American Archivist,* **67** (1), 107-22.

Shovlin, J. (2004) Naomi V. Jelish archive website: www.naomivjelish.org.uk/homepage.htm.

Smith, M. (2006) Journeys, Documenting, Indexing, Archives, and Practice-based Research: a conversation with Susan Pui San Lok, *Art Journal*, **65** (4), 18–35.

Smith, M. (2008) Why 'What is Research in the Visual Arts?: Obsession, archive, encounter'?, in Holly, M. A. and Smith, M. (eds), *What is Research in the Visual Arts? Obsession, archive, encounter*, Clark Studies in the Visual Arts, Sterling and Francine Clark Fine Art Institute, x–xxvi.

Spandoni, C. (1984–5) In Defence of the New Professionalism: a rejoinder to George Bolotenko, *Archivaria*, **19**, 191–5.

Spencer, T. T. (1983–4) The Archivist as Historian: towards a broader definition, *Archivaria*, **17**, 296–300.

Spieker, S. (2008) *The Big Archive: art from bureaucracy*, MIT.

Spooner, R. (2006) 'Rough Notes', www.axisweb.org/atSelection.aspx?SELECTIONID=15395 (with thanks to Rebecca Spooner for providing me with a CD of the project).

Steedman, C. (1998) The Space of Memory: in an archive, *History of the Human Sciences*, **11** (4), 65–83.

Steedman, C. (2001) *Dust*, Manchester University Press.

Steedman, C. (2006) 'Something She Called a Fever': Michelet, Derrida, and Dust (Or, in the Archives with Michelet and Derrida). In Blouin jr., F. X. and Rosenberg, W. G., *Archives, Documentation, and Institutions of Social Memory: essays from the Sawyer Seminar*, University of Michigan Press.

Stone, L. (1992) History and Post-Modernism, *Past and Present*, **135**, 189–94.

Taylor, H. (1977) The Discipline of History and the Education of the Archivist, *American Archivist*, **40**, 397–402.

Taylor, H. (1984) Information Ecology and the Archives of the 1980s, *Archivaria*, **18** (Summer), 25–37.

Taylor, H. (1997) The Archivist, the Letter and the Spirit, *Archivaria*, **43**, 1–16.

Thompson, P. R. (1978) *The Voice of the Past: oral history*, Oxford University Press.

Vaisey, B. T. (1983–4) Archivist-Historians ignore Information Revolution, *Archivaria*, **17**, 305–8.

Williams, R. (1976) *Keywords: a vocabulary of culture and society*, Croom Helm.

Woods, H. (2000) The Fetish of the Document: an exploration of attitudes towards archives, in Procter, M. and Lewis, C. P. (eds), *New Directions in Archival Research*, LUCAS.

Wright, P. (2007) Who are You and What do You Think You've Been Doing All These Years?, Patrick Wright interviewed by Noel King (Department of Media, Macquarie University, New South Wales, Australia). Based on a conversation recorded on 5 May 2005 at Birkbeck College, London. Revised and rewritten May 2007, www.patrickwright.net.

Yee, S. (2007) The Archive. In Turkle, S. (ed.), *Evocative Objects: things we think with*, MIT, 31–5.

Zinn, H. (1971) Secrecy, Archives and the Public Interest, reprinted in *The Zinn Reader: writings on disobedience and democracy*, Seven Stories Press.

Part 2
Shaping a discipline

4

Structural and formal analysis: the contribution of diplomatics to archival appraisal in the digital environment

Luciana Duranti

Introduction

'Analysis is the essence of archival appraisal' (Schellenberg, 1956a, 45 [277]). All those who have written about appraisal, regardless of their perspective, beliefs and context, agree that the key to the accurate assessment of the value of records is a systematic and rigorous analysis of their context, interrelationships, form, content and/or use. They may disagree on the methodology for, or on the object of, analysis but, since the mid-19th century, the idea that appraisal could be based on intuition has all but disappeared, being replaced by the conviction that appraisal can only result from a scientific process of analysis, regardless of the interest being served and the criteria being followed.

Structural analysis

Structural analysis was introduced in the discourse on appraisal in the 20th century by German theorists. Although many archivists in Germany still supported the primacy of content analysis aimed at determining the usefulness of records for future historical research (Zimmerman, 1959), structural analysis began to dominate appraisal methodology, mostly as a consequence of the widespread international acceptance of the principle of provenance as the theoretical basis of archival arrangement. If meaning is derived from context, then an understanding of the administrative structure of a records' creator should be able to guide not simply arrangement, but also appraisal (Heredia Herrera, 1987, 123). To German archivists, the destruction of copies and transitory records was still the proper thing to do, because they were extraneous to the understanding of context and structure (Doehaerd, 1950, 325), until, in 1939, Hans O. Meissner re-issued and developed the systematic appraisal standards formulated in 1901 by Georg Hille. His primary contribution to appraisal methodology was the use of structural analysis to gather an understanding of the organization, functions and activities of the records-creating body. However, he believed that such analysis had to be combined with that of subject content in order to be able to identify records of value (Klumpenhouer, 1988, 52). In 1940, Hermann Meinert endorsed Meissner's standards arguing though that the value of records depends primarily on the significance of a records' creator within an administrative hierarchy, which can be determined through an analysis of its position in such a structure, of the nature of its activities, and of their relationship with those of superior and subordinate administrative units (Schellenberg, 1956b, 137). This was the first articulation of the now generally accepted proposition that records must be appraised in their administrative context. In 1957, Georg Wilhelm Sante (1958, 93) stated that the process of appraisal must begin with the functional analysis of the creator and then proceed to an assessment of the significance of each function and of the administrative body carrying it out.

This German confidence in structural analysis as the best means of establishing value continued until the 1980s. However, in the 1960s, its object began to shift from the creator of the records to the body of records. Johannes Papritz (1964, 220) expressed his belief that scientific principles should guide appraisal and that knowledge of the structural form of the record body would serve as a precondition because, by creation and meaning, the record body constitutes a logical unit in which each document exists in relationship to the entire body of records. Several years later, Hans Booms (1987, 90), in his seminal article 'Society and the Formation of the Documentary Heritage', stated that structural analysis derives from an implicit and excessively ideological assumption of the ultimate value of the public realm over the private and dismissed the validity of Papritz's assertions saying that value cannot logically flow from the structural form of the record body, in contrast with the widespread belief in the rest of Europe that there is a direct link between structure and value. Champion of such a belief was the Italian archival theorist Elio Lodolini (1987, 214), who insisted that the importance of structural analysis resides in the fact that it reflects a theoretical understanding of the organic nature of the archival *fonds* and therefore supports the maintenance of the integrity of series through the empirical process of appraisal.

This idea that the protection of the nature of the record had to be at the heart of any appraisal process was only implicit in the concept of structural analysis as it developed in Germany and was received in Italy, while it was central to the British views on appraisal and the consequent procedures. While the principle of provenance was never explicitly referred to in connection with appraisal, the use of structural analysis was linked to the consideration of administrative use as the key to appraisal and its equation with historical value. In 1954, the Grigg report accepted Jenkinson's principle that the authenticity, impartiality and interrelatedness of the records must be protected in the process of appraisal, but took the view that a structural analysis of the body of records using the functions and activities of the records' creator as point of reference would ensure that the appraiser maintain an objective stance (United Kingdom, 1954, 30). Michael Cook (1987, 52) noted in 1987 that the broad correspondence between administrative and research value established by the Grigg report had not been seriously challenged since it was first advocated. Indeed, the use of the principle of provenance in appraisal through structural analysis not only preserves the archival and evidentiary nature of the documents, but subsumes the content analysis inherent in the principle of pertinence, thereby resolving the conflict between the two principles.

The endurance of the concept of structural analysis was also due to the fact that it relied on an argument hard to contest, that records do not merely refer to their creator's activities but are material parts of them and directly connected to them (Jenkinson, 1937, 3). This explains why the concept is also found in American writings, which are not as concerned as the European ones with the protection of the nature of the records. The first to discuss the use of structural analysis in appraisal was Philip Brooks (1940, 226), who linked it to proper records management strategies: 'The whole appraisal function . . . can best be performed with a complete understanding of the records of an agency in their relationships to each other as they are created rather than after they have lain forgotten and deteriorating for twenty years.' Brooks advocates a two-fold analysis of the administrative structure and functions of the records' creator and of the relationships of the records to each other. He focuses on the relationships that exist between records as written evidence of functions and activities of the creating agency, and uses provenancial information to create an objective framework in which value is related to the accuracy with which the records represent the records' creator (Brooks, 1940, 231). Brooks's methodology of appraisal has had quite an impact in North America, filtered as it was in the 1950s through the writings of Schellenberg.

Arguing from the perspective of the principle of provenance as understood in the German tradition, Schellenberg identifies structural analysis of the administrative context of records' creation as the primary means for ascertaining evidential value, which is directly related to the hierarchical position of each office in the administration, the functions performed by each office, and its activities in the execution of each function. 'The archivist must know how records came into being if he [*sic*] is to judge their value for any purpose' – he states. But the aim is to preserve the records that most effectively document the substantive functions of the organization (Schellenberg, 1956a, 243–53). In fact, when it comes to informational value, Schellenberg is no longer so much interested in structural analysis as he is in formal analysis. He identifies form among the three tests by which informational value may be judged and states that formal analysis is meant to identify records that are in the most complete, usable and concentrated form available (Schellenberg, 1956a, 256–7). Schellenberg's emphasis on the importance of structural and formal analysis was not challenged for at least three decades, and subsequent writers on appraisal have considered a given that records must be appraised in context. In the mid-1980s, however, 'functional analysis' became quite popular, and in the early 1990s Samuels (1992, 20–4) explicitly contrasted it to structural analysis, stating that the latter was made obsolete by the fluidity of organizational structures and that functions had to be examined independently of where they occur. Regardless, the methodology of such analysis, as well as that of structural and formal analysis, has not been discussed further in the USA.

Functional analysis

By contrast, in Canada, structural and formal analyses have been the focus of attention of most writers on appraisal. 'Archivists must . . . look at the processes and functions behind records creation. In this first and most important phase of appraisal, they must understand why records were created rather than what they contain, how they were created and used . . . and what formal functions and mandates they supported' (Cook, T., 1991, 38). And, 'the interaction of structure and function together articulates the corporate mind (or programme) of the records creator' (Cook, T., 1992, 46). Cook's emphasis on relating the processes and functions of administrative structures to the circumstances of creation, supporting the centrality of provenancial information in appraisal, was complemented by Craig's focus on the analysis of the records:

> The reality of the record base must be an indispensable component of all acts of appraisal. Without an understanding of documents and records, of their forms and of their functions, and of how they were created and used, a plan can be so easily upset by the attractiveness of concentrating on information divorced from the realities of its documentary expression...., it is the record which is our special area of knowledge; it will be a sad day and a dangerous step when faith in planning replaces the study and knowledge of records.
>
> (Craig, 1992, 179)

Finally, in 1998, Lemieux (1998, 32–85) suggested that, on the basis of the organizational configurations identified by Mintzberg, one could determine which functions are 'organizationally significant' without the need to analyze the actual functions, and that would lead to the identification of the 'sites of archivally significant records'.

Yet, none of the Canadian writers – similarly to European and American writers – discussed how to gain that understanding of the records' context (i.e., structure and/or functions and activities) and of the records themselves, an understanding that is identified by all of them as the essential pre-requisite to sound appraisal. At least, not explicitly, until this author identified in diplomatic criticism the most appropriate methodology for conducting structural and formal analysis of records' creators and the related bodies of records for the purposes of appraisal:

> The relationship between the records and the actions from which they derive, as embedded in the records intellectual forms and in their forms of aggregation, which tend to be very repetitive, will enable us to identify which functions and activities generated them, and their relative significance. Record forms will guide

us to meaning, context and value, and so will the processes and procedures, the functions and activities of records creators.

(Duranti, 1991, 26)

The only other writer who considered form the key to a full understanding of the record was Peter Sigmond (1991–2, 141–7), the leader of a project called 'Commentaries on Sources', undertaken in the Netherlands in the mid-1980s. This project had the objective of identifying and describing the procedures and record types used by Dutch government bodies during the 19th century to carry out their mandates. The researchers focused on the identification of recognizable patterns of action starting from a diplomatic analysis of the records, rather than relying on the logical breakdown of functions and activities resulting from the study of the organizations' mandates without examining any existing aggregations of records. This work was very successful within the limits that it had defined and provided evidence of the continuing validity of diplomatic criticism. However, it did not have much resonance because the research was carried out on records that were a century old – therefore, relatively few in number – and on paper – therefore, fixed in form and content, structured, and manifestly interrelated. By contrast, the proposal made by this author that diplomatic criticism be used on contemporary and even yet to be created electronic records, that is, in a prospective way rather than only in a retrospective way (Duranti, 1990), attracted much attention, particularly as it came in response to a clear emergency call on the part of electronic records' experts.

With few exceptions, electronic records' experts have generally appreciated the use of structural analysis. In 1984, Naugler proposed a two-tiered approach to the appraisal of electronic records that combined structural and content analysis with technical analysis. In 1990, the United Nations Advisory Committee for the Co-ordination of Information Systems (ACCIS) recommended an analytical process that begins at the design phase of the information system that is expected to make or receive and maintain a creator's record, thereby endorsing both Brook's position that the appraisal process must begin as early as possible in the records life cycle, and the concept of structural and formal analysis as it was developed by Western archival theorists in the course of the 20th century. But the ACCIS report went much further in the explicit concern that it manifested for the protection of the nature of the record as, to that purpose, it recommended interference with the records creation process. In fact, it stated that design decisions must determine, for all records to be produced in the course of significant transactions, record layout, the linkage of records to each other and to those in other systems, and the function that each type of record fulfils. Although this author appreciated at the time the emphasis put by the ACCIS report on the identification of the entities in the system that are records in order to conduct an appraisal that is effective and efficient, she also felt that the report went too far in its recommendations and that the structural and formal analysis should be used differently in support of the appraisal function and should be guided by the methodology of diplomatics (Duranti, 1990, 12; Duranti, 1997).

The science of diplomatics

Diplomatics was developed as a science for the purpose of determining the authenticity of records of unproven origin. Thus, it comprises a body of concepts about the nature of records, their characteristics, components, effects and relationships, and the requirements for their trustworthiness and genuineness, and a methodology for identifying the entity record and assessing its authenticity in any context. The methodology involves detailed sub-methods for analysing the juridical-administrative system in which the records are created, the records' creators, their functions and activities, their procedures and processes, their recordmaking and recordkeeping systems, and their records. These methods are of a comparative nature in that they create models and templates representing the ideal record, the ideal procedure, the ideal structure of a record system, etc., based on past knowledge, and bounce unknown or new situations against them. In the course of this analytical process the researchers learn about the situation under study by recognizing what is known and describing what is new, and develop new models and templates on the basis of the acquired new knowledge. While diplomatics originated from the need to discover, understand and assess what exists, and is still used that way by professional diplomatists, the body of knowledge it has accumulated over the centuries can be easily used for determining the features of what will exist, by designing records forms, structuring procedures, developing records systems, and for supporting several archival activities, including appraisal, in ways that no other discipline can offer.

Twenty years after the ACCIS report, the need for structural and formal analyses supported by the methodology of diplomatics has become evident and urgent. Its importance has been demonstrated by the research conducted in the past ten years in the context of the InterPARES project, an international multidisciplinary collaborative project aimed at the development of theory, methods and practices for the long-term preservation of electronic records (www.interpares.org). Some of the findings of InterPARES regard appraisal, and specifically its methodology. With digital records, appraisal has changed in four fundamental ways: first, the preserver must assess the authenticity of the records considered of continuing value; second, the preserver must determine the feasibility of the preservation of authentic records; third, the disposal decision must be made very early in the life of the records; and, fourth, the preserver must constantly monitor the records of the creator and, if warranted by the changes that they have undergone through time, revise the disposal decision (Eastwood, 2004, 202–8; InterPARES Project, 2001b). Of these new activities involved in appraisal of digital records, two in particular are based on formal and structural analysis: the determination of the authenticity of the records and the monitoring of the records from the moment that they are created to the time that they become inactive. However, before discussing these activities and the methods for carrying them out, the most significant issue presented by appraisal of digital records needs to be discussed: the identification, in each given case, of the object of appraisal, the records. Increasingly, archivists feel unable to find records in digital systems, as they appear to contain only data. When such a situation occurs, archivists must determine, on the basis of the creator's functions and activities, whether a record should exist, and, if this is the case, must then help the creator to redesign the system to enable it to create records that can be preserved and can serve either a memorial or an evidential function. This is quite difficult when, for reasons primarily of social and professional responsibility, but also of transparency and accountability, records must be created that contain a certain type of data and must be kept for the same use for which they are created, probably for a very long time. In such cases, the assessment of the value of specific data sets is conducive to the definition of the form of the records that should contain them and of the digital presentation that will allow for their long-term use, accessibility and preservation.

Although appraisal ends up serving a creation purpose and is followed by the actual creation of new documentary forms, it does not affect the impartial, involuntary nature of the resulting records, as the data sets already exist and the records that come to contain them are used in the usual and ordinary course of business by the creator for its own purposes, rather than being generated for research purposes.

Diplomatics in the digital age

In order to demonstrate the problems presented by digital systems in terms of the identification of the entities to appraise, the concept of digital record as formulated by diplomatics should be presented. The diplomatic concept of digital record identifies the following necessary characteristics: 1) a fixed form; 2) an unchangeable content; 3) explicit linkages to other records within or outside the digital system, through a classification code or other unique identifier; 4) an identifiable context of creation; 5) the involvement of five identifiable persons, that is, i) an author – the person responsible for issuing the record, ii) an addressee – the person for whom the record is intended, iii) a writer – the person responsible for the articulation of content, iv) an originator – the person responsible for the space from which a record is sent or in which it is generated and saved, and v) a creator – the person in whose *fonds* or archive the record exists; and 6) an action, in which the record participates or which the record supports either procedurally or as part of the decision-making process (Duranti, 2009). With complex digital systems, the characteristics that create the most problems are the first two: fixed form and stable content. We can say that a digital record has a fixed form if its binary content is stored so that the message it conveys can be rendered with the same documentary presentation it had on the screen when first saved, even if its digital presentation has been changed, for example, from Word to PDF (portable document format). We can also say that a digital record has a fixed form if the same content can be presented on the screen in several different ways but in a limited series of pre-determined possibilities: in such a case we would have different documentary presentations of the same record (e.g. statistical data viewed as a pie chart, a bar chart or a table). The latter situation brings forth the issue of 'stored record' versus 'manifested record'.

A stored record is constituted of the linked digital component(s) that are used in re-producing the record, which comprise the data to be processed in order to manifest the record (content data and form data) and the rules for processing the data, including those enabling variations (composition data). A manifested record is the visualization or materialization of the record in a form suitable for presentation to a person or system. Sometimes it does not have a corresponding stored record, but is re-created from fixed content data when a user's action associates them with specific form data and composition data (e.g. a record produced from a relational database). If the same user's action produces always the same documentary presentation with the same content, we can say that the manifested entity, even when it does not have a corresponding stored record, has fixed form and stable content and, if all other records characteristics are present, is a record. In contrast, when one stored record may result in several documentary presentations, as mentioned above, it is an appraisal decision to determine whether the entity to keep as the record of an activity is the stored one or one or more of the manifested ones, and such a decision is made when the entity identified as the record is assigned a retention period. There may also be situations in which a stored record is never manifested, as is the case with software patches that enable the playing of electroacoustic music, or with interacting business applications, workflow generated and used to carry out experiments, analyses of observational data carried out by interpreting software, etc. Also in this case, it is an appraisal decision to determine which enabling entities should be retained with other records of the same activity, manifested or not. Clearly, these decisions require both structural and formal analyses of functions, activities and records, as aggregates and as individual entities. These analyses necessitate the use of diplomatic theory and methodology, also when the matter to be studied is not only contextual and formal, but also content-related. And this takes us to the concept of stable content.

A digital entity has stable content and can be considered a record if all other conditions are satisfied and if the data and the message in it are unchanged and unchangeable, meaning that data cannot be overwritten, altered, deleted or added to. However, there are cases in which we consider as having stable content entities that demonstrate bounded variability. A digital entity has bounded variability when changes to its form are limited and controlled by fixed rules, so that the same query or interaction always generates the same result, and when the user can have different views of different subsets of content, due to the intention of the author or to different operating systems or applications. While the former definition of stable content applies to static digital entities, the latter is significant when the entities we are looking at are interactive.

A static digital entity is one that does not provide possibilities for changing its manifest content or form beyond opening, closing and navigating, for example e-mail, reports, sound recordings, motion video, and snapshots of web pages. These entities, if all other conditions are satisfied, are records because they have fixed form and stable content. An interactive digital entity, instead, presents variable content, form, or both, and the rules governing the content and form of presentation may be either fixed or variable. Interactive entities may or may not be records, depending on whether they are non-dynamic or dynamic. Non-dynamic entities are those for which the rules governing the presentation of content and form do not vary, and the content presented each time is selected from a fixed store of data. Examples are interactive web pages, online catalogues, and entities enabling performances: if the other conditions exist, they are records. Dynamic entities are those for which the rules governing the presentation of content and form may vary: they are potential records, in that they become records if either the digital system in which they exist is redesigned in such a way that the rules do not vary any longer, or they are moved to another system that only maintains digital records (i.e. static or non-dynamic entities). Examples of dynamic entities are: entities whose variation is due to data that change frequently (e.g., the design permits updating, replacement or alterations; it allows data collection from users or about user interactions or actions; or it uses the data to determine subsequent presentations); entities whose variation is due to data continually received from external sources and not stored within the system; entities produced in dynamic computing applications that select different sets of rules to produce documents, depending on user input, sources of content data and characteristic of content (e.g. weather sites); and entities produced by evolutionary computing where the software generating them can change autonomously (e.g. scheduling and modelling of financial markets; edutainment sites), etc. (Duranti and Thibodeau, 2006).

The question that immediately comes to mind is: 'Why cannot we simply re-design in some standardized way each type of system to enable it to produce and keep static or interactive but non-dynamic entities?' The answer is simple: because the way in which each system is designed entirely depends on the function that the system fulfils in the context of the records' creators and/or uses over time. The InterPARES research project has proven through many case studies that solutions to these issues are specific, in addition to being dynamic. For example, a Geographic Information System (GIS) used by a public body to make decisions on the basis of the data available at the time of the decision itself, probably would require that the data sets are time stamped so that an auditor can see not necessarily what a decision maker *saw* at a given point in time but what they *would have been able to see* if they had followed the required procedure, and be able to hold the decision maker accountable on that basis. In contrast, a GIS used by a private research team to carry out testing might need to be able to stabilize and fix all the users' interactions and their effects, not by time, but by type of action or by type of material on which the action was carried out. In another example, a relational database of a public office having high interoperability with the digital systems of functionaries in other public offices, and incorporating a Public Key Infrastructure (PKI) for continuous authentication and extreme assessment of integrity of data, may need to provide access to the material attesting public transactions and to periodically transfer them to a public archives. However, the database does not contain any records, even if it is non-dynamic (i.e. the database itself is a record), thus the only way of making the material available, given the reasons for doing so, might be to define an EXtensible Markup Language (XML) schema which may serve as a translation device between the complex data model used by the database, and a less complex model, to be defined, sufficient to satisfy the needs of users. The content of each data set could then be exported to a file according to the XML schema and imported into a parallel relational database sufficiently simple to be maintained for purposes of access and preservation (e.g. Microsoft Access). All these decisions are indeed appraisal decisions about what to select, why, and in which form, and need to be based on a structural analysis of the functions and activities of the creating body as well as on a structural and formal analysis of the system containing the material in question and of each digital entity in the context of the entire records system (digital and otherwise) in which they belong.

Once again, the knowledge necessary to carry out such analyses derives from diplomatics.

Diplomatics and appraisal of digital records

However, as mentioned earlier, the need for diplomatics knowledge in conducting appraisal of digital records is not limited to the identification of the records to be appraised and to a consequent decision based on their characteristics, purpose and use, and to the re-design of digital systems when it is needed to have records where data sets should be embedded in records, but also for assessing the authenticity of the records to be appraised for continuing preservation and to monitor the records and the system in which they exist during the period between the initial assessment of value and the implementation of the final appraisal decision (e.g. the transfer to an archival institution).

Traditional appraisal literature has never concerned itself with the authenticity of records. Yet, authenticity does represent a great challenge for the appraiser of digital records. In 1922, Sir Hilary Jenkinson identified authenticity as one of the characteristics of archival material, and linked it to the procedures of creation, maintenance and preservation. Archival documents (i.e. records) are trustworthy as statements of fact because those who generate them need to rely on them for action or reference, and they are trustworthy as records because that same need of the creator and its legitimate successor ensures that proper guarantees are put into place to keep them intact over time, both in the short and the long term (Jenkinson, 1922, 8–9, 39). With digital records, a presumption of records authenticity based on the reliance on them by their creator and on a legitimate chain of unbroken custody is no longer possible. Because of their manipulability, vulnerability and fragility, the authenticity of digital records is constantly at risk, especially when they are transmitted across space and time and when they are migrated from an obsolescent system to a new one. Thus, authenticity cannot be considered a characteristic of all digital records, but only of those whose processes of creation, maintenance and preservation respect certain pre-established authenticity requirements. In all other cases, authenticity must be verified.

An authentic record is one that is what it purports to be. According to diplomatics, record authenticity comprises identity and integrity. 'Identity' refers to the attributes of a record that, together, uniquely characterize it and distinguish it from other records. These attributes include: the names of the persons concurring to its formation; its date(s) of creation and transmission; an indication of the matter or action in which it participates; the expression of its archival bond, that is, of its relationships to the other records within the same *fonds*; as well as an indication of any enclosure(s). These attributes may be explicitly provided by formal elements of the record (e.g., a signature, a subject line, or a classification code) or by information linked to the records (e.g., a register entry), or may be implicit in the various contexts of the record (i.e., administrative, provenancial, procedural, documentary or technological). 'Integrity' refers to the wholeness and soundness of a record. A record has integrity if it is intact and uncorrupted, that is, if the message that it is meant to communicate in order to achieve its purpose is unaltered. Its physical integrity (e.g., in a digital record, the proper number of bit strings) may be compromised, provided that the articulation of the content and its required elements of form remain the same. Integrity may be demonstrated by evidence found on the face of the record, in information related to the record, or in one or more of its contexts.

In light of these definitions, in order to assess the authenticity of a record, one has to establish its identity and demonstrate its integrity. However, the question arises of who should be responsible for such an assessment, the archivist or the researcher. Traditionally, archivists have rejected such responsibility. In cases of demonstrable legitimate unbroken custody, archivists have presumed authenticity, but even so, if asked to declare a record authentic, they would only go as far as to declare that a record in their custody was as authentic as when transferred to the archives. In a 1949 article, Herman Kann (1949, 363) wrote that, if a researcher were to request a declaration that a record is authentic, the archivist should firmly refuse to issue it, because this kind of interpretation is not part of their responsibilities. Thus, the assessment of records authenticity is traditionally a responsibility of the researcher. This is perfectly consistent with archival theory and the impartiality that it accords to the professional archivist. The only important role that archivists have with respect to authenticity is to describe the records in their custody in context, by making explicit, stabilizing and perpetuating their relationships with their creator and among themselves; this elucidation of the records in their various contexts is one of the primary instruments of any researcher who wishes to assess the authenticity of the records. Indeed, archival description is a collective attestation of the authenticity of the records of a *fonds* and of all their interrelationships, as made explicit by their administrative, custodial and technological history, the illustration of their scope and content, and the hierarchical representation of the records aggregates. The unique function of archival description is to provide a historical view of the records and of their becoming while presenting them as a universe in which the individuality of each member is subject to the bond of a common provenance and destination. Beyond archival description and certification of the authenticity of copies of records in their custody, archivists have traditionally held no other role with respect to the authenticity of records, especially when it came to appraisal.

Archival theory accepts appraisal only in the measure in which it respects – by not interfering in the process of assigning value – the characteristics of the records, that is, their naturalness, impartiality, authenticity, interrelatedness and uniqueness. In other words, as long as the archivist does not import into their function elements of personal judgement, then the selection of records for permanent preservation is regarded as a legitimate archival endeavour. In this context, the assessment of the authenticity of records is an activity that risks compromising the impartiality of the records by alerting the creators to their inherent value, interpreting the records formal elements, and evaluating their processes of creation and maintenance. Also archival practice has traditionally rejected the assessment of the authenticity of the records as part of appraisal, on the grounds that it would make appraisal far too laborious and time consuming. However, this common stance of archival theorists and practitioners could be held only because, with traditional records, the documents entering an archival institution or programme were the same that were made or received and set aside by their creator or legitimate successor and evaluated by the archivist in the appraisal process. Thus, the assessment of authenticity could be easily delegated to future researchers, who would be able to analyse the records under scrutiny in their original instantiation, that is, in the same form and status of transmission (i.e. degree of perfection: draft, original or copy) they had when first made or received and set aside. This is no longer the case.

Digital records undergo several changes from the moment that they are generated to the moment that they become inactive and are ready for the implementation of the appraisal decision made while they were still used by the creator. Some of those changes are intentional. Information technology is in a constant state of development. Records' creators continually update their systems and the live digital entities contained in them; at times with minimal consequences for the form, functionality, organization and metadata of the records, and at other times with dramatic consequences. The latter situation is more likely to occur when records generated in an obsolete system are migrated to a new one. In addition to intentional changes, inadvertent changes occur, simply because of the fact that it is impossible to keep a digital record; it is only possible to store its digital components in a way that it can be reproduced when needed.

A digital component is a digital object that contains all or part of the content of an electronic record, and/or data or metadata necessary to order, structure or manifest the content, and that requires specific methods for storage, maintenance and preservation. It is distinguished from the extrinsic and intrinsic elements of form, which are those parts of a record that constitute its external appearance and convey the action in which it participates and the immediate context in which it was created, because a digital component is simply a unit of storage, not meaningful *per se*. Every time a digital record is reproduced from its digital components, it is slightly different from the previous time. This happens because there are three steps in the reproduction of a digital record. The first is to reassemble all the record's digital components in the correct order. The second is to render the components, individually and collectively, in the correct documentary form or presentation (if we are dealing with a manifested record). The third is to re-establish the relationships between the digital components of the record in question and all of the other records that belong in the same archival aggregate (e.g., series, file). This requires, first, to recreate the structure of the archival aggregate, and then to fill it with the records that belong to it. Each step involves a margin of error. Considering that the processes of storage and retrieval by re-production imply transformations, both physical and of presentation, the traditional concept of unbroken custody must be extended to include the processes necessary to ensure the unaltered transmission of the record through time, and must therefore become an 'unbroken chain of preservation', which begins when the records are created respecting established authenticity requirements, and continues with the documentation of all the changes to the records and of the processes of appraisal, transfer, reproduction and preservation. However, the most important consequence of this situation is that the appraisal function must include appropriate activities aimed at ascertaining the authenticity of the records considered for selection, monitoring it, and attesting it.

The appraisal of digital records, therefore, more then ever, must rely on a diplomatics-based structural and formal analysis. This analysis is also necessary for establishing whether the digital components embodying the essential elements that confer identity to and ensure the integrity of the records can be preserved, given the current and anticipated technological capabilities of the archives. This determination process comprises of three steps. The appraiser should identify the record formal elements that provide informational content and those that need to be preserved according to the authenticity requirements that constitute the specific terms of reference for the designated preserver. Then, the appraiser should identify where these crucial record elements are manifested in the digital components of the record. Finally, the appraiser should reconcile these preservation requirements with the preservation capabilities of the organization that is responsible for the continuing preservation of the body of records being appraised. The appraisal decision comprises of two parts: a determination of what must be transferred to the archives, including the list of the digital components of the records, and a determination of how and when this should happen, including the identification of acceptable digital presentations or formats (especially for stored records that do not have corresponding manifested records) and methods of transmission to the archives (InterPARES Project, 2001b). One key component that must remain inextricably linked to the record is the metadata, the presence of which constitutes the key authenticity requirement for any digital record.

Diplomatically, records metadata can be divided into identity metadata and integrity metadata. The former include, at a minimum, the identity attributes identified earlier: the names of the five persons concurring in the record creation; the date(s) and time(s) of issuing, creation and transmission; the matter or action in which the record participates; the expression of its archival bond; the record documentary presentation, or form; its digital presentation, or format; the indication of any attachment(s); and the presence of a digital signature. The latter include data related to responsibility for the record and to changes made to the record and, at a minimum: the name of the juridical person responsible for the record; the name(s) of the person(s) handling the record over time; the name of the person responsible for keeping the record; an indication of annotations; an indication of technical changes; an indication of the presence or removal of a digital signature other than that with which the record was received; the time of planned removal from the system; the time of transfer to a custodian; the time of planned deletion; and the existence and location of duplicates outside of the system. Metadata that need to be added by the appraiser and the preserver for the purpose of providing additional grounds for the authentication of the records over time can be determined on the basis of the structural and formal analysis of the records. The presence of identity and integrity metadata is just one of the factors the appraiser needs to assess in order to declare a presumption of authenticity for the digital records under examination. The others are that the digital materials being appraised are protected from unauthorized action using physical security, access privileges and blocks on modifying records once filed pursuant to a classification plan; that they are protected from accidental loss and corruption using daily back-ups; and that steps have been taken by the creator to prevent hardware and software obsolescence by upgrading and migrating to new technology and retaining relevant documentation for long-term preservation (InterPARES Project, 2001a). A protection of the records entrusted to digital authentication technology is not sufficient to ensure their authenticity and indeed the appraiser should advocate the removal of any type of digital signature to guarantee the continuing preservation of the records.

It is one of the most important contributions of diplomatics to the trustworthiness of the records to have differentiated authenticity and authentication, which is defined as a declaration of authenticity, resulting either by the insertion or the addition of an element or a statement to a record. In a diplomatic analysis of the extrinsic elements of electronic records, digital signatures are identified as examples of electronic seals, being functionally equivalent to medieval seals, which were not only a means of verifying the origin of the record and the fact that it was intact, but also made the record indisputable and incontestable, that is, had a non-repudiation function. The analogy is not perfect, because the medieval seal was associated exclusively with a person, while the digital signature is associated with a given person *and* a specific record, and because the former was an expression of authority, while the latter is only a mathematical expression. However, it is essential to remember that authenticity is a property of the record that accompanies it for as long as it exists; while authentication is a means of proving that a record is what it purports to be at a given moment in time.

Once the appraiser has concluded their structural and formal analysis, a presumption of authenticity can be issued, based upon the number of requirements that have been met and the degree to which each has been met. If the presumption of authenticity is too weak, a verification of authenticity will be necessary. A verification of authenticity is the act or process of establishing a correspondence between known facts about the records and the various contexts in which they have been created and maintained, and the proposed fact of the authenticity of the records. It involves a detailed diplomatic examination of the records in all their contexts, and of reliable information available from other sources (e.g., audit trails, back-ups, copies preserved elsewhere), and, if needed, even a textual analysis. The resulting assessment may affect the determination of the value of the records. This information is also crucial to understanding and using the records once they have been transferred to the preserver. Future users of the records must know how well founded a declaration of authenticity of the records is and what information that declaration is based on in order to make their own assessment, long after the fact, at a time when accumulating relevant information will be difficult, if not impossible. If the appraiser has good reason to suspect that the records no longer reflect what they were at the time of their creation and primary use, they may decide not to preserve them (InterPARES Project, 2001b; InterPARES 2 Project, 2008a).

Once the initial appraisal is concluded, the records selected for long-term preservation must be continually monitored until the day of the transfer to the designated preserver, mostly for changes in their technological context and characteristics, but also for changes to their function, use, and consequently value. In most cases, monitoring produces minor revisions to the documentation on their appraisal and to the terms and conditions of transfer. In some cases, however, it may be necessary to repeat the appraisal because of changes that can affect the feasibility of preservation of the selected records in the archival environment, or because of changes that can affect their identity.

The InterPARES 2 report Modeling Digital Records Creation, Maintenance and Preservation states:

> Because there may be changes in the way records are generated or organized, in the technology the creator uses to create them, or in the preserver's preservation capabilities, part of appraising digital records involves monitoring records that have already been appraised to identify any necessary changes to appraisal decisions over time. As well, because the creator's organizational mandates and responsibilities may change over time, as might the way those responsibilities are carried out, such that data accumulated in formerly appraised systems may be put to new uses, it is possible that systems that did not initially contain records may be upgraded to do so, especially in organizations with hybrid paper and electronic recordkeeping systems. Likewise, it is likely that the preserver's preservation capabilities will change over time, as might its organizational mandates and responsibilities. Therefore, in addition to monitoring changes to the creator's appraised records, it is also necessary for the preserver to keep track of appraisal decisions in relation to subsequent developments within the creator's and/or preserver's operations that might make it necessary to adjust or redo an appraisal, such as substantial changes to: (1) the creator's organizational mandate and responsibilities, (2) the creator's recordmaking or recordkeeping activities or systems, (3) the preserver's records preservation activities or systems and/or (4) the preserver's organizational mandate and responsibilities.
>
> (InterPARES 2 Project, 2008b, 35)

Several InterPARES case studies have demonstrated such necessity. For example, a university student registration system underwent three migrations to new and more complex technologies. The first system had a current and a historical part, the latter containing the records of *alumni*, which would be accessible but impossible to modify, delete or add to. The designers of the second system eliminated the historical component so that all information on students and *alumni* was kept live. Both systems contained, about each individual, the data sets required by the registrar office to carry out its specific functions. The third system was much more complex and allowed for manipulating data in ways that could support activities that were not the responsibility of the registrar, but of other university offices, such as recruitment of new students, and planning of university events, which could be carried out using the data sets in the registration system if they were enriched with additional data and manifested in several additional ways. Thus, the registrar's office began asking the students to provide upon registration more information about themselves – as detailed by the interested university offices which were going to use the system – and the system was configured to produce manifested records pre-defined by those offices in order to exhibit the relevant data sets in such a way that they could be used to carry out their functions.

Clearly, the retention and disposition decision made for the first iteration of the university registration system was no longer valid for its second and third iteration. Furthermore, the methodology for conducting appraisal now required beforehand a structural analysis of the university offices using the system and the functions and activities that they so fulfilled. On that basis, the data sets used in the course of each activity as content of each manifested record had to be identified by formal analysis and put into relation with the other records produced by the same activity and residing outside of the registration system. Following this analytical process, a determination had to be made as to the relative value of each data set contained within the registration system with respect to each function carried out by each user office and to the other records/data sets created in the process, and then an appraisal decision had to be linked to each data set. If a data set was linked to multiple appraisal decisions, the decision requiring the longest retention period would override any other. Certainly, a redesign of the system based on the structural analysis of its users and the formal analysis of the records aggregates used and added to by each would allow for proper control of the records and a better appraisal. Such a system would have embedded into it integrated business and documentary procedures for each user office, an integrated classification system and retention schedule consistent with that of the office of primary responsibility for each type of manifested records, and appropriate identity and integrity metadata sets.

However, redesigning digital systems is a very expensive endeavour and not one likely to take place until a time when users encounter some serious legal problem seeming to require it. And a long time will pass before knowledgeable records professionals will be asked to participate in the initial determination of requirements and specifications for the design of recordmaking and recordkeeping systems, and this means that our knowledge of diplomatics will have to continue to be used retrospectively

– analyzing the characteristics and behaviour of what records/data exist, rather than prospectively – analyzing records' creators' functions and activities to determine what form the records yet to be generated should take, be they manifested or stored, static or interactive. While we wait for that time to come, we need to continue to develop the science of diplomatics and its methodological tools so that the appraisal of the next complex forms of digital records (e.g. holographic) in the context of the new activities that will use them will not find us unprepared.

References

Advisory Committee for the Co-ordination of Information Systems (ACCIS) (1990). *Management of Electronic Records: issues and guidelines*, United Nations.

Booms, H. (1987) Society and the Formation of a Documentary Heritage: issues in the appraisal of archival sources, (trans. Joldersam, H. and Klumpenhouer, R.), *Archivaria*, **24**, 69–107.

Brooks, P. (1940) The Selection of Records for Preservation, *American Archivist*, **3** (4), 221–34.

Cook, M. (1986) *The Management of Information from Archives*, Gower Publishing Co.

Cook, T. (1991) *The Archival Appraisal of Records Containing Personal Information: a RAMP Study with Guidelines*, UNESCO General Information Program and UNISIST. PGI 91/WS/3.

Cook, T. (1992) Mind Over Matter: towards a new theory of archival appraisal. In Craig, B. L. (ed.), *The Archival Imagination: essays in honour of Hugh A. Taylor*, Association of Canadian Archivists.

Craig, B. (1992) The Acts of the Appraisers: the context, the plan and the record, *Archivaria*, **34**, 175–80.

Doehaerd, R. (1950) Remarks on Contemporary Archives, *American Archivist*, **13** (4), 323–8.

Duranti, L. (1990) Diplomatics: new uses for an old science (part II), *Archivaria*, **29**, 4–17.

Duranti, L. (1991) ACA 1991 Conference Overview, *ACA Bulletin,* July.

Duranti, L. (1997) The Thinking About Appraisal of Electronic Records: where we have been and where we are going, *Janus,* International Council on Archives (ed.), 47–67.

Duranti, L. (2009) Diplomatics. In Bates, M., Maack, M. N. and Drake, M. (eds), *Encyclopedia of Library and Information Science*, Marcel Dekker.

Duranti, L. and Thibodeau, K. (2006) The Concept of Record in Interactive, Experiential and Dynamic Environments: the View of InterPARES, *Archival Science,* **6** (1), 13–68. Also online: http://dx.doi.org/10.1007/s10502-006-9021-7.

Eastwood, T. (2004) Appraising Digital Records for Long-term Preservation, *Data Science Journal*, **3**, 202–8. www.jstage.jst.go.jp/article/dsj/3/0/202/_pdf.

Heredia Herrera, A. (1987) *Archivistica General: Teoria y Practica*, Deputacion Provincial de Sevilla.

InterPARES Project. (2001a) Authenticity Task Force Report, www.interpares.org/book/interpares_book_d_part1.pdf.

InterPARES Project. (2001b) Appraisal Task Force Final Report, www.interpares.org/book/interpares_book_e_part2.pdf.

InterPARES 2 Project. (2008a) Methods of Appraisal and Preservation, www.interpares.org/ip2/display_file.cfm?doc=ip2_book_part_4_domain3_tas k_force.pdf.

InterPARES 2 Project. (2008b) Modeling Digital Records Creation, Maintenance and Preservation, www.interpares.org/ip2/display_file.cfm?doc=ip2_book_part_5_modeling_tas k_force.pdf.

Jenkinson, H. (1937) *A Manual of Archive Administration*, 2nd edn, reprint, Percy Lund, Humphries & Co. Ltd (originally published 1922).

Kann, H. (1949) A Note on the Authentication of Documents, *The American Archivist*, **XII** (4), 361–5.

Klumpenhouer, R. (1988) *Concepts of Value in the Archival Appraisal Literature: an historical and critical analysis.* Unpublished MAS thesis, University of British Columbia.

Lemieux, V. (1998) Applying Mintzberg's Theories on Organizational Configuration to Archival Appraisal, *Archivaria*, **46**, 32–85.

Lodolini, E. (1987) *Archivistica: Principi e Problemi*, Franco Angeli.

Naugler, H. (1984) *The Archival Appraisal of Machine-Readable Records: a RAMP study with guidelines*, UNESCO.

Papritz, J. (1964) Zum Massenproblem der Archive, *Der Archivar*, **17**, 213–20. Quoted in Booms, 94.

Samuels, H. (1992) *Varsity Letters: documenting modern colleges and universities*, Society of American Archivists and the Scarecrow Press, Inc.

Sante G. W. (1958) Behorden – Aktn – Archive. Alte Taktik und Neue Strategie, *Archivalische Zeitschrift*, **54**, 90–6, quoted in Klumpenhouer, 134.

Schellenberg T. R. (1956a) The Appraisal of Modern Public Records, *Bulletins of the*

National Archives 8, October, 5–46 [237–78].

Schellenberg T. R. (1956b) *Modern Archives: principles and techniques*, University of Chicago Press.

Sigmond, P. (1991–2) Form, Function and Archival Value, *Archivaria*, **33**, 141–7.

United Kingdom (1954) *Committee on Departmental Records Report*, Sir James Grigg, Chair, Cmnd. 9163. (Referred to in the text as 'Grigg Report'.)

Zimmerman, F. (1959) Wesen und Ermittlung des Archivwertes: Zur Theorie einer Archivalischen Wertlehres, *Archivalische Zietschrift*, **54**, 104–7.

5

Archivistics: science or art?

Eric Ketelaar

Introduction

L'archivistique est-elle une science ou un art? was the question put by Bruno Delmas at the conference Archival Science on the Threshold of the Year 2000 held in 1990 at the University of Macerata (Italy), and he repeated the question in the first issue of the journal Archival Science, published in 2001. However, while his original question can be translated as the title of this chapter, Delmas used in the Archival Science article a different term, asking 'Is archiving a science or an art?' The difference is not just a slip of the pen while translating: the contrast reflects the distinction between archivage (archiving) and archivistique (archivistics or archival science) which through time and in different places has been interpreted differently.

Many people would regard archiving an art, if an art is 'something which can be achieved or understood by the employment of skill and knowledge' (OED, 2010a). Surely most, if not all, aspects of archiving necessitate the employment of skill and knowledge. Sorting, for example, was considered by the great Hilary Jenkinson (1922, 75) as an art: 'one of the most difficult which the most skilled archivist could undertake'. His Canadian colleague W. Kaye Lamb (1962) called appraisal and selection of archives 'the fine art of destruction'.[1] Archival description invokes skills of interpretation and creative talents. One can therefore appreciate that early 19th-century Spanish manuals described the *'arte de archiveros'* (the archivists' art).[2]

Considering the archivist's work as an art, does not preclude considering archivistics as a science. Börje Justrell (1999, 46) wrote: 'Some of the matters that archivists deal with in their professional work are not of any concern to archival science, and some problems of archival science are not of any concern to the archival profession.' I do not share the second part of this statement. Theory informs the archivist's methodology and practice, but that practice is not *driven* by theory. However, *archivistica applicata* and *archivistica pura* are not opposites, they follow naturally from one another (see Ketelaar, 2007). Both are connected by what Anne Gilliland-Swetland (2000) has called the archival paradigm: 'a set of assumptions, principles, and practices that are common to the archival community and are a model for its activities and outlook'. Archive professionals are 'by nature pragmatic', but nevertheless they have to reflect on new challenges and need to find innovative solutions beside the beaten path. Then and there the practitioner will meet the theorist who has been wrestling with the archival paradigm, questioning the received assumptions, principles and practices.

Theory should have an important place in the professional education. The 'Guidelines for a Graduate Program in Archival Studies' of the Society of American Archivists state that archival education:

> should teach the fundamental concepts concerning: the nature of archives, records and papers, and archival functions (archival theory); the techniques for performing archival functions (archival methodology); and the implementation of theory and method in archival institutions (archival practice). Instruction should cover the history of archival theory and methods and their articulation in the professional literature (archival scholarship).
>
> (Society of American Archivists, 2002)

Early definitions: the Dutch Manual, Jenkinson, Schellenberg

The German archival theorist Wolfgang Leesch (1956, 14) traced the individuality of archival science back to 1898. In that year the Dutch Society of Archivists published the *Manual for the Arrangement and Description of Archives* by the trio Muller, Feith and Fruin (2003). Schellenberg (1956, 12) considered the Dutch Manual 'from the point of view of its worldwide contribution to archival science the most important manual written on archives administration.' Its purpose was to provide a methodology resulting in a logical and scientific arrangement of archives.[3] One may assume that 'scientific' was understood as 'the application of scientific methods in fields of study previously considered open only to theories based on subjective, historical, or undemonstrable abstract criteria' (OED, 2010b). Similarly, when Hilary Jenkinson in 1922 referred to 'Archive Science'[4] he must have meant 'science' as 'A branch of study which is concerned either with a connected body of demonstrated truths or with observed facts systematically classified and more or less colligated by being brought under general laws, and which includes trustworthy methods for the discovery of new truth within its own domain' and not, as often today, 'as synonymous with "Natural and Physical Science", and thus restricted to those branches of study that relate to the phenomena of the material universe and their laws' (OED, 2010b).

To avoid confusion with the natural and physical sciences I personally prefer the term 'archivistics', being the equivalent to the term in other European languages. Even before the Dutch *Manual* was published, Charles-Victor Langlois (1895–6, 2) proposed the French *archivistique* (as a noun) as equivalent to 'la science des archives'. The Italian Eugenio Casanova who published his *Archivistica* in 1928, was the first writer to use a term that uniquely referred to the new science (cited in Duranti, 1997).[5] In Dutch we use *archivistiek*, which is equivalent to the German *Archivistik*, the Polish *archiwistyka*, the French *archivistique*, the Spanish *archivistica*, the Portuguese *arquivistica*, etc. In Spanish and Portuguese these terms have replaced *archivologia* and *arquivologia* (Duranti, 1997, 5). However, in Mexico *archivística* is the *practical* application of the technical and theoretical principles of *archivonomia*, the latter concept being equivalent to archivistics (*archivística*) in Spain (Archvivo General de la Nación, 1997). Yves Perotin (1966, 9) chose as equivalent for the French *archivistique* the English 'archivology', 'archiveconomy' being in his view a virtual barbarism and having no real place in either English or French. Jenkinson used the term 'Archive Economy', but in a larger sense than his colleagues on the continent did, where *archivéconomie* was restricted to arrangement and description of archives.[6] The term was used by the Belgians Cuvelier and DesMarez at the Brussels congress (1910), and in the French edition (co-translator Cuvelier) of the Dutch *Manual*. Jenkinson's 'Archive Economy' is equivalent to archive administration. In that sense, Waldo Leland (1909, 342, 345) the American champion for the archival enterprise, used the term 'archive economy' as early as 1909.[7]

Luciana Duranti (1997, 5) stated that the Dutch *Manual* articulated 'systematically the concepts and methods that find their validity in archival theoretical ideas with internal logic and consistency, rather than in their historical, legal, or cultural context'. Indeed, the *Manual* is based on an analysis of ideas about what archives are, their essential characteristics and common properties – in short on archival theory.[8] There had been manuals for managing records and archives before, as early as the 16th century.[9] Ever since there have been professionally managed archives archivists have been applying methods and techniques. These practices were not a Dutch invention, as neither was the principle of provenance or the principle of respect for original order of Dutch origin. However, what the Dutch trio did was give the practices and principles a theoretical basis:

> The pioneering work of the *Manual* lies in defining the archival fonds; in the formulation of the connection between the archive and the functions of those who create it, and in making archivists aware that the boundaries and structure of an archive need to be respected and that the components of which an archive consists can only be comprehended within their original context.
>
> (Horsman, Ketelaar and Thomassen, 2003, 258)

Terry Cook (1997, 22) has called the *Manual* 'very important precisely because, for the first time, it codified European archival theory and enunciated a methodology for treating archives which has widely influenced our collective theory and practice'.

The theory thus codified formed the basis for the two great manuals for use in the English-speaking world, written by Jenkinson and Schellenberg. The former, however, developed his own theory, that is he allowed the few great principles which govern the making and handling of archives 'to emerge from an independent examination into the nature, the evolution, and the stages in transmission of Archives' (Jenkinson, 1922, 19). Jenkinson (being British) advocated combining 'a sound theory with ordinary common sense and both with practical experience'. His book *A Manual of Archive Administration* (1922) goes beyond arrangement and description, and deals also with 'archive making'. Schellenberg, after having published *Modern Archives* (1956), dealt in his *The Management of Archives* (1965) explicitly with archival methodology, rather than with theory. Still, Schellenberg proposed in both books 'principles and techniques', covering more ground than the Dutch trio and Jenkinson. Where Jenkinson's 'archive administration' was restricted to 'archive keeping' and 'archive making',[10] parts II and III of Schellenberg's *Modern Archives* dealt more extensively with different aspects of records management and archival management (including, among others, appraisal, preservation, publication programmes and reference service). Thus, what Schellenberg mainly wrote about was what in current US archival terminology is defined as 'archives management' (or 'archival administration'): 'The general oversight of a program to appraise, acquire, arrange and describe, preserve, authenticate, and provide access to permanently valuable records.' as The Society of American Archivists' Glossary of Archival and Records Terminology explains:

> Archives administration includes establishing the program's mission and goals, securing necessary resources to support those activities, and evaluating the program's performance. Archives management is distinguished from library, museum, and historical manuscripts traditions by the principles of provenance, original order, and collective control to preserve the materials' authenticity, context, and intellectual character.
>
> (archivists.org/glossary/term_details.asp?DefinitionKey=525)

Archival science

These principles were codified in the *Manual* of 1898 as the basis for arrangement and description. However, the principles of provenance and original order have a broader value in what Angelika Menne-Haritz (Germany) and Bruno Delmas (France) have called 'a functional archival science'. (see for example Ketelaar[8]) Functional archival science replaces descriptive archival science. Only by a functional interpretation of the context surrounding the creation of documents can one understand the integrity of the *fonds* and the functions of the archival documents in their original context. Functional archival science obliges the archivist to look through the records to their contextual history, leading Tom Nesmith (1999, 146) to a new formulation of 'provenance', consisting 'of the social and technical processes of the records' inscription, transmission, contextualization, and interpretation which account for its existence, characteristics, and continuing history'. For Theo Thomassen (Netherlands) descriptive archival science cannot meet the modern paradigm that centres 'process-bound information' as the object of archival science; that is both the information itself and the processes that have generated and structured that information.[11] Archival methodology is not restricted to the description and arrangement of (historical) archives, but 'provides the basis for the establishment of functional requirements for record-keeping systems' (Thomassen, 2001, 382).

Duranti has stressed the importance of archival science as a self-contained whole. For a long time, according to Duranti (1997, 7), the purpose and focus of archival science have been 'removed from its internal system of ideas and brought outside, in the realm of history'. Moreover, due to the dichotomy between records and archives, existing in the USA and elsewhere, archival enterprise focused on archives as historical sources and as part of the cultural heritage, putting the archivist at the end of the life cycle of records, literally at the dead end, in the archival graveyard where the life of the record ended. Archival theory and methodology were primarily justified

> from the point of view and in the interests of preserving archival documents for historical research . . . .Thus, the values governing thinking about archives were drawn both from outside the established precepts of archival science and from outside the milieu of records creation. Moreover, these values and ideas imported into archival knowledge from sociology, librarianship, and the like were applied to individual elements of the archival system, with the result that it broke down into separate areas with no coherent theory connecting them.
>
> (Duranti, 1997, 8)

Duranti explains how, in the 1990s, the principle of provenance and the respect of archival structure have been renewed by Australians, rediscovered by Canadians, revived in Scandinavia and The Netherlands. Thereby, archival science has regained its independence from ideas formulated in the context of other disciplines, retrieving 'its cohesion, its global vision, and ultimately its scientific rigor, systematic organization, and disciplinary unity' (1997, 7, 9–13). Just in time, since today, more than ever, archival science is necessary. Our Information Society can only survive if we can trust information. That trust has to be based upon a functional interpretation of the context in which information originates. And that is precisely what archival science is all about, and what the 'archival turn' in other disciplines tends to overlook (see Chapter 3).

Not that archival science is not interested in what other disciplines have to say about 'the archive' – quite to the contrary. Duranti ends her article by proposing a three-step process for the further development of archival science. Following the re-establishment of archival science would come, first, an opening to links with other disciplines such as organization theory, communication theory, library and information science, and, second, the adoption of useful elements from them, which should be made compatible with archival theory and methodology, followed by, third, the reconnection of archival science with the knowledge areas that have played a part in the development of archival science, such as law, philology, administrative history and political science. Although I do not believe that these steps should be taken one after another, but rather simultaneously and coherently, I agree with Duranti (1997, 14) that all of these disciplines should become involved or re-involved with archival science. Thereby, archival ideas 'would constantly be used to meet new challenges . . . and the results of this continuous testing would infuse the archival system.'

'What would happen,' Tom Nesmith asks:

> if we opened this line of inquiry much further into the relationship between archival thought and the larger world? What might become of archival theory and the key concepts of archives? The concern of archival theory would then shift emphatically to incorporate wider study of various understandings of that broader world. This would reorient some archival theorizing (such as Livelton's) from a focus on what the classic archival texts say an archives, a record, or a public record is in 'nature,' to a study of how human perception, communication, and behaviour shape the archives, records, and public records we actually locate and create as archivists and records creators. That would bring us closer to understanding what archives, records, and public records, as well as other remaining features of archives, are and have been, though would still not completely establish their full 'nature.' . . . . Widening openings to the larger world would allow far more hypotheses, information, and perspectives to enter archival thinking and challenge accepted views.
>
> (Nesmith, 1999, 142)

Such widening, opening and challenging is typical of what John Ridener (2009) has recently labelled the 'Questioning Archives paradigm'. Ridener, in his examination of 'how archivists have engaged with theory through the tension between keeping records that reflect objective history "as it happened" and subjective decision making in the archive' deals with the *records organizers* (the Dutch trio), the *keepers of records* (Jenkinson), the *records selectors* (inspired by Schellenberg), and, finally, the *records questioners* working in a new, postmodern context. Archivists working in the 'Questioning paradigm' have, according to Ridener (2009, 117), conceived of archival theory as a theory of communication: 'The transmission of information from archival document to user, from *fonds* to archivist, from record creator to an active document, are all examples of areas in which communication takes place in the archival context. Within each step of communication lies the possibility for interpretation between transmission and reception of information.'

Through that communication and interpretation, in contexts which are always changing in time-space, the record is continuously activated, a 'mediated and ever-changing construction' (Cook, 2001, 10). To understand that agency, archivistics needs to ally with and be challenged by other disciplines who study human perception, communication, and behaviour. Scholars of archivistics 'are learning (or relearning) from anthropologists, sociologists, psychologists, philosophers, cultural and literary theorists, learning to look up from the record and through the record, looking beyond – and questioning – its boundaries, in new perspectives seeing *with* the archive, to use Tom Nesmith's (1997) magnificent expression, trying to read its tacit narratives of power and knowledge' (Ketelaar, 2001, 132).

Conclusion

Is archivistics a science or an art? It might be both. An archivist may well process archives by employing skill and knowledge, not caring about archival theory.[12] Still, every practitioner starts from hypotheses and ideas. The practitioner (other than the theorist) often accepts these hypotheses straightaway as true. The practitioner is thus concerned with the operational side. Yet at some point he or she will have to address more fundamental questions to prevent archives' management from becoming routine and in order to find answers to changing technologies and challenges. Practitioners can be theorists too, only they do not realize the fact. As Luciana Duranti (1998) has written: 'When they dwell on a new idea and develop and test it in the context of archival understanding, they are theorists in action.' Aren't these 'theorists in action' not practicing an art – applying creative skill and imagination?

References

Archvivo General de la Nación (1997) Hacia un Diccionario de Terminología Archivística.

Cook, T. (1997) 'What Is Past Is Prologue': a history of archival ideas since 1898, and the future paradigm shift, *Archivaria*, **43**, 17–63.

Cook, T. (2001) Archival Science and Postmodernism: new formulations for old concepts, *Archival Science*, **1** (1), 3–24.

Delmas, B. (2001) Archival Science Facing the Information Society, *Archival Science*, **1** (1), 25–37.

Duranti, L. (1997) Archival Science. In Kent, A. (ed.), *Encyclopedia of Library and Information Science*, **59**, suppl. 22.

Duranti, L. (1998) The Future of Archival Scholarship. Keynote address at the conference *Cyber, Hyper or resolutely Jurassic? Archivists and the millennium*, University College Dublin, 2–3 October, www.ucd.ie/archives/html/conferences/cyber1.htm.

Gilliland-Swetland, A. (2000) Enduring Paradigm, New Opportunities: the value of the archival perspective in the digital environment, Council on Library and Information Sources, www.clir.org/pubs/reports/pub89/contents.html.

Horsman, P., Ketelaar, E. and Thomassen, T. (2003) New Respect for the Old Order: the context of the Dutch manual, *American Archivist*, **66** (2), 249–70.

Jenkinson, H. (1922) *A Manual of Archive Administration*, Clarendon Press.

Justrell, B. (1999) *What is this Thing we Call Archival Science? A report on an international survey*, National Archives of Sweden.

Ketelaar, E. (2001) Tacit Narratives: the meanings of archives, *Archival Science*, **1** (2), 143–55.

Ketelaar, E. (2007) Archives in the Digital Age: new uses for an old science, *Archives & Social Studies: a journal of interdisciplinary research*, **1** (0), 167–91, http://socialstudies.cartagena.es/images/PDF/no0/ketelaar_archives.pdf.

Lamb, W. K. (1962) The Fine Art of Destruction. In Hollaender A. E. J. (ed.), *Essays in Memory of Sir Hilary Jenkinson*, The Society of Archivists.

Langlois, C. V. (1895–6) La Science des Archives. In *Revue Internationale des Bibliothèques, des Archives et des Musées*, **1**, 7–25.

Leesch, W. (1956) Methodik, Gliederung und Bedeutung der Archivwissenschaft. In *Archivar und Historiker. Studien zur Archiv- und Geschichtswissenschaft, Zum 65, Geburtstag von Heinrich Otto Meisner*, Staatliche Archivverwaltung. Schriftenreihe; vol. 7, Rutten, 14.

Leland, W. G. (1909) *American Archival Problems*, Annual Report of the American

Historical Association.

Muller, S., Feith, J. A. and Fruin, R. (2003) *Manual for the Arrangement and Description of Archives*, translation of the second edition by Leavitt, A. H. with new introductions, Society of American Archivists.

Nesmith, T. (1997) *Seeing with Archives: the changing intellectual place of archives*, Paper, presented at the annual meeting of the Association of Canadian Archivists, Ottawa, 6 June.

Nesmith, T. (1999) Still Fuzzy, But More Accurate: some thoughts on the 'ghosts' of archival theory, Archivaria, **47**, 136–50.

OED (2010a) 'art, n¹', *OED Online*, Oxford University Press.

OED (2010b) 'science', *OED Online*, Oxford University Press.

Perotin, Y. ed. (1966) *A Manual of Tropical Archivology*, Mouton & Co.

Ridener, J. (2009) *From Polders to Postmodernism: a concise history of archival theory*, Duluth.

Schellenberg, T. R. (1956) *Modern Archives: principles and techniques*, University of Chicago Press.

Schellenberg, T. R. (1965) *The Management of Archives*, Columbia University Press.

Society of American Archivists (2002) *Guidelines for a Graduate Program in Archival Studies*, http://archivists.org/prof-education/ed_guidelines.asp.

Thomassen, T. (2001) A First Introduction to Archival Science, *Archival Science*, **1** (4), 373–85.

Notes

1   This has been echoed by other authors, see for example, Wilson, I.E. (2000) The fine art of destruction revisited, *Archivaria*, **49** (Spring) 124–39, and Cook, T. (2004) Macro-appraisal and Functional Analysis: documenting governance rather than government, *Journal of the Society of Archivists*, **25**, 5–18.

2   Ruiz, F. F. (1996) Los Inicios de la Archivística Española y Eeuropea, *Revista General de Información y Documentación,* **6***,* 43–77, here 51–4. Ruiz refers, among others, to Froilán Troche y Zúñiga who published in 1828 *El Archivo Cronológico-topográfico: instrucción de archiveros...* In the title of the second edition (1835) *Instrucción de Archiveros* was replaced by *Arte de Archiveros*.

3   Feith, M. and Fruin, R. *Manual,* explanation to paragraph 64. Other places where the Manual refers to 'scientific' are the explanations to paragraphs 10 and 12. In the German and French editions the Dutch 'wetenschappelijk' was translated as 'wissenschaftlich' and 'scientifique'.

4   Jenkinson, H. (1922) *A Manual of Archive Administration,* Clarendon Press, 9, 16, 17, 21, 178. He included as Appendix II an 'Outline for a Bibliography of Archive Science'.

5   See also Lodoloni, E. (1998) *Archivistica: principi e problem,* Franco Angeli, Milano, 391–404. Roger Ellis (1986), in his review of the first edition of Lodolini's book, considered 'archivistica' untranslatable: it 'comprehends both the primary tasks of the archivist and the intellectual and philosophical basis of the principles which guide him' (*Journal of the Society of Archivists,* **8** (2), 151).

6   See Cuvelier, J. and Stainier, L. (1912) *Congrès de Bruxelles 1910 : Actes,* Bruxelles, 5, 301, 305, 656, 665. Cuvelier gave a course of archiveconomie and Fruin taught the same subject at the Dutch Archiefschool. See Munden, K. (1967) (ed.) *Archives and the Public Interest: selected essays by Ernst Posner,* Public Affairs Press, 35.

7   See also Jimerson, R. C. (2006) 'American Historians and European Archival Theory: the collaboration of J. F. Jameson and Waldo G. Leland', *Archival Science,* **6,** 299–312.

8   Ketelaar, E. (1996) 'Archival Theory and the Dutch Manual', *Archivaria,* **41** (Spring) 31–40, repr. in Ketelaar, E. (1997) *The Archival Image: collected essays,* Hilversum, 55–65; Muller, Feith and Fruin, *Manual,* IX.

9   See, for example, Delsalle, P. (1990) *Une Histoire de l'Archivistique,* Presses de l'Université du Québec, 144–51; Gilliland, A. and White, K. (2009) Perpetuating and Extending the Archival Paradigm: the historical and contemporary roles of professional education and pedagogy, *InterActions: UCLA Journal of Education and Information Studies,* **5** (1), Article 7: http://repositories.cdlib.org/gseis/interactions/vol5/iss1/art7.

10 The term 'archivation' was first used in the 1990s by the French philosopher Bernard Stiegler: Chabin, M-A. (1999) *Je Pense Donc j'Archive,* L'Harmattan, 66. French archivists, however, used the term as equivalent to 'archivéconomie' or 'archivage': Delmas, B. (2001) 'Archival Science Facing the Information Society', *Archival Science,* **1** (28). As Paul Ricoeur and Jacques Derrida use the term *archivation,* it is writing down the oral testimony and then setting aside, assembling, and collecting these traces: Ricoeur, P. (2000) *La Mémoire, l'Histoire, l'Oubli,* Éditions du Seuil, 209, 211. Ricoeur's translators translated *archivation* by *archiving:* Ricoeur, P. (2004) *Memory, History, Forgetting,* (trans. Blamey, K. and Pellauer, D.), University of Chicago Press, 167. Derrida's *archivation* became *archivization* in the English translation, *archiviazione* in the Italian edition, and *Archivierung* in the German edition: Derrida, J. (1996) *Archive Fever,* (trans.

Prenowitz, E.), University of Chicago Press; Derrida, J. (1996) *Mal d'Archivio: un' Impression Freudiana*, (trans. Scibilia, G.), Filema Napoli; Derrida, J, (1997) *Dem Archiv Verschrieben: einde Freudsche Impression: ubers: Hans-Dieter Gondek und Hans Naumann*, Brinkmann + Bose.

11 See, for example, Thomassen, T. (1999) The Development of Archival Science and its European Dimension, in *The Archivist and the Archival Science: seminar for Anna Christina Ulfsparre...*, Landsarkivet, 67–74; Thomassen, T. (2001) A First Introduction to Archival Science, *Archival Science*, **1** (4), 373–85.

12 Mortensen, P. (1999) The Place of Theory in Archival Practice, *Archivaria*, **47** (15), 19–20; Ketelaar, E. (2000) Archivistics Research Saving the Profession, *American Archivist*, **63** (2), 322–40.

Part 3
Archive 2.0: archives in society

6

Archons, aliens and angels: power and politics in the archive[1]

Verne Harris

Introduction

Etymologically the English word 'archive' derives from the classical Greek word *arkheion*, which meant the place, or residence, of the superior magistrates, the *archons*, those who held and signified political power. The root of this word was *arkhé*, a word rich in meanings – beginning, origin, command, power. In classical Greece the concept of 'archive' was indissociable from the location and the exercise of power. Although the citizenry – a social category excluding women, slaves, foreigners and other 'aliens' – could gain access to certain records in the archive, the state generated the archive, kept custody of it, and controlled the use of it. This approach built on a tradition developed over two millennia in societies of the near East (Mesopotamia, Egypt, Persia), where archives were created by rulers and kept by them to support the exercise of rule.

The West had to wait until the French Revolution and its aftermath for the emergence of the interlinked notions that archives had uses beyond those associated with the exercise of rule and that they were for 'the people' rather than for a small elite. (Arguably, by then the latter notions had long histories in uncolonized societies outside of the West – societies not restricting their concepts of archive to places of custody and to accumulations of written records [Harris and Hatang, 2000]. Nonetheless, these histories demonstrated in different ways the unavoidable and indelible imprint of power on any archive.) The 19th century saw the establishment in Europe of public archives services and the growth of public rights of access to them. A deepening of Western democracy in the 20th century brought with it public services shaped increasingly by accountability, participation and 'freedom of information'.

Archives influenced by this deepening have spread – through colonialism and neocolonialism – to many parts of the world. In the analysis of Jacques Derrida, such archives can be seen – should be seen – as an expression of democratization:

> Effective democratisation can always be measured by this essential criterion: the participation in and the access to the archive, its constitution, and its interpretation.
>
> (Derrida, 1996, 4)

As this chapter will seek to demonstrate, application of this 'essential criterion' to archives of different countries, different traditions and different conceptual underpinnings – in both Western and non-Western contexts – finds them wanting in greater or lesser measure. Always the indelible imprint of power either marginalizes or excludes (in terms of both 'content' and 'access') the weak, the poor and the outcast – society's aliens. This chapter will argue, following Derrida, that this has to do with the reality that 'there is no political power without control of the archive' (Derrida, 1996, 4). So that democratization – always a 'process' imperfectly realized and always drawing on powers, formations and energies which Derrida names 'archontic' (3) – can never fully remove the *arkhon* from the *arkheion*. Consequently the call of justice in relation to the archive is a call to activism – a call to open the archive in a fundamental way to those alienated, or estranged, in it and by it; to open the archive to the alien, the stranger, the *xenos*. In the memorable words of Nelson Mandela, at the inauguration of his Centre of Memory and Dialogue: 'we want it to dedicate itself to the recovery of memories and stories suppressed by power. That is the call of justice' (Nelson Mandela Foundation 2005, 98). The activists – those who heed the call, who hear the message, disseminate it and act on it – are, in the terminology of this chapter, 'angels', from the Greek *aggelos*, meaning messenger.

Power and the archive

It is relatively easy to understand the importance of archives for the exercise of power in classical Greece, in Rome, and in the ancient near East. Archivists in these contexts were the right-hand to emperors, kings and princes, and their well resourced storehouses were critical instruments of rule. On the face of it, the contrast with polities of the 21st century could not be starker. Even in countries where archivists have successfully re-imagined themselves as auditors of state recordkeeping, or as institutional knowledge managers, or as purveyors of national and local narratives, their purchase on power seems slight. With few exceptions, even premier archival institutions find themselves straining to make their voices heard in higher level policy making and decision making. They find themselves struggling to secure adequate resources. Their influence on public discourses usually requires the mediation of journalists, scholars, human rights activists or politicians. Whether as structures of the state, branches of corporations or organs of civil society, archives are seldom able to divest themselves of a Cinderella status.

However, 'the archive' is bigger than the sum of all institutions calling themselves 'archives' and of all practitioners calling themselves 'archivists'. To the extent that these institutions and practitioners – and the broader 'archival' professions and disciplines – resist this idea, they impoverish both their discourse and their practice. For 'the archive' is to be found whenever and wherever information is marked, or recorded, on a substrate through human agency. It is to be found whenever one person shares a story with another, and a trace – a configuration of brain particles, a patterning of energy pulses, no one is sure – is left in the psychic apparatus of that other. It is to be found in the conjoining of paint and rock created by hunter-gatherers in many parts of the world. It is to be found in a plethora of markings on the human body, from circumcision to facial scarification, from tattoos to amputations. It is to be found in carvings on stone, inscriptions in clay, writing on paper, imprints of light on film, and the patterning of bits and bytes on computer hard drives. 'The archive', in short, is all around us; it is on us and inside us. It is the stuff of daily life. And it is the source of what Bruno Latour calls 'an essential power':

> We take for granted that there exist, somewhere in society, macro-actors that naturally dominate the scene . . . . The problem is that these entities could not exist at all without the construction of long networks in which numerous faithful records circulate in both directions, records which are, in turn, summarized and displayed to convince.

(Latour, 1986, 28–9)

Everyone has access to this power, but the degree of access is determined by the contours of privilege, marked across any number of continua – physical ability and disability, levels of literacy, wealth and poverty, geographical closeness and distance, degrees of security clearance, and so on. In this reading the powerful in society, the macro-actors, are those who have a more or less privileged capacity to construct and to access long networks of (more or less faithful) records.

The domination of a 'scene' by macro-actors, for Latour, is never natural. It is constructed. In the following passage he elaborates the argument in relation to a specific case:

> The 'rationalisation' granted to bureaucracy since Hegel and Weber has been attributed by mistake to the 'mind' of (Prussian) bureaucrats. It is all in the files themselves . . . . Economics, politics, sociology, hard sciences, do not come into contact [with each other] through the grandiose entrance of 'interdisciplinarity' but through the back door of the *file*. The 'cracy' of bureaucracy is mysterious and hard to study, but the 'bureau' is something that can be empirically studied, and which explains, because of its structure, why some power is given to an average mind just by looking at files: domains which are far apart become literally inches apart; domains which are convoluted and hidden, become flat; thousands of occurrences can be looked at synoptically . . . . In our culture's 'paper shuffling' is the source of an essential power, that constantly escapes attention since its materiality is ignored.
>
> (Latour, 1986, 28)

'"Paper shuffling" is the source of an essential power.' There is a growing literature on oppressive regimes – from Nazi Germany to apartheid South Africa, from the communist German Democratic Republic to the Pol Pot regime in Kampuchea – which seems to substantiate this thesis. Equally, there is a growing literature on the power of 'paper shuffling' in democratizing societies. Of course, the structure of the 'bureau' has been revolutionized by electronic technologies since this analysis by Latour. Paper shuffling has been superseded – although not yet replaced – by bit crunching. In this realm the functionalities named by Latour – to bring distant domains together, to flatten convoluted and hidden domains, to view masses of occurrences synoptically, to circulate records along networks, to summarize and to display them – have been enhanced exponentially and joined by functionalities undreamed of two decades ago. Here is the source of an essential power drawing on virtuality rather than materiality – frightening in its deployment for the surveillance of citizens or the prosecution of war, invigorating in its deployment for the provision of public services or the combating of disease.

Latour foregrounds the capacity of the archive to structure cognition. In each of the binaries he posits – 'the mind' and 'the files', the 'cracy' and the 'bureau' – the latter is privileged as determinative: 'it is all in the files'; 'the "bureau" . . . explains . . . why some power is given'. This is to underplay, or to miss entirely, the very condition for the unleashing of the power which Latour describes so eloquently – the structuring of the archive. Power flows from merely 'looking at files' precisely because looking is preceded by a whole range of interventions – from the structuring of information in documents to the gathering of documents into files, from the classification of files in terms of a system to the preparation of finding aids – and because every act of looking becomes an intervention more or less structurally determined but at the same time carrying restructuring potential. In Latour's own terminology, the structure of the archive is never natural; it is constructed, by human cognition. So while he is right that the 'cracy' of bureaucracy – and, by extension, the 'mind' of bureaucrats – 'is mysterious and hard to study', the real mystery and the real challenge to analysis lies in the bi-lateral structuring always already at work between archive and cognition. Human beings – whether Prussian bureaucrats or African storytellers, whether medieval scribes or television journalists, whether scientists analysing data or schoolchildren surfing the internet – process information by ordering it, categorizing it, selecting, referencing, preserving and connecting it to other information. In the words of Geoffrey Bowker and Susan Leigh Star (2000, 230), a 'mutual process of constructing and shaping differences through classification systems is crucial in anyone's reality'. Information never speaks – discloses meaning and significance – for itself; it speaks through the classification systems in which it is embedded and by which it is processed. *Here* lies an essential power. A power held by the custodians of classification systems. As Bowker and Star argue:

> Each standard and each category valorizes some point of view and silences another. This is not inherently a bad thing – indeed it is inescapable. But it is an

ethical choice, and as such it is dangerous – not bad, but dangerous.

(Bowker and Star, 2000, 5–6)

The power at play here – and its concomitant dangers – becomes clearer when the analyses of Latour, Bowker and Star are exposed to the broader layers of context within which information is embedded and processed. These layers range from the idioms, languages and psychologies of those generating information to the contingencies of place and time informing information retrieval, from the biographies of information managers to the modes of knowledge construction available to the users of information. Indeed, in principle there can be no limit to this form of layering. In the words of Derrida (1988, 137): 'the finiteness of a context is never secured or simple, there is an indefinite opening of every context, an essential nontotalisation'. It is in understanding the role of contextualization, engaging its mystery and probing its complexity, that the nature and the contours of power – any power – begin to emerge. Scholars and commentators from many disciplines and many countries, working with a range of theoretical and epistemological frameworks, have revealed how the exercise of political power hinges on control of information. Noam Chomsky, for instance, has offered searing critiques of democracy, in the USA especially, demonstrating how elites depend on sophisticated information systems, media control, surveillance, privileged research and development, dense documentation of process, censorship, propaganda, and so on, to maintain their positions (cited in Mitchell and Schoeffel, 2002).

But it is Derrida and Michel Foucault who offer the most convincing readings of the logic, even the law, underlying these phenomena. And they do so precisely by insisting on the contexts within which information discloses meaning and significance. In Foucault 'the archive' is the assemblage of all discursive formations existing in a given society. It is discourse as system: 'The archive is first the law of what can be said' (Foucault, 1992, 129). And *when* it can be said, *how*, and *by whom*. In Derrida 'the archive' is a tracing – the consigning of information, of text, to a substrate, an exterior surface, a place (and it can be a virtual place) of consignation (Derrida, 1996). Structurally, tracing, or consignation, is all about contextualization, in relation to the process and to the place. As Derrida (1988, 136) has put it, there is nothing outside context. And contextualization, in turn, cannot avoid the exercise of (archontic) power. The archive, in short, is the law determining contexts. For both Foucault and Derrida, then, the archive is a construction, one which issues from and expresses relations of power, and which is the condition for any engagement with information and any exercise of power. It is here, beneath the surface whirl and clatter of information, that the instruments of power are forged. Instruments which in their most fundamental of operations create and destroy, promote and discourage, co-opt and discredit, *contexts*. Archivists have conceptualized what they do around their special expertise in context. But it is the archon, the one who exercises political power, who is the purveyor of context and who is the archetypal archivist. In this reading politics is archival, and the archive is the very possibility of politics.

The archive, in these conceptualizations of it, reaches *everywhere* – across the geopolitical spread of an empire, into the depths of an individual's unconscious. As do, commensurately, the instruments of power. This can be illustrated by counterpointing recent studies of European imperialism with a deconstructive reading of the human psyche. During the last 30 years, scholarship on the age of European empire has been transformed by what Ann Stoler (2002, 87) calls 'an archival turn'. Scholars like Stoler, Edward Said, Richard Thomas, Gayatri Chakravorty Spivak and Premesh Lalu, all influenced in greater or lesser measure by the work of Derrida and Foucault, have foregrounded the role of archive in the exercise of colonial rule. In their work the archive is not simply a storehouse of information and records; rather, it is a technology of rule, an apparatus producing and reproducing forms of subjection. It consists of rules of formation which establish labels, categories and hierarchies (Lalu, 2009, 30). Understood thus, the colonial archive is an instrument more fundamental than guns, ships and railways. It reaches into the psyches of both rulers and ruled, and can continue working there long after the removal of the cruder instruments of subjection. In the formulation of Lalu (2009, 24), the archive continues to regulate much of what can be said in the wake of colonialism, and is therefore critical to an understanding of the resilience of colonialisms long after formal processes of decolonization.

There are extensive and quickly growing literatures on human memory – collective and individual – and on the imprint of archive in the human psyche. Arguably, the latter is the most mysterious terrain of all; the most difficult to study. And, by extrapolation, it is the location of archive most difficult to penetrate. Derrida (1996, 2002b), again, this time reading Freud, takes us furthest. In his reading (which constitutes but one strand amongst many in his thinking of archive and the psyche), the act of remembering by an individual human being does not involve a space we can name 'archive': 'the archive doesn't consist simply in remembering, in living memory, in anamnesis; but in consigning, in inscribing a trace in some external location – there is no archive without . . . some space outside' (Derrida 2002b, 42). That 'space outside' could be someone else's psyche – in sharing one's remembering, one's living memory, with another or with others, one inscribes a trace in (an) external location(s). But Freud revealed for the first time another 'external' location in his probing of the human psychic apparatus' complex architecture – the 'unconscious', which Freud named as an external space located deep inside:

> Freud's contribution consists in saying that the psyche is structured in a way that there are many places in which traces are kept, which means that within the psyche there is an inside and an outside.
>
> (Derrida, 2002b, 42)

So, the unconscious – a world of dreams; of forgotten or repressed memories, narratives and images; of languages and idioms difficult or impossible to grasp; of aliens – is a 'space outside' bearing traces; a form, therefore, of archive; and, therefore, the source of an essential power. In the work of a myriad scholars since Freud – from Lacan to Derrida, from Jung to Hillman – all of it more or less inscribed, or determined, by that archive we can name 'Freud', is to be found engagement with this power.

Politics and the archive

Power – wherever it is found, whatever its contexts – can be used for good and for ill. It can liberate people; equally, it can oppress people. In polities claiming the mantle 'democracy' the critical debate, it could be argued, is around how power can be extended more effectively to people at the same time as containing its potential for abuse. Two contrary energies then – on the one hand, an opening of space for power to play in, a pushing back of boundaries, an extending of freedoms; on the other, a regulating of space, a tightening of boundaries, an elaborating of responsibilities and obligations. Two contrary energies apparently delineating – and emanating from – a binary opposition: liberatory power as opposed to oppressive power. Beneath the surface appearance, however, as with all binary oppositions, there is a profounder contradiction at play. For in the 'liberatory' there is always to be found the seeds of the 'oppressive', and vice versa. In the terminology of Derrida (1996, 11), the archontic is always accompanied by what he calls the anarchontic. This can be illustrated quickly – at the risk of over-simplification – in the archive. To provide four examples:

1   The files of the German Democratic Republic secret police, the
    Stasi files, were demonstrably key instruments in the oppression of a
    citizenry. And yet, today, these same files are being used by people to
    liberate themselves from that oppressive past (Ash, 1997).
2   Over four decades the apartheid state in South Africa removed black
    South Africans from land designated for 'white' occupation, in both
    urban and rural environments. Today the state records which
    documented these removals are being used in land restitution
    processes to provide the victims and their descendants with
    reparation (Harris, 2007, 107–8).
3   The archives of South Africa's liberation movements document
    generations of struggle for freedom in the country. A close reading
    of them, however, demonstrates how they replicate what can be
    called the oppression of women within that struggle.[2]
4   The South African History Archive, a small non-governmental
    organization which emerged as a more or less underground
    structure in the 1980s, is dedicated to documenting struggles for
    justice in the country through the apartheid era and into the present.

Analysis would reveal the extent to which a particular metanarrative has shaped the privileging of certain voices and the marginalizing of others within its holdings.[3] The same pattern, the same imprint, can be found in whatever societal spacing is subjected to scrutiny. A highly regulated economy can be instrumental in liberating the underclasses. 'Free enterprise' can be a euphemism for an unfettered exploitation of the same classes. State surveillance of citizens can be critical to their protection from reactionary forces. At the same time, such surveillance circumscribes the rights of citizens and can be used to oppress individuals.

Power – archontic, anarchontic – is always already at play in the archive. And how this power is used, how it is deployed, is always already a question of politics. In common usage the word 'politics' refers usually to processes in what could be typified as a high-level domain – a jostling of power, authority and status in public life, especially in the upper reaches of the state, of government, of corporations, of diplomacy. But the word can also be used in relation to processes in 'lower level' domains – as in 'office politics', 'family politics', 'sexual politics', and so on. In this chapter the word is used to signify the engagement of power with principle, across orders of the public and the private, the collective and the individual. The engagement is unavoidably messy, seeming to invite in the manoeuvre, the strategic intervention, the half-truth. Derrida (2002a, 39), following Hannah Arendt, goes as far as suggesting that 'politics is a privileged space of lying'. Understandably, then, the word, especially in its application to 'lower level domains', is usually used pejoratively. However, there are also benign, even affirmative, senses to its use. For in the real world principle must reckon with the harsh reality of power at play. Politics is necessary to achieve a convergence of principle (what is right) with the pragmatic (what is possible) and the popular (what is supported). The call of justice is not to eschew politics – to keep one's hands clean – for that would be to abandon the terrain, any terrain, to power. It would also be to abandon common sense – as defined above, the political is unavoidable, whether in the home, the office or the public domain. The call is to dirty one's hands in the mess of the political, reaching always for a politics which is just.

Politics, then, is always already at play in the archive. This can be demonstrated by observing more closely sites – or scenes – of archive formation, or, to use a different terminology, sites of recordmaking.[4] In the following paragraphs six sites (why six? why *these* six? what are the politics of this selection, of *any* selection?) are observed: i) the government correspondence file; ii) the state-sponsored truth commission; iii) the oral record of a small collectivity; iv) the family archive; v) the marking of 'private parts'; and vi) the psychotherapist's consulting room.

The most frequently found record in conventional Western archival repositories is still the hard copy government correspondence file – usually two or three centimetres thick, filled with correspondence and correspondence-related documentation (reports, minutes of meetings, notes, diagrams, maybe photographs, and so forth) related to a particular function or subject, and covering an extended period of time. A record comprising of records, all fraught with politics. Who authored or generated the individual records on the file? What were their purposes? What perspectives or values shape their arguments and observations? What are they hiding? What do they fail to see? If the file happens to be that of a security police service, how much of the content is deliberate misinformation?[5] Which office, which registry, which officials managed the file through the period before its deposit in the repository? Does it bring together all relevant documentation? It could be that other relevant records were placed on other files. It could be that material was never filed officially, but rather kept informally by officials and subsequently disposed of. Documents, even whole files, may have been removed or destroyed to protect the interests of the office or of certain individuals. How have archivists arranged and described the file? Why did they choose to preserve it? What related records did they choose not to preserve? How have they documented the process of selection? What restrictions on public access apply to the file? How have archivists applied these restrictions? Which parts of the file are accessible, and which are not? How have they used the file or parts of it in public programming activities – in exhibitions, on websites or in publications? In all these interventions by archivists, what narratives have been constructed or reinforced, and what users have been privileged? How have users interpreted and mediated the file in public discourses? How has their reading of it been determined by a long history of recordmaking which they may or may not be fully aware of? In what ways does their continuing making of the record determine the meanings and significances attributed to it? The questions are endless. Each one, it is being suggested, delineates a space suggesting, inviting, or demanding, the adjective 'political'.

Over the last two decades the state-sponsored truth commission has become ubiquitous globally – from Argentina to South Africa, from Guatemala to Sierra Leone, from Canada to Kenya – as an instrument enabling polities to deal with oppressive pasts (Wilson, 2001, xv–xix). It aims to find the nexus between truth, justice and reconciliation as a source of healing for societies negotiating often complex transitions to democracy. It is, in all its forms, quintessentially an archival intervention.

How is the commission appointed? Is there public participation in its appointment and in the mandate given to it? What interests are privileged in its composition? What elements of the past are foregrounded or obscured by the mandate? What other instruments of reconciliation are in place, and how does the commission relate to them? How do decisions on reparation and amnesty shape the narrative which emerges? How is the commission resourced? What powers are accorded it? How independent is it? How are its research and investigation priorities determined? How transparent are its operations? To what extent is the media enabled to disseminate, critique and popularize its work? Are there public hearings? How are testimonies gathered? Who is selected to give oral as opposed to written testimony? What are the criteria for such decisions? What obstacles does the commission experience in accessing records? What is the nature and the scope of its report and the broader institutional archive generated by it? Who is the custodian of this archive? How accessible is it? How is it used and by whom after the commission's work is completed? Again, these are but a few of a multitude of questions jostling for attention. Again, the answers to them will identify voices, experiences, stories and histories either privileged (given space, foregrounded, allowed special significance, and so on) or disadvantaged (marginalized, ignored, excluded) by the process. Again, what is being delineated is the role of the political in the formation of archive.

The third site is a less conventional one (from orthodox archival perspectives): the oral record of a small collectivity. The collectivity might be as small as a clan or village community, or as large as a grouping of clans or a community defined by a district-level authority. In this scenario the collectivity is given coherence and overseen by 'traditional' or 'indigenous' authority, and is located outside of mainstream urban areas. It may be permeated by literacy and access to a range of 'modern' media. It may have allowed its oral record to be converted into material custody through one or more oral history projects conducted by 'outsiders'. But it continues to hold its history, which might go back many centuries, through the telling and re-telling of it from generation to generation. Who are the custodians of this history? The elders? The *male* elders? How is the telling regulated? Who are the storytellers? What are the specific roles of various layers of authority, of praise singers, of healers? What are the ceremonies at which stories are told, what are their specific configurations and linkages to physical sites? How do the stories shift in relation to these configurations and linkages? How does the world outside the collectivity impact on its rituals of storytelling and on the content of the history? If outsiders are allowed into the rituals, how does their presence impact on what is told and how it is told? If the outsiders take away recordings, who determines how those recordings are used and in what contexts? How do the recordings impact on the archive held by the collectivity, and on the collectivity itself? How do those who use the recordings subsequently relate them to the collectivity and its archive? What is the impact of outsiders seeking access to the archive through individual members either temporarily or permanently outside of the collectivity? Does access to 'non-elders', to women, to youth, provide new views on the archive, or does it constitute the formation of a different archive? Who are the archons in this scenario? Who are the aliens? And who are the angels? These and many other questions, it is argued, convene a play of politics in the archive.

To narrow the focus further, what of the family archive? More specifically, the nuclear family archive. In this scenario the nuclear family is located in a 21st-century, Western, urban context, with high levels of dependence on literacy and the full gamut of recordmaking technologies. Here the rules of archive formation are less tightly controlled and the loci of authority less rigidly defined than in the previous scenario. As the children grow older they become less confined by parentally determined recordmaking scenes – the family gathering, the dinner table, the family outing, the group portrait, the scrapbook, the family photo album, and so on. But within that shifting space of confinement, who determines which stories are told and which are not? In which contexts do the stories get told? Who determines the idiom, the register, the framework of signification, for the telling? Who determines which texts and images are recorded on shared external surfaces? And how they are labelled or otherwise contextualized, if at all? What are the rules of engagement with these external surfaces? How, at what pace, in what order, and by whom, are members inducted into that space designated 'private' or 'secret'? How is the extended family constellated around the nuclear family, and how does that constellation impact on the formation of archive? Which stories are kept secret forever, and which are passed on only after certain milestones are passed? Who determines the milestones? What is the impact of a record, whether a single document or an accumulation of documents, being bequeathed to one or more members? Who decides whether it is one or more? How are the modalities different when that record is lodged in a repository outside of the family? Or when the record is discovered more or less accidentally as opposed to being deliberately passed on?[6] Clearly, understanding 'family archive' is dependent on understanding family politics.

With the marking of 'private parts', the focus becomes narrower yet and the site even less conventional. In many countries and in many traditions boy children are circumcised to mark a milestone. Female circumcision is common in fewer countries and traditions. Whether male or female, the circumcised one is left with an archive on their body (an archive, precisely, of absence) telling a story of their initiation into a socially determined state, or spacing, or grouping. It marks them, separates them, as initiated. Who decides on the act of circumcision? Who determines when and how? Who tells the stories of and around the act? What is the impact on the circumcised one? What are the consequences of refusing the initiation? What are the modalities of individual and group circumcisions? What are the dynamics of disclosure? Related to circumcision, although arguably of a different archival order altogether, is the determination in girl children of whether they are sexually active or not by the presence or absence of the hymen. As with circumcision, the marking represents an initiation, and the archive it leaves is one of absence. Again, who decides when and how? Who tells the stories of and around the act? What is the impact on the initiate? And so on. In some traditions what is called 'virginity testing' is an integral part of preparation for marriage. Who is authorized to do such testing? What rights does the bearer of the archive have? What are the consequences of refusal? What are the consequences of a hymen either broken by causes other than sexual activity or abnormally resistant to breakage? The politics of the archive in this site are particularly harrowing.

Harrowing also, finally, are the politics of the psychotherapist's consulting room. For on the one hand the analyst – the well qualified analyst, the effective analyst – has access to the deepest secrets of analysands, and the tools with which to expose the secrets not even consciously recognized as such by analysands – the repressed or suppressed stories, lodged in the unconscious and attested to by symptoms, signs, figures, metaphors and metonymies. On the other, the analysand is usually emotionally vulnerable, or even in the consulting room involuntarily – thus the intricately woven ethical codes that inform the work of analysts. But who determines these codes? How conversant with them should the analysand be? Who constructs the broader psychoanalytical archive from which individual analysts draw in their practice? How accessible is this archive to laypersons? How can laypersons begin to judge the relative merits of competing psychoanalytical archives? Who should carry the responsibility of moving stories from the unconscious to consciousness? What are the consequences of this shift? Who can determine what a particular dream signifies, today, or tomorrow, or to others? Who can begin to understand the reach of a particular collective unconscious, if a collective unconscious exists at all?[7] Who can predict what shadows will be thrown by the shining of light into dark psychic spaces? What is the impact on those close to the analysand of the latter's experience of psychotherapy? Who takes responsibility for these consequences? Who decides on 'health' in these contexts? How are the interactions between analyst and analysand documented? Who has access to this record and under what conditions? Who are the recordmakers in this scenario? Who are the archons? Who are the aliens? And who are the angels? A myriad questions here, as with any and every site of archive formation.

This more or less cursory observation of six sites of archive formation has sought to demonstrate that politics is always already at play in the archive. The observation in each case identifies a series – a series without limit other than an arbitrary one – of questions delineating a space which suggests, invites, or demands, the adjective 'political'. Each question provokes a play of what is right, what is possible, and what is supported, or supportable. Each question is unavoidable for the players in archive, the recordmakers – *as* players they are implicated in the question, by the question. And always the answers to these questions are contested, in fact, and contestable in principle. What is being described is the mess of the political in archive. And what is being argued is that getting one's hands dirty is unavoidable.

Conclusion

In the dominant archival discourses today, either explicitly or implicitly, politics is something to be kept at bay.[8] Ethical standards are codified as a bulwark against the intrusion of politics (Harris, 2007, Section 3). In this chapter an argument has been made which suggests that such views – and their concomitant strategies – are misguided and irrelevant. Politics is the messy warp and woof of the archive. And the archive, perhaps, is the very possibility of politics. The relevant question becomes how to find a *just* politics; how to find an ethics which constitutes not a codification of principle, but a praxis providing guidance on how to ask the right questions and on what to do with them in the hurly-burly of action in the archive. For those schooled in the dominant discourses this might appear to be a confusion of the political with the ethical. If it is a confusion, then it is a deliberate one. For the ethical, in the argument of this chapter, is precisely about the reaching for a just politics. As Derrida puts it:

> every time the ethical and the political are caught in a knot, in an irreducible intrication, this does not mean that they are simply tangled, but that what seems not to have to be negotiated politically . . . is . . . subject to political transaction: and this political transaction . . . is not an accident, a degeneration, or a last resort; it is prescribed by ethical duty itself.
>
> (Derrida, 2002c, 304)

It is beyond the scope of this chapter to explore what a just politics of the archive might look like. But its trajectory, to return to the note sounded at the outset and reinforced throughout, has to be determined by the imperative to open the archive in a fundamental way to those alienated in it and by it. This is a call to what could be termed 'a fundamental hospitality'. The embrace of which for Derrida is the closest approximation to a definition of ethics.[9]

Like the 'love' of the poet Leonard Cohen (1984), the 'archive' is 'so vast and shattered it will reach you everywhere'. We engage it, and are engaged by it, every day. It sounds at every level of our being, speaks to and of every persona and every identity we adopt. It is the source of an essential power. It oppresses us and it liberates us. We play in it and with it. It is a resource to every individual and to every collectivity. It belongs to us all. It belongs to the archons – including the *arkhon* inside each one of us – who control the archive's formation and regulate its use. To the aliens – including the *xenos* inside each one of us – who strain to be heard in it. To the angels – including the *aggelos* inside each one of us – who reach for justice and proclaim the message of hospitality.

References

Ash, T.G. (1997) *The File: a personal history*, Flamingo.

Bowker, G. and Star, S.L. (2000) *Sorting Things Out: classification and its consequences*, Massachusetts Institute of Technology.

Byatt, A.S. (1990) *Possession*, Chatto and Windus.

Cohen, L. (1984) Heart with no Companion. In *Various positions*, Columbia, New York.

Cooley, M. (1998) *The Archivist*, Abacus.

Derrida, J. (1988) *Limited inc*, Northwestern University.

Derrida, J. (1996) *Archive Fever: a Freudian impression*, University of Chicago Press.

Derrida, J. (1997) *Politics of Friendship*, Verso.

Derrida, J. (2002a) *Without Alibi*, Stanford University Press.

Derrida, J. (2002b) Archive Fever in South Africa. In Hamilton C. et al. (eds), *Refiguring the Archive*, David Philip.

Derrida, J. (2002c) *Negotiations: interventions and interviews 1971–2001*, Stanford University Press.

Derrida, J. and Dufourmantelle, A. (2000) *Of Hospitality*, Stanford University Press.

Foucault, M. (1992) *The Archaeology of Knowledge and the Discourse on Language*, Pantheon.

Govender, P. (2007) *Love and Courage: a story of insubordination*, Jacana.

Hamilton, C. et al., (eds) (2002) *Refiguring the Archive*, David Philip Publishers.

Harris, V. (2000) *Exploring Archives: an introduction to archival ideas and practice in South Africa*, 2nd edn, National Archives of South Africa.

Harris, V. (2007) *Archives and Justice: a South African perspective*, Society of American Archivists.

Harris, V. and Hatang, S. (2000) Archives, Identity and Place: a dialogue on what it (might) mean(s) to be an African archivist, *The Canadian Journal of Information and Library Science*, **25** (2–3), 41–60.

Holland, T. (2007) *The Archivist's Story*, Bloomsbury.

Johnson, S. (2006) *The Native Commissioner*, Penguin Books.

Lalu, P. (2009) *The Deaths of Hintsa: postapartheid South Africa and the shape of recurring pasts*, HSRC Press.

Latour, B. (1986) Visualization and Cognition: thinking with eyes and hands, *Knowledge and Society*, **6** 1–4.

Mitchell, P. and Schoeffel, J. (eds) (2002) *Understanding Power: the indispensable Chomsky*, The New Press.

Nelson Mandela Foundation (2005) *A Prisoner in the Garden: opening Nelson Mandela's prison archive*, Penguin Books.

Saramago, J. (1999) *All the Names*, The Harvill Press.

Stoler, A. (2002) Colonial Archives and the Arts of Governance: on the content in the form. In Hamilton, C. et al. (eds), *Refiguring the Archive*, David Philip.

Vassanji, M.G. (1994) *The Book of Secrets*, McClelland and Stewart.

Wilson, R.A. (2001) *The Politics of Truth and Reconciliation in South Africa: legitimizing the post-apartheid state*, Cambridge University Press.

Notes

1   In preparing this chapter I have been mindful of the injunctions given to contributors by the editor. Two, in particular, are worth noting here. First, contributors were requested not to use the first person in their texts (footnotes, mercifully, were excluded from this constraint). For me this constitutes more than a stylistic modelling. Use of the first person came to me relatively late in my writing career, and when it did it had to overcome years of schooling in an academic discourse which discouraged the practice. In retrospect I understand that schooling to be part of an apparatus of knowledge construction which forbade admissions of subjectivity and indications of a subject–object divide which is necessarily and unavoidably porous. The chapter's absence of self-reflection and its claims to third person authority are, in large measure, the consequence of this constraint. Second, contributors were enjoined to write with a view to the book's primary purpose – to be a reader for postgraduate students. I'm not entirely sure how this has impacted on my writing, but I have consciously endeavoured to find an accessible register and to avoid 'at the edge' deconstructive exploration. I have attempted to pull together and elaborate on my own work over 20 years in the terrain I have named 'the play of power and politics in the archive'. I have used as a point of departure the rather similar commission I fulfilled in preparing *Exploring Archives*, a short textbook designed primarily for students of archive in South Africa in 1997 (first edition) and 2000 (second edition). With a northern hemisphere audience in mind, I have eschewed the strong South African signature in that work as far as possible, although the signature should remain evident – it defines who I am and how I see the world. As in

Exploring Archives, I have referenced thinkers and writers from various epistemological traditions, but this should not hide the fact that I work within an unashamedly deconstructive framework. Acknowledgement of this, and of my particular indebtedness to Jacques Derrida, is necessarily oblique in the text given the editorial commitment to use of the third person. My reading of Derrida's life and work has found a powerful resonance with my life experiences in South Africa in its transition from apartheid to a still fledgling democracy, issuing in a belief that the call of justice in relation to archive is to make it at once a weapon of liberation, an evidentiary stimulus to and limit on human memory and imagination, and a space for play. This is a belief informed by a faith that every human being is ultimately an alien, tempted by the allure of the archon but called to become the angel that destiny insists on. Faith, of course, is another dimension of knowledge construction frowned upon in present-day scholarly discourses, and I have kept it under tight rein for this project. I am also indebted to Kerry Harris, Shadrack Katuu and Professor John Wright, who offered me close and critical readings of the chapter's first draft, and to Jennie Hill, whose thoughtful editorial interventions concentrated my thinking and improved the text substantially.

2   Many of the witnesses at South Africa's Truth and Reconciliation Commission testified to this form of oppression. As has Pregs Govender in her autobiography *Love and Courage* (2007).

3   This judgement is based on the experience I gathered over three years as Director of the South African History Archive.

4   I have defined recordmaking as that huge and messy realm in which what are conventionally called records' creators, records' managers, archivists, users, and so on, negotiate, contest and narrate the contents, the contexts and the meanings of what are conventionally called 'records'. For an extended argument substantiating this definition, see Chapter 9 of my *Archives and Justice.*

5   Timothy Garton Ash provides a compelling account of disinformation and related dimensions of the security police file in his *The File* (1997).

6   Tracing the biography of the bequeathed or discovered record has become almost a genre in 'fiction'. To name a few of the more significant novels: A.S. Byatt's *Possession* (1990), M.G. Vassanji's *The Book of Secrets* (1994), José Saramago's *All the Names* (1997 in Portuguese, 1999 in English), Martha Cooley's *The Archivist* (1998), Shaun Johnson's *The Native Commissioner* (2006) and Travis Holland's *The Archivist's Story* (2007). The genre can even be found in movies – for example, *The Bridges of Madison County* (1995).

7   Here I'm signalling the work of Carl Jung and those, like James Hillman, who have been influenced by him.

8   While I was preparing this chapter a powerful example landed in my e-mail inbox. The Secretary General of the International Council on Archives (ICA), David Leitch, intervened in an ICA listserv discussion with the following warning: 'One of the strengths of the ICA network is that it encompasses many different cultures and traditions. As ICA is an organization for archive professionals, it is not appropriate to use the list-serv for the expression of political opinions. There are many other forums that are available for this purpose' (communication dated 9 January 2009).

9   Derrida made this argument in numerous texts. See, for example, Derrida, J. (1997) *Politics of Friendship* and Derrida, J. and Dufourmantelle, A. (2000) *Of Hospitality*, Stanford University Press. In the last decade of his life, from the 1994 publication in French of Politics of Friendship, Derrida repeatedly engaged the theme of hospitality.

7

Interactivity, flexibility and transparency: social media and Archives 2.0

Kate Theimer

Introduction

Today it is impossible for most people to imagine the world without the world wide web. This year's 'Mindset List', which annually compiles a list designed to reveal the world as the year's college freshmen know it, noted that for these students 'WWW has never stood for World Wide Wrestling' (Beloit College, 2009). Although the term 'internet' was first applied to the ARPANET (Advanced Research Projects Agency Network) system in 1974, it wasn't until it was opened to 'commercial interests' in 1988 that the public began to have access to (text only) services such as e-mail and bulletin boards (Wikipedia, accessed 2009). However, the date 6 August 1991, when Tim Berners-Lee first used hypertext in conjunction with the infrastructure provided by the internet, is generally credited as the birth of the world wide web (Wikipedia, accessed 2009). With the introduction of the first web browser, Mosaic, in 1993, most of the pieces of 'Web 1.0' were in place.

Beginnings of the world wide web

Most archives saw the value of using the web to publish information about themselves and their collections – usually in the form of putting finding aids online. In his 1995 article, 'Archival Outreach on the World Wide Web', William Landis (1995, 129, 133) reviewed four 'fairly mature Web sites', although he noted that an online list contained links to over 600 sites from 'around the world'. Also appearing in 1995 was David Wallace's 'Archival Repositories on the World Wide Web: A Preliminary Survey and Analysis', which reviewed 15 archival websites. Both Landis and Wallace conclude their articles by considering the value the web provided to archives. For Wallace, the value lay in the possibilities presented by 'data interchange standards':

> Since it is only through such standards that seamless virtual archives will cease to be institution-based and become user-driven. If the promise of hypertext and hypermedia is achieved, users will be able to leap from one site and collection to the next, tracing their unique research, education, and accountability needs across state and national borders without having to punch in a new URL [Uniform Resource Locator] or conduct stop-and-start searching.
>
> (Wallace, 1995, 168)

Like Wallace, Landis (1995, 145) envisioned one of the most significant aspects of the web to be the possibility to create 'a "seamless web" of digital information about repositories and their collections'. Both authors stressed the need to examine the intended (or potential) audience for an archives' website, but Landis went further:

> Taking traditional paper guides and inventories, research protocols, and ideas about how collections ought to be used and simply translating them into a digital environment seems like a tragic mistake. Such strategies may offer a place to begin, but it is crucial for this profession that archivists remain alive to the possibilities that this new environment offers. It is quite clear from developments over the past few years that historical materials have an immense fascination for people generally and that there are those who are ready to exploit that fascination in whatever way they can. Archivists have something to offer this potential audience, but the audience also has something to teach archivists. We risk quite a bit by failing to grasp the realities and possibilities of the digital world and by failing to educate future generations of archivists about those realities and possibilities.
>
> (Landis, 1995, 146)

In the early days of the web, interaction with users was most often demonstrated by the growing phenomenon of e-mail reference. In her article in the *American Archivist*, again from 1995, Helen Tibbo provided guidance on how to address reference requests received via 'electronic mail'. Interestingly, Tibbo (1995, 309) noted that: 'Recent comments on the

Archives and Archivists listserv indicate that many repositories that offer electronic mail reference tend to treat it just the same as postal service reference. This is unfortunate, as so much more is possible.' It was the potential for increased interaction with the researcher implicit in e-mail which Tibbo was advocating.

These early commentators saw the power inherent in the web for the sharing of information about collections and for interaction with audiences. However, as late as 1999 the possibilities for users locating relevant materials directly via searching the web were still unrealized according to the findings published in a Pease award-winning article in the *American Archivist*:

> The findings of this study suggest that the Internet is too large and heterogeneous a search ground in which to locate archival holdings information by commonly used Internet searching practices and tools . . . . The findings also suggest that electronic finding aids may not be well suited to serve as pointers to archival collections. Instead, they may be more appropriate as resources for researchers who have already located a repository's on-line resources through other means.
>
> While the ability to place archival holdings information on the Internet and to make that information electronically searchable is certainly an invaluable development for archives and their users, this study provides evidence of the continuing necessity of expertise and professional assistance in the traditional means of locating archival materials, whether through a logical, provenance-based search or through the use of subject guides.
>
> (Feeney, 1999, 224)

The search engines used in Feeney's study were AltaVista and HotBot. In 1998 Google – the search engine that would transform the way people accessed information on the web – was launched. By December 2008, Google had reached a worldwide market share of 82.7% among search engines (Wikipedia, accessed 2009). For most archivists, hearing 'I found you on Google' from users became a common refrain.

Google and its increasingly effective search algorithms gave archives a means of connecting searchers to collections – if Google could search your descriptions, users could find them without the need for a specialized database or union catalogue. This opened the discovery of archival collections to people across the world who probably never would have had the motivation or knowledge to look for them. But because information about archival collections is now showing up in the results pages of Google searches, it is likely that we are experiencing the beginnings of the democratization of archives users – although as yet we have no hard evidence of these changes. Prior to the web, only a small number of people (usually scholars) were ever aware of the existence of most archival collections; now at least the existence of most collections is discoverable on the web by anyone who enters the right search terms.

Web 2.0 tools

The web experienced another kind of revolution with the developments that have come to be known as 'Web 2.0'. The origins of the term are somewhat disputed, but its most prominent early use was by O'Reilly Media, which sponsored the 'Web 2.0' conference in 2004 (Wikipedia, accessed 2009). The term '2.0' refers to the system used by software developers to signify new versions of software – that is, by assigning a new number (rather than using, say, 1.8 or 1.9), the developers signal that this software release has significant changes and differences. 'Web 2.0' was used to signify that the web had begun a fundamental change in the way that people were able to use it.

There is no standard definition of Web 2.0. While O'Reilly Media may have popularized it, the term was not created by one company or one type of software. Rather, it describes a confluence of changes in web design and functionality that resulted in fundamental differences in the ways that developers and users approach the web. The most significant of these changes were:

- ■ 'Network as platform' or 'cloud computing' – applications and data 'live' on the web, not on your local computer, and so applications and data can be accessed from anywhere you have an internet connection.
- ■ Openness in technical interfaces and standards – the use of open standards and open source in software development and the use of open application programming interfaces (APIs) meant that websites and tools could interact with each other in new ways.

- Creation of syndicated content – use of 'really simple syndication' (RSS) allowed websites to 'push' customized content out to users, rather than users having to visit individual sites to 'pull' content out of them.
- Customized web experience for users – websites draw on user profile information to create customized views for each user.
- Broad use of interactivity – websites allow (and encourage) users to interact with posted content, using features such as commenting, tagging, ranking, making lists, and allowing many options for redistribution and sharing.
- Prevalence of user-created content – the rise of sites such as Wikipedia, Flickr, and YouTube, and tools like podcasting and blogging, which allow users to publish and share content made individual people just as much a force in publishing on the web as traditional information providers.
- Integration of user-to-user connection – a broad-based use of the web as a way to connect people to each other, not just to information sources.

Taken together these changes have transformed the way that people expect to access and interact with information on the web. While initially many archives were reluctant to commit resources to these kinds of 'frivolous' and 'faddish' outlets, the permeation of sites such as YouTube, Flickr, Twitter, Wikipedia, and Facebook into the public consciousness and the use of these tools by institutions such as the Library of Congress in the US and the National Archives in the UK have resulted in a rush of archives participating in social media. (For a listing of archives using Web 2.0 tools, see the Archives 2.0 Wiki at http://archives2point0.wetpaint.com.)

The Web 2.0 tools most commonly used by archives today for outreach are blogs, micro-blogging (Twitter), podcasting, image sharing (Flickr), video sharing (YouTube), social networking (Facebook), and wikis. Below are brief descriptions of each major Web 2.0 tool and a discussion of how they are being used by archives.

A blog is a web page or site created by software that allows material to be easily published in the same manner that log – or diary – entries are written in a journal. However, in a blog when a new entry is published, it appears at the top of the web page, moving older entries down, and eventually off, the site's first page. Because blog software is so simple, it is open to a wide range of uses. For example, the Dickinson College Archives has created a blog that provides a public listing – discoverable via search engines – of all their reference requests (http://itech.dickinson.edu/archives). This enables other users searching for the same topics, places, or people's names to discover that the college holds materials of possible interest to them.

Archives are also using blogs to virtually open some of their 'hidden' collections. Many archives have successfully implemented blogs that document the processing of a single collection, such as 'Processing the Chew Family Papers' from the Historical Society of Pennsylvania (http://chewpapers.blogspot.com). One recent blog has also documented the process of assembling an archival exhibit (http://atkinslibraryspecialcollections.wordpress.com). Several archives have begun using blogging software to create simplified online catalogues (or 'catablogs'), most prominently the 'UMarmot' blog created by the University of Massachusetts, Amherst (www.library.umass.edu/spcoll/umarmot). Many private collectors, as well as archives, have had success publishing date-based content, such as diaries and letters, via blogs, allowing the public to subscribe to the feed and follow along with the story. For example, you may now follow 'Scott's Last Expedition' on both Twitter (@scottslastexp) and a blog (www.spri.cam.ac.uk/museum/diaries/scottslastexpedition). Sponsored by the Scott Polar Research Institute, both the tweets and blog posts share entries exactly 99 years after they were written in a diary kept by Captain Robert Falcon Scott during the British Antarctic Expedition in 1910–12 (his last and fatal expedition).

However, the most basic and common type of archives blog is a means of publishing general information about the repository – such as changes in hours, collections acquired or open for research, and announcements about public programmes. Many archives have adopted blogging as an integral part of their overall outreach programme. For example, in the 'Historical Notes from OHSU' blog (http://ohsu-hca.blogspot.com), the relatively obscure collections of the Oregon Health and Science University (OHSU) have found a worldwide audience. Archivist Sara Piasecki writes:

> The results have been far more positive than I could ever have imagined when I conceived the blog. Patrons we never would have reached before now stumble

across us in Web searches. Readers from all sorts of communities (historians, librarians, archivists, healthcare workers, genealogists) have contacted us because of something they saw in some post or other of mine. We've received donations of materials from as far away as New York and Arizona. Awareness of our collections and services among the OHSU community has risen exponentially, and though that has come about in combination with other outreach efforts, the blog is definitely a part of it. Another wonderful aspect of blogging is the ability to tap into extramural expertise: when we posted about some mysterious Russian LPs [long-playing record albums] we had received, two readers quickly responded with translations of the jacket text.

(cited in Theimer, 2009, 39–40)

Perhaps because of their ease of use and flexibility, blogs are probably the most popular Web 2.0 tool currently used by archives. They were also among the first tools available, and are now a stable medium for sharing a wide variety of information. Blog software allows for sharing text posts – of any length – as well as images and embedded audio or video files.

Archives, like people, organizations, and businesses everywhere, have recently flocked to the microblogging site Twitter. Microblogging is, as it sounds, blogging on a very small scale. In the case of Twitter, users publish updates limited to 140 characters at a time. Twitter's limitations, however, are also its strengths, allowing archives to quickly and efficiently share information and interact with their followers. The Nova Scotia Archives (@NS_Archives) uses Twitter to both push out information about their activities and to interact with other regional cultural organizations, as well as their over 1800 followers. Archives are using Twitter to publish excerpts from diaries and letters in their collections, such as the Massachusetts Historical Society's account for John Quincy Adams (@JQAdams_MHS), which shares line-a-day diary entries, beginning with his journey to Russia on 5 August 1809. The National Archives of the Netherlands created an innovative Twitter account written from the point of view of the 'Schaghenletter' (@Schaghenletter), a 17th-century letter about the purchase of Manhattan, which travelled to New York in 2009 for an exhibition. The letter's tweets share information about the exhibition in a charming and quirky way.

Perhaps because it requires more technological expertise and infrastructure, archives have been slower to begin podcasting. Podcasting is the publishing of audio or video files, usually as an ongoing series to which people can subscribe, which are available for download to personal media players, such as iPods. Among the most prominent podcasters among archives is The National Archives (of the UK), which produces a very successful series that captures the wide range of public programmes and lectures sponsored by the archives (www.nationalarchives.gov.uk/rss/podcasts.xml). Using podcasting is an ideal means to extend the benefits of their already ongoing lecture series. The podcasts' producers wrote, 'while 20 to 100 people attend the regular talks and events at The National Archives in Kew, there are over 5,000 downloads of each talk' (Theimer, 2009, 62). Podcasting is also an ideal way to disseminate digitized audio and video material from an archives' holdings. The State Archives of Florida uses podcasting to make available one-of-a-kind recordings from its Folklife collections, including recordings of musical performances unavailable from any other source (www.floridamemory.com/collections/folklife/sound_pod.cfm). The Los Alamos Historical Society has built a surprisingly large following for its podcast series of excerpts from its oral history collections, featuring material highlighting the personal experiences of people associated with the Manhattan Project (www.losalamoshistory.org/pods.htm).

Perhaps no Web 2.0 tool is a better example of the potential that the web now has for sharing archival materials than Flickr. Using Flickr, anyone can upload digital images (or short videos) and share them with people around the world. Archives can allow users to add tags, notes and comments to images, as well as allowing them to be posted on blogs, added to Flickr galleries and group image 'pools'. While most archives have developed internal capabilities for posting digital images on their websites, those images are often not widely accessed by the general public and most internal systems have few of the social media functionalities provided by Flickr. 'Normal' accounts on Flickr are free, although a 'pro' account, with enhanced features, is also available at a very low cost. By sharing images on Flickr, archives are following the strategy of 'going where the users are', usually to great success. In January 2008, the Library of Congress posted two collections (totaling 4,615 images) on Flickr, classifying their participation as a 'pilot'. In the final report on that pilot, they observed that:

- As of October 23, 2008, there have been 10.4 million views of the photos on Flickr.
- 79% of the 4,615 photos have been made a 'favorite' (i.e., are incorporated into personal Flickr collections).
- Over 15,000 Flickr members have chosen to make the Library of Congress a 'contact,' creating a photostream of Library images on their own accounts.
- 7,166 comments were left on 2,873 photos by 2,562 unique Flickr accounts.
- 67,176 tags were added by 2,518 unique Flickr accounts.
- 4,548 of the 4,615 photos have at least one community-provided tag.
- Less than 25 instances of user-generated content were removed as inappropriate.
- More than 500 Prints and Photographs Online Catalog (PPOC) records have been enhanced with new information provided by the Flickr Community.
- Average monthly visits to all PPOC Web pages rose 20% over the five month period of January–May 2008, compared to the same period in 2007.

(Springer, et al., 2008, iv)

While few archives can match the scale of the Library of Congress' experience, the increased exposure for archives participating in Flickr, and the increased access to the digital images shared there has been a great benefit to cultural institutions, at very little cost.

The popular video-sharing site YouTube operates in much the same way as Flickr. For no cost, users post digital video files, which are then accessible to anyone visiting the YouTube site – which means millions of people each day. Like Flickr, YouTube provides users with the ability to interact with and share video content, for example by commenting on videos, adding them to playlists, rating them, and posting video responses. However, while the majority of archives use Flickr to share digitized images from their collections, YouTube provides a platform for more diverse uses. For example, Purdue University Archives has created original videos describing items from their collections and providing examples of how to date historic photographs (www.youtube.com/user/PUarchives). In an effort to educate users about how archives work, The National Archives of the UK has created a series of videos explaining topics such as 'The life of a document', 'Preparing to research', 'Using the catalogue', 'How records are arranged' and 'Ordering documents' (www. youtube.com/user/NationalArchives08). Other archives, such as the State Records Office for New South Wales and the University of Manitoba Archives, have created videos that are essentially animated slide shows of still photographs, accompanied by music or explanatory audio. Of course, a wide range of archives are also using YouTube to disseminate digitized archival video content – including the National Archives and Records Administration (US) (www.youtube.com/user/usnationalarchives) and the National Library of Scotland (www.youtube.com/user/ NLofScotland).

Most Web 2.0 sites or applications incorporate social networking features – such as tagging, commenting, sending messages, creating networks, marking 'favorites,' sharing content, etc. – but social networking sites, like Facebook, MySpace, and Ning, exist purely to provide a space for creating social networks. Facebook has emerged as the pre-eminent social networking site, attracting millions of users across all age groups. In its early development, Facebook was used primarily by individuals, including archivists, to create informal networks, to share information, and to use formal groups for networking. However, as its growth skyrocketed, Facebook added more capabilities for organizations, such as archives, to share information through the creation of 'fan pages'. Fan pages allow archives to push updates out to their network of 'fans', as well as to post links, videos and pictures and host discussions. Facebook also facilitates easy sharing of content posted on other Web 2.0 sites, such as Twitter, YouTube and Flickr, meaning that an organization's Facebook page can become a virtual dashboard, or place for 'one-stop shopping' for Web 2.0 content sharing on many sites. With Facebook content now visible to non-members as well as members and discoverable via Google searches, a Facebook page has become an essential part of most archives' social media strategies.

The Coca-Cola Archives uses its Facebook page to share new blog posts, as well as posting videos and behind-the-scenes pictures (www. facebook.com/CokeArchives). The Bancroft Library (the primary special collections library at the University of California, Berkeley) posts a 'digital object of the day' on their Facebook wall, (www.facebook. com/pages/Berkeley-CA/The-Bancroft-Library). The Alabama Department of Archives and History has 900 fans of its Facebook page, and makes frequent posts to its 'wall', as well as hosting albums of images and a number of 'fan photos' (www.facebook.com/pages/Montgomery-AL/Alabama-Department-of-Archives-and-History/129258533071).

Because of the popularity of Wikipedia, most people who use the web are somewhat familiar with how wikis work. Wiki software allows for the collaborative building and editing of websites, as well as preserving a record of how the site content has been changed over time. An important aspect of wikis is that they allow you to track which user made which changes to any given web page, and they allow administrators to adjudicate those changes, rejecting spurious ones and returning the site content to its earlier state. Wikis can be relatively easy to launch – either through downloading software (such as MediaWiki) onto local servers or by using a commercially hosted site (such as PBWorks or WetPaint). However, perhaps because editing and contributing to a wiki does require a few hurdles, archives have been slower to embrace wikis than they have been to post content on blogs, Flickr, Twitter or Facebook. One notable exception to this is the 'Your Archives' wiki hosted by The National Archives (UK) (http://yourarchives.nationalarchives.gov.uk). This site, created by archives staff and contributed to by both staff and the public, was established to provide a forum (outside of the formal collections catalogue) for the collection and dissemination of information about the historical topics pertinent to the archives' collections. Several colleges and universities in the United States, such as the College of William and Mary (http://scrc.swem.wm.edu/wiki/index.php/Main_Page), and the University of Massachusetts, Amherst (www.library.umass.edu/spcoll/youmass/doku.php), have created wikis to capture commonly requested and used information in one easily accessible and updatable online location. Wikis are also used internally by archives staff to share administrative information and track project progress. In one innovative example, the University of Pittsburgh's Archival Service Center used a wiki to collect and share information on the processing of an intriguing series of records – the Allegheny County Coroner's Case Files (http://coronercasefile. pbworks.com), but also made the wiki available to the public, providing detailed information about the materials in addition to the formal finding aid for the collection.

While these Web 2.0 tools are currently the most popular among archives on the web, they are certainly not the only options available. For example, there are other social networking sites (such as LinkedIn and MySpace) and there are other kinds of online opportunities, like the virtual world, Second Life. However blogs, Twitter, podcasting, Flickr, YouTube, Facebook and wikis are by far the most commonly used and it appears that they will continue to be so for at least some time to come.

The impact of Web 2.0 on archives

The use of these kinds of new web tools is both evidence of change in the archival mindset and a catalyst for bringing those changes about. These changes in the way that archives operate and think about themselves are sometimes referred to as 'Archives 2.0' – reflecting the influence of Web 2.0 on the profession and representing a shorthand way of indicating a new 'version' or generation of the archival profession. While there are many ways to characterize this change in mindset, it is clearly typified by a desire for interactivity, flexibility and transparency. While there are clearly overlap and dependencies between these concepts, it is important to understand how each of them is affecting the profession today and how the changes themselves are dependent on Web 2.0 technologies.

One of the most obvious changes made possible by Web 2.0 applications is the opportunity to invite users to interact directly with both archival materials and archivists. Prior to the web – and to Web 2.0 in particular – communication and access were limited almost exclusively to formal mechanisms. Archival materials were accessed through visits to the research room or viewing by microfilm. Responses or discoveries about the materials were shared with the archivist alone or with the scholarly community through publications. Visits to the repository (or telephone calls) were the exceptional opportunity for 'real time' interactivity between visitors and the archivist, and were usually limited to professional historians, intrepid family historians or private scholars.

One aspect of the interactivity that Web 2.0 brought to archives is clearly the opportunity to make images of archival materials available through sites like Flickr and YouTube. These sites allow for the antithesis of the pre-web scenario. Anyone with an internet connection may now access these materials at any time – no appointment necessary. Podcasting of digitized archival material – such as the oral histories made available by the Los Alamos Historical Society – allow users to take the archival experience with them wherever they go with their MP3 player. Some archives are taking the next natural step and are creating applications that are designed to run on mobile devices (such as the popular iPhone), giving people opportunities to interact with archival collections from virtually anywhere. Among the first of these applications are those from The National Archives (UK) and Duke University which allow users to easily browse images from the digital collections via their iPhones.

Just as social media sites provide a framework for making archival materials more accessible on the web, they also mean that the archivist can be more accessible as well. By actively using tools like blogs, Twitter and Facebook, many archivists have opened up the virtual door to their own offices, just as other tools open up the virtual doors to their storage areas. Being 'available' through these kinds of social media provides users with a chance to exchange opinions with, or ask questions of, archivists without the formal mechanisms that were previously required. The Nova Scotia Archives' use of Twitter, as well as Facebook, is exemplary in this regard because of the way that they have created a friendly and approachable online persona. The US National Archives and Records Administration's (NARA) 'NARAtions' blog (http://blogs.archives.gov/online-public-access) regularly invites user input on how NARA should approach social media, posing questions such as 'We are considering starting an ongoing mini interview feature with selected NARA archivists – what questions should we ask them?' and 'What tools and processes do you suggest we use to transcribe NARA's billions of pages of handwritten documents quickly and efficiently?'

The use of these kinds of tools to increase interactivity between the archives and users is not just the result of new technological opportunities; it also represents a change in philosophy and thinking. Sites like Flickr don't just allow archives to publish collections – they also enable users to add notes and comments and tag images with their own keywords. Opening up collections to this kind of public interaction is antithetical to the ideas held by many archivists in the past about controlling how collections are catalogued, described and accessed. Sites such as The National Archives' 'Your Archives' wiki, which exist primarily as a vehicle for soliciting information and contributions from the public, typify this change in how the relationship between the archives and the public is framed.

Perhaps it is not surprising that commercial sites that feature archival materials – such as Footnote and Ancestry – have taken the lead in providing opportunities for users to interact with online materials. These commercial sites have a more focused audience (primarily genealogists and family historians), access to more resources for developing the technology necessary to support interaction, and a driving need to provide tools that give them a competitive advantage in their marketplace. Given how many people access archival materials primarily or exclusively through commercial sites, anyone looking for insight into what kinds of services archives might be providing in the future should pay attention to the options available on these kinds of sites. For example, Footnote allows you to annotate documents (maybe to help transcribe difficult handwriting), add comments (perhaps to make a note of any inaccurate information in the document), create galleries of content that interests you, create your own 'pages', create a 'spotlight' on a particularly interesting document or area of a document, create 'connections' between online content (documents and images) and upload images to share publicly. This is certainly more interactivity than any archive is currently able to provide, and studying how these features are used could provide insight into what kinds of interactivity users value most.

However, it is not just the level of interactivity that is different for archives with Web 2.0 – it is also the kind of interactions. The kinds of archival materials being posted, the places in which they are posted, and the ways that they are published are, in many cases, designed to appeal to a general, non-scholarly (and often a non-genealogical) audience.

Publishing historic diaries and letters on blogs or Twitter is a means of drawing in people who want to follow a narrative – a story. Rarely in the past have archives been tellers of stories; more often they have relied on others to share the stories found in the collections. This appeal to people's need for entertainment or emotional connection is seen even more clearly in the kinds of reactions that people have to images and videos posted on social media sites. These materials amuse, trigger personal recollections, and often evoke a 'wow' response. Often today's audiences seek out archival materials online because they want to have an interaction with 'the past', not because they are looking for specific historical information. Increasingly archives are recognizing that these kinds of interactions have just as much value for their institutions as more traditional, scholarly efforts.

This discussion of the new interactivity of archives using Web 2.0 tools has also demonstrated another characteristic of 'Archives 2.0' – flexibility. In addition to having reputations as 'closed' or restrictive places, many archives (and archivists) were also traditionally characterized as being rigid and inflexible. While not justified in many cases, this stereotype reflects that all too often in the past archivists adhered too strictly to ideas about what constituted appropriate use of their collections and were reluctant to explore new ways of making collections accessible to the public.

This new flexibility can be seen in the willingness to separate archival material from its original context and give up strict limits on control by sharing materials on sites such as Flickr and YouTube. Being open to letting these materials stand on their own, outside of the traditional archival framework, allows the archives to put their materials where the audience is already going. This flexibility allows the materials to be present where the people are, not either passively waiting for users to come to the archives or trying (in vain, almost certainly) to promote the materials in a way that is competitive with popular social media sites.

It should be noted that the willingness to be a part of popular commercial sites is often itself evidence of a new flexibility. Establishing a 'fan page' on a social networking site like Facebook or starting a Twitter account may have once seemed like something that was beneath the dignity of a prominent archival institution; but more and more archives understand that this is the level of interaction much of today's public expects from all cultural heritage institutions. This willingness to share materials through social media is itself a way of acknowledging that there is a broad diverse popular audience for archival materials, beyond the traditional audiences of historians, scholars and genealogists.

The flexibility to share materials through sites where people can post comments and share information also demonstrates a new openness to encouraging the contributions of others – and in many cases the contributions of non-scholars. This kind of 'crowd sourcing', acknowledging the expertise that exists in the population of web users, is what built Wikipedia, arguably the most commonly used reference site on the web. Allowing Flickr users to tag images can result in some inaccurate, silly or even incomprehensible tags being applied, but that in itself can be informative, and it also results in more correct tags being applied than the archives have time to add. This willingness to open up the collections and allow people with specific subject matter expertise – for example, knowledge of a different language, specific location or local culture, or a familiarity with the details of a historic event – to share their knowledge builds on the general trend in Web 2.0 towards harnessing the possibilities inherent in a truly world wide web.

Another aspect of 'Archives 2.0' made possible by technology, but not created by it, is the flexibility to find new ways of doing things. The 'catablog' is a perfect example – the archivists who started the UMarmot catablog wanted to quickly and easily publish descriptive information on the web without creating complete finding aids or utilizing an online catalogue. They wanted to be able to update or change their descriptions, sort them, add tags, and allow the public to find the descriptions via search engines and to comment on them. Their solution was to use blogging software to create a new kind of online catalogue. Similarly, several archives, including the Amsterdam City Archives and the National Archives of Australia, have implemented systems that allow users to request that archival materials be scanned for them. This 'scan on demand' business model allows users to have remote access to the materials that they desire (for a small fee) while enabling the archives to increase the amount of materials scanned – and ensures that the materials being scanned are the ones that users most want. Projects like these, which involve changing traditional business practices, may be made possible by technology but they are not driven by technology. They are the work of archivists who are open to new ways of problem solving and have the flexibility to adapt their processes to most effectively meet their users' needs.

One of the most creative people writing about the impact of the web, David Weinberger, wrote, 'Transparency is the new objectivity' (referring to the differences between print and web journalism). While one can argue whether this statement is true with regards to journalism, it certainly is an idea that should be considered in the archival context as well. In the past, archivists were trained to strive for objectivity in their work – both in how they processed collections and in how they treated researchers. Today most people agree that true objectivity is almost impossible; everyone has inherent biases, even if they are not malicious or even conscious. Weinberger wrote:

> Objectivity used to be presented as a stopping point for belief: If the source is objective and well-informed, you have sufficient reason to believe. The objectivity

of the reporter is a stopping point for reader's inquiry. That was part of high-end newspapers' claimed value: You can't believe what you read in a slanted tabloid, but our news is objective, so your inquiry can come to rest here. Credentialing systems had the same basic rhythm: You can stop your quest once you come to a credentialed authority who says, 'I got this. You can believe it.' End of story.

(Weinberger, 2009)

Archivists were trained to think that they should (and could) create objective archival descriptions – we were that kind of 'credentialed authority'. What we provided might not be complete, but it was objective. However, in his discussion of archival description in *Archives Power: memory, accountability, and social Justice* (2009), Randall Jimerson observes:

> As they engage with the archival record, both within governmental, business, academic, and other institutional archives and in manuscript collecting repositories, archivists also manipulate the past, either deliberately, or, far more often, subconsciously. Tom Nesmith observes that in both description and reference, archivists 'significantly shape what counts as meaningful context.' This considerable power 'can clearly influence readings by users of archives.'
>
> (Jimerson, 2009, 309–10)

Jimerson argues that the solution to this for archivists is to 'recognize their unavoidable influence on the process and to make their actions as transparent as possible' (Jimerson, 2009, 311). One strategy proposed to make the work of the archivist more transparent is the addition of more information about the circumstances of processing, or 'colophons'. In their 2002 article in the *American Archivist*, Tom Hyry and Michelle Light presented an argument that archivists should incorporate two changes to the traditional finding aid: colophons (including, for example, additional information about the processing and processors of the collection) and annotations (notes added to the finding aid by researchers, references archivists, and others who use the collection) (Hyry and Light, 2002). Looking back after seven years, the notion that the finding aid is the right vehicle for this kind of transparency is debatable, but Hyry and Light's conclusion still rings true, perhaps even more so as we consider how social media tools can help make their recommendations a reality:

Colophons and annotations represent suggestions for shifts in archival methodology as a response to postmodern criticism. If employed, they would allow us to be more open about our techniques, to incorporate multiple perspectives about the content of collections, and to provide a structure for recording growth in meaning of collections. They would also force researchers to acknowledge the value we add to collections and spark more dialogue between the keepers and users of archives, which in turn will lead to greater understanding of the historical record. By revealing the nature of our decisions and opening them up to a broader community for further interpretation, we fulfill to a greater extent our responsibility and role in the transmittal of culture and social memory.

(Hyry and Light, 2002, 239)

Processing blogs, which often document the context and decisions related to processing a collection, help achieve many of these aims. They can also 'spark more dialogue' – as can other kinds of blogs and other forms of social media. However, in addition to the need for more transparency surrounding the processing and description of archival collections, increasing transparency can also mean lifting the veil that has previously separated archivists from the public. Often part of the means of preserving the objectivity or neutrality of the archivist was that he or she should try to be as invisible as possible. Unfortunately, this has resulted in a public – and at times even a scholarly public – that does not understand what the role of the archivist is, or what it is exactly that we do. Tools like blogs and podcasts and sites such as Twitter and Facebook allow archivists to talk directly to the public about what they are working on, sharing the excitement of new discoveries or acquisitions, and the occasional horrors of archival work, such as flooding or insect infestations. Using these kinds of Web 2.0 tools allows the voice of the archivist to come through and be personal; they encourage a non-corporate presence, with humour, enthusiasm, or whatever kind of quirkiness the archivist chooses to convey. Communicating in this way is not only a means of publishing information, it is also a way of informing the public about the nature of archival work and of putting a human face on the person who previously existed only behind the scenes.

Using the tools of social media – blogs, Twitter, Facebook, Flickr, wikis or whatever comes next – to ask the public for its input also demonstrates that the process of creating descriptions of archives is iterative. This kind of transparency, also demonstrated in products like catablogs, opens up the process of creating description. Rather than hiding behind a shield of anonymity (and hence presumed expertise and neutrality), inviting the public to share in the process of creating descriptions and contributing ideas for the archival programme as a whole (as NARA does on its blog) invites collaboration with users. These kinds of collaborations, however informal and uncontrolled they are, may result in users with a greater appreciation for archival collections and a greater sense of investment in the archives. In this regard, transparency is not merely or only professionally responsible (as Jimerson and others argue), but constitutes a form of advocacy for the archives. By opening up more and more aspects of archival practice to the public for their entertainment, education and participation, the archives can create a public with greater understanding and emotional connection to the archival mission.

Conclusion

One common thread that runs through these increases in interactivity, flexibility and transparency is a new focus on the users of archives. While not directly caused by the evolution of web technology, this emphasis on the researcher has coincided with the rise of social media tools that also emphasize user participation. Therefore it is no surprise that today's archivists are increasingly taking advantage of social media to reach more potential users, share more materials, seek out user contributions and demystify the archival endeavour.

These kinds of changes are not without risk, as Joy Palmer (2009) points out in her article 'Archives 2.0: if we build it, will they come?' Palmer discusses the possibilities that users may not embrace the opportunities for interaction that archives are building with Web 2.0 tools, as well as the thorny issues related to archival authority in this environment. If archives were to turn exclusively to social media tools for outreach and interactions with patrons, there would also be a risk of leaving behind those who do not have internet (and particularly high-speed internet) access. Concerns about the so-called 'digital divide' must be taken into account, particularly if the archival materials pertain to a community that traditionally does not use the web for communications and research. Another challenge is that there is as yet no established method of preserving many social media products; any archive that wishes to permanently preserve the Web 2.0 products it creates does not have a suite of tools and processes to turn to for preservation. There are, however, options available for preserving most Web 2.0 content (although they may not be ideal from an archival point of view) and research in this area is underway by both archivists and those with a commercial interest in preserving social media.

But despite these risks, the tools of Web 2.0 are supporting and complementing the current shift in the archival profession away from a focus on the primacy of our materials to practices that focus first on the users of archives, and that is a shift that can only benefit our profession. At least in the United States, during much of the 20th century the archival profession focused most of its attention on establishing and implementing professional standards and establishing physical and intellectual control over archival collections. Only recently has the research community and the profession as a whole begun to seriously consider who are users are, who they could be, how they want to use our materials and what they have to contribute. The development of 'Archives 2.0' and the embrace of Web 2.0 tools by the profession, both in the US and around the world, is an indication of a new user-centred approach.

It is worth returning to William Landis' observations from 1995, perhaps just as true now as they were then:

> It is crucial for this profession that archivists remain alive to the possibilities that this new environment offers . . . . Archivists have something to offer this potential audience, but the audience also has something to teach archivists. We risk quite a bit by failing to grasp the realities and possibilities of the digital world and by failing to educate future generations of archivists about those realities and possibilities.
>
> (Landis, 1995, 146)

Based on the evidence of their approach to using Web 2.0 tools, it appears that the archival profession is indeed 'alive to the possibilities' of our current environment. And, as Web 2.0 is surpassed by 3.0 and 4.0 and whatever comes next, let us hope that we continue to be open to those possibilities and that we are successful in not only educating future generations, but ensuring that they too recognize that archives must always be places valued for the services they provide in preserving and making available to the public information of enduring value.

References

Beloit College (2009) Mindset List, Beloit, Wisconsin, www.beloit.edu/mindset/2012.php.

Feeney, K. (1999) Retrieval of Archival Finding Aids Using World-Wide-Web Search Engines, *The American Archivist*, **62** (2), 206–28.

Hyry, T. and Light, M. (2002) Colophons and Annotations: new directions for the finding aid, *The American Archivist,* **65** (2), 216–30.

Internet (2009) Wikipedia, http://en.wikipedia.org/wiki/Internet (accessed 26 August 2009).

Jimerson, R.J. (2009) *Archives Power: memory, accountability, and social justice*, Society of American Archivists.

Landis, W. (1995) Archival Outreach on the World Wide Web, *Archival Issues*, **20** (2), 129–47.

Palmer, J. (2009) Archives 2.0: If we build it, will they come?, *Ariadne,* **60** (July), www.ariadne.ac.uk/issue60/palmer.

Search Engine (2009) Wikipedia, http://en.wikipedia.org/wiki/Web_search_engine (accessed 1 December 2009).

Springer, M., Dulabahn, B., Michel, P., Natanson, B., Reser, D., Woodward, D. and Zinkham, H. (2008) For the Common Good: The Library of Congress Flickr Pilot Project, Washington, The Library of Congress, October 30, www.loc.gov/rr/print/flickr_report_final.pdf.

Tibbo, H. (1995) Interviewing Techniques for Remote Reference: electronic versus traditional environments, *The American Archivist,* **58** (3), 294–310.

Theimer, K. (2009) *Web 2.0 Tools and Strategies for Archives and Local History Collections*, Neal-Schuman Publishers.

Wallace, D. (1995) Archival Repositories on the World Wide Web: a preliminary survey and analysis, *Archives & Museum Informatics*, **9** (2), 150–69.

Web 2.0 (2009) Wikipedia, http://en.wikipedia.org/wiki/Web_2.0 (accessed 25 May 2009).

Weinberger, D. (2009) Transparency is the New Objectivity, Joho the Blog, 19 July, www.hyperorg.com/blogger/2009/07/19/transparency-is-the-new-objectivity.

World Wide Web (2009) Wikipedia, http://en.wikipedia.org/wiki/World_Wide_Web (accessed 26 August 2009).

8

The impact of independent and community archives on professional archival thinking and practice[1]

Andrew Flinn

Introduction

In 2004 the Archives Task Force (ATF), established by the UK Museums, Libraries and Archives Council (MLA) to consider the state of the archive sector in the UK, issued a report that concluded that 'archives in the community [were] as important to society as those in public collections' and should therefore be 'accessible to everyone' (ATF, 2004, 43). This statement represented for the first time wider public and professional recognition of the existence and significance of archival collections held outside of professionally staffed archives. The existence of these collections was in itself not new but the acknowledgement of their wider public significance was unusual. Such recognition carried with it implications for professional archival practice and perhaps thinking. If these collections were now deemed so important, how was their accessibility and sustainability to be guaranteed? Indeed what right was there to guarantee the accessibility of privately held collections to everyone (Hopkins, 2008, 88) and what might be the role for archival (and other heritage) professionals in seeking to support these preservation and access imperatives?

The ATF report was just one example of a growing awareness of the independent, personal and community archival activity occurring to a large extent outside the ambit of professional practice as well as a better appreciation of the significance of such activity. In the UK this appreciation was expressed in a variety of ways including the growth of professional interactions with independent and community archivists (either on the ground or via advisory bodies such as the Community

Archives and Heritage Group [CAHG]), the development of policy and guidance relating to these archives emanating from government and heritage sector bodies, and a range of journal articles, books and research projects looking at the origins, motivations, impacts and challenges of independent community archives and heritage activity. Internationally countries including (but surely not exclusively) South Africa, Australia, New Zealand and the USA have held conferences and produced guidance materials discussing independent and community archival activity.[2] This chapter will seek to take stock of these developments by examining some of the meanings, history and context which lie behind the 'community archives movement', distinguish between different types of activity, and then explore how these activities have impacted on professional archival thinking and practice. The chapter will conclude by observing that independent and community archives have much in common with private or personal archival activity and thus does not so much provoke new ways of thinking about archival theory and practice as suggest a further undermining of the already unsustainable tenets of objectivity, neutrality and custody in professional thinking in favour of broader, more inclusive and diverse approaches.

Definitions, scope and history

An essential starting point for discussion of the implications of independent and community archival activity for the dominant principles of archival theory and practice is to examine the history and attempt to clarify what we mean by independent and community archives. The term 'community archive' is one which has come to prominence in the UK in the early part of the 21st century, and is used in other countries as well. However it is also a term capable of varied interpretation and its use is subject to some controversy and debate. Problems with the term include concerns over the correct usage of the words 'community' and 'archive' as well as with the external designation as 'community archive' those organizations and initiatives that may not themselves use or even recognize the term.

Unease regarding the use of 'community' centres on the lack of clear understanding of what the term actually means despite its ubiquity in contemporary discourse. Particular disquiet is expressed about the narrow and frequently essentialized usage in public policy-speak where it is often represented as either an unalloyed and frequently unexplored 'good' (as in 'building community spirit' or 'community cohesion') or as a way of 'othering' a specific group in society (as in 'the black community', 'the Asian community' or 'the gay community'). In this latter case, the word 'community' can be seen as a euphemism employed to dismiss or disparage the activities of a group of activists as a 'minority' concern, not reflective of the interests of the broad mainstream of society (Alleyne, 2002; Waterton and Smith, 2010). In light of these objections it may be more appropriate to refer to these initiatives as independent archives or at least as independent community archives (Flinn and Stevens, 2009, 5).

Questions about the appropriateness of the usage of the terms 'archive' and 'archives' to describe these organizations and their collections are important ones to which this chapter will return in more detail later. In brief there has been some objection by professional archivists to use of the terms to describe these initiatives. Indeed the materials collected and made available by bodies which identify themselves or have been otherwise denoted as community archives almost always include a range of material such as copied and actively created documentary matter, objects, books, oral history testimonies, photographs and other audiovisual materials, organizational and personal ephemera, clothes and works of art, all of which would usually be excluded from traditional professional definitions of an archive. This has provoked a rather defensive reaction among some archivists, perhaps fearing an undermining of their professional status. As a consequence even some sympathetic observers have argued that it would have been less contentious if these terms had not been used to refer to these collections and their custodians (Maher, 1998, 254; Jenkins, 2009). This chapter will reflect further on these definitional questions later but it does suggest that independent and community archives transcend traditional barriers between museums, libraries and archives (as well as calling into question the appropriateness of too rigid distinctions between 'the amateur' and 'the professional', 'the producer' and 'the consumer').

This leads to the final point of critical examination of the terminology employed, the external designation of bodies as community archives. Whilst there are many initiatives in the UK and elsewhere that have actively associated themselves with the term 'community archive', there are a large number of other organizations which have been identified by others as belonging to this category without necessarily recognizing or using the term themselves. Whilst it is clearly problematic and potentially misleading to categorize activities from outside, I would argue that as long as much of the content and activity of independent archives and libraries, oral history projects, local heritage groups, community museums, community resource and archive centres is similar to those self-identifying as community archives, then it is more useful to view them as diverse expressions of a similar activity rather than emphasize the differences. Especially when those differences may in some cases only mirror the often arbitrary and artificial divisions of the professional heritage world. In the view of this chapter, what is ultimately more significant is the activity itself (and the motivations which inspire the activity) rather than the terminology that is used to describe it.

As a rule, discussion in the UK has acknowledged these difficulties and has focused on the activity rather than the form. The accepted definitions or descriptions of independent community archives have tended to be broad and inclusive, emphasizing diversity and variety rather than being prescriptive and dogmatic. So, for instance, the CAHG (2009) notes that 'community archives and heritage initiatives come in many different forms and seek to document the history of all manner of local, occupational, ethnic, faith and other diverse communities'. They do this 'by collecting, preserving and making accessible documents, photographs, oral histories and many other materials which document the histories of particular groups and localities'. On the associated Community Archives website (www.communityarchives.org), which seeks in part to provide a directory of UK community archives, the definition is an even simpler one. A community archive is one in which 'the subject-matter of the collection is a community of people. The classic example is a group of people who live in the same location, but there are "communities of interest" as well, such as people who worked in a certain profession' adding only the proviso that 'the process of creating the collection has involved the community'.

Within this inclusive framework it is important to acknowledge the huge variety of independent community activity, whether it be in terms of the size and resources, the length of time established, the physical, virtual or hybrid status, the materials collected, the community or group represented, or the level of autonomy or independence. Despite advocating the utility of inclusive definitions when thinking about community archive activity, three of these distinctive criteria (on collections; independence; and motivation and objectives) deserve brief further reflection. First, collections. As has already been noted, community archives frequently hold materials that transcend traditional archival definitions, including items that have been actively created or which are more frequently regarded as being museum objects, library materials or of ephemeral quality. Within the context of community archives, such distinctions are largely irrelevant, but it is important that there are collections of some sort, and that the collection and creation of largely primary source materials is a fundamental objective of the archive. It is the collection of source materials which distinguishes the community archive from, for example, the local history society, which is primarily concerned with holding meetings, hosting lectures and producing publications. If, however, the history group in addition to the above also records oral testimonies, collects photographs, encourages the writing and preservation of individual unpublished memoirs, and makes copies (digital or transcriptions) of rare documents, then its work might also be considered akin to that of a community archive (McKay, 2005, 134–5). The originality and uniqueness of the materials is not so much the crucial factor – as in time such copies may become the only copies, or at least the only accessible copies – rather it is the very act of collecting which ultimately defines the community archive.

Scope

The next criterion worthy of examination relates to different levels of autonomy and independence, of community participation and perhaps cultural ownership. Some definitions of independent community archives focus on the content of the collections (material which is about a specific group or community) without necessarily stipulating that the materials should be created, collected or owned by members of that community. A UK report by Jura Consultants (2009, 12) for MLA suggested that community archives could be located anywhere on a scale between projects which were 'initiated by statutory organisation[s]' with limited involvement from the community concerned, and those archives which were formed as part of a grassroots movement and owned by the social group or community that they describe. The generally accepted position within the UK (including by the CAHG) is to acknowledge those archival activities that are largely inspired by a mainstream heritage or other government body as long as there is clear community involvement and the creation or collection of archival material, as well as those which emerge more organically as grassroots initiatives. Others, including the present author, believe that whilst not necessarily wholly disengaged from government agencies, independent community archives are better understood as those bodies substantially inspired, owned and controlled by the group or the community whose history they seek to represent (Flinn, Stevens and Shepherd, 2009, 73).

The extent to which a community archive must be independent and community owned is clearly one that is open to debate but it is nevertheless beyond argument that one key to understanding a specific organization or initiative is the extent to which the project is motivated by a sense of grassroots empowerment and community action as opposed to being the result of the initiative of a state or heritage body. A South African conference on community archives convened by the Gay and Lesbian Archives of South Africa and the South Africa History Archives concluded that 'a key premise of community archiving is to give substance to a community's right to own its own memories' and that 'community participation is a core principle of community archives' (Eales, 1998). Those archives whose history and activities closely approximate this definition are likely to differ substantially in their approaches to archival thinking from those projects which result from an external impetus. In some cases, such as the principles of autonomous 'radical archiving' developed by the Lesbian Herstory Archive in New York (www.lesbianherstoryarchives.org), grassroots control ('the community should share in the work of the Archives') can imply complete independence from mainstream funding ('funding is sought from within the community the Archives serves, rather than from outside sources') and paradigms ('archival skills shall be taught, one generation of Lesbians to another, breaking the elitism of traditional archives') (Loeb, 1981, 2). In some cases, notions of 'community' ownership extend to seeking to retain physical custody over the collections; in other cases physical custody may be relinquished if a substantial degree of intellectual ownership and control can be guaranteed.

Understanding the importance of community participation and ownership in different independent and community archives, lies at the root of the final criterion discussed here, between those initiatives which we might describe as 'serious leisure' heritage activities (Finnegan, 2005, 6) and those which are motivated by political and cultural concerns and might be better understood not as heritage bodies at all, but as social movements seeking to achieve some measure of social and political transformation. Most community archives, including those seeking to document a local area or a workplace are motivated by the desire to recover hidden histories absent from (perhaps geographically removed) mainstream heritage institutions or to preserve memories of occupations and skills before they are consigned to obscurity. However for the politically motivated archives, as social movements, their commitment is even more pronounced, emphasizing both the absence of material from mainstream archives and museums and then the benefits which preserving and using this material brings to individuals and to the group. Politically motivated archives, whether they are constituted around race and ethnicity, class, gender or sexuality are uniformly 'more overt in [their] mission to include those fragments and perspectives that ordinarily would not be recognised as valid or worth preserving by a more conventional repository' (Eales, 1998). Furthermore in these cases, the collection and preservation of such materials is not about "serious leisure" but about their use for political and educational purposes, either as tools in contemporary struggles (Sivanandan, 2008, 28; Nestle, 1990, 91), or to remember and commemorate past lives whose achievements were disfigured by trauma and discrimination (Ajamu X, Campbell and Stevens, 2009, 283–4), or to combat the alienation and disempowerment of those, particularly the young, denied access to their own history (Garrison, 1994, 238–9; Fullwood, 2009, 247–8). One does not have to judge one archive or initiative better than another to realize that it is important to acknowledge these distinctions and the extent to which the motivations and objectives which underlie the archives fundamentally inform the way they approach their work and how they think about what they are doing and what they are trying to achieve.

History

A further sense of the distinctions between the archive as community heritage and the archive as social movement (and how they have subsequently cross-fertilized each other) can be determined by briefly examining the history of independent community archives in the UK.[3] As the accounts of Hunt (2005), Drake (2005) and Mander (2009) all testify, amateur or non-professional, non-academic antiquarian, archaeological and local history groups have been in existence, collecting and creating local historical collections for over 300 years. Many of these societies have long since disappeared with their collections ending up in local museums, libraries and archives, or indeed in some cases evolving into those museums and archives (Shepherd, 2009, 177–8). Some, however, have remained in existence for over a hundred years or more and particularly, but not only, in rural areas at some distance from the nearest conventional heritage body have continued to collect and preserve materials of local historical interest (Mander, 2009, 30; Flinn, 2007, 155). Interest in local history (and hence in the collection of local history materials by local groups) was further stimulated by the work of the Workers' Educational Association and university extra-mural departments after World War 2.

From the 1960s onwards, interest in local, 'community' histories was further transformed and expanded through the impact of 'new' social history and New Left politics, including history from below, identity histories, oral history and the History Workshop movement. This resulted in both a renewed interest in local, grassroots histories (in particular a large number of oral history initiatives to recover 'hidden histories') but also in a sustained critique of what was held, collected and displayed by conventional archives and museums. In reaction to a perception of a lack of interest in these histories (Francis, 1976, 183) and a generalized distrust of state institutions, including heritage bodies (Martin, 2005, 197–8; Hopkins, 2008, 89–92), the 1970s, 1980s and 1990s witnessed the establishment of a number of regional and national independent working-class, women's, black, gay and lesbian archives, libraries and other history bodies. Given the difficulties of sustaining such independent institutions over time, some of these collections now reside in professional repositories. However others, such as the Black Cultural Archives, the George Padmore Institute and Archives and the Working-Class Movement Library, have retained some or all of their independence and direct control over the resources for the production of their histories (Flinn, 2007, 156– 7; Flinn and Stevens, 2009).

More recently, the 1990s and early 2000s do appear to have seen something of an 'explosion' in the numbers of independent community archives in the UK. This growth was partly encouraged by streams of public funding for 'community' based archive and heritage projects and by developments in technology (including initially software such as Comma and latterly participatory, social networking sites such as Flickr) which enabled and popularized the easy digitizing, disseminating and sharing of local and community memory materials across the internet to great success. However it also reflected continued interest in history and in particular in individuals and communities researching and telling their own histories. For politically motivated archival activists, the critique of conventional heritage narratives and archival collections has not lessened in the 21st century. In fact it has in many ways been sharpened by a more general questioning of the authority of all mainstream institutions to represent the stories of others that is now common across society. Whilst such critiques now sometimes advocate engagement with, and intervention into, the mainstream rather than complete autonomy, they do so from a position which seeks to subvert and transform conventional representations and retain control and ownership of the intellectual product of such interventions (Ajamu, Campbell and Stevens, 2009, 292–3).

What we have termed 'serious leisure' community archival activity also reflects this growing interest in telling one's own histories. Closely linked to the continued popularity of family history, local or community history is often associated with loss or change. Community archive activity is often at its strongest and most sustained in those areas or communities which are in a state of flux, having been through dramatic and perhaps traumatic change such as deindustrialization and the destruction of occupational communities (steel mills, the docks, the mines) or migration and rapid population shifts. In these circumstances, community histories and archival activity might be not only nostalgic and backward looking but also might help the community to understand the reasons for the change and help it to mould the present. It is this potential which particularly interests public policy agencies concerned with 'neighbourhood renewal' or 'sustaining communities' but it may also happen independently and as part of a radical, grassroots response to these changes. In both Butetown in Cardiff and on the Isle of Dogs in London, the recording and preservation of community histories was seen as a way of confronting the redevelopment of dockland areas and of seeking to sustain previously tight-knit communities in an era of profound and rapid change (Jordan, 2009; Hostettler, 2009). Similarly, an archive like Eastside Community Heritage (www.hidden-histories.org.uk) has worked since the early 1990s on documenting the lives and experiences of the working classes of East London, seeking not only to preserve the hidden histories of those communities but also to empower those same individuals and communities through participating in the process of history making.

Independent and community archives: challenging professional archival thinking and practice?

Following on from the ATF's declaration that independent, community archives are 'as important to society' as public archives, various studies have sought to demonstrate, even quantify, this importance. Focusing on the process and practice of community archiving rather than on their content, both the Community Archives and Development Group's impact review (CADG, 2007) and the Jura Consultants' (2009) sustainable communities report suggested that participating in community archive activities could result in a wide range of positive outcomes for individuals and communities. These impacts included building up cultural and social capital, supporting lifelong learning, community empowerment, digital inclusion, health and well-being, and a sense of place and belonging.

Rather than examining the whole rich variety of independent and community archive activity, research at University College London (UCL) (https://www.ucl.ac.uk/infostudies/research/icarus/community-archives) concentrated in more detail on independent activist archives that were mainly (but not exclusively) concerned with the history and experiences in the UK of people of African, Asian and other heritages. Whilst problematizing the sometimes superficial connections made by policy bodies between independent archives and 'identity' and their impact on concepts such as 'community cohesion', the research was able to demonstrate clear evidence that working with, and engaging with, the materials held in these archives could have a significant impact on individuals by stimulating a dialogue about identities and identifications as fluid, dynamic and multifaceted. As Mike Featherstone (2006, 594) has noted, these archives offer the possibility of a space in which to 'engage in imaginative and creative work to form new collective memories' where the archive becomes 'an active aspiration, a tool for reworking desires and memories, part of a project for sustaining cultural identities'. Although these endeavours are often inspired by one or two key individuals, the building of these archives and the subsequent history-making activities are often interactive and collaborative processes, drawing in a range of volunteers and supporters inspired by these aspirations.

In addition to challenging and acting as a corrective to the absences and mis-representations in some dominant heritage narratives, these archives can also encourage in some individuals who engage with the materials a greater sense of self-belief and esteem:

> People did not have a sense of pride or self-worth about who they were because they don't see themselves in a positive light . . . . So people tend to have low self-esteem as a result of the social conditions that they grow up in . . . one way to combat that, to give people something, something more positive to think about themselves, is to show that they were part of a story or a history that links them to better things.
>
> (Swadhinata Trust, 2009)

Whilst acknowledging that some independent community archive and history-making activities might be directed towards sustaining and strengthening reactionary or closed identifications (Cox, 2009, 259), the UCL research found little evidence of such narrow or reified approaches amongst the archives studied or interviewed.

Recognizing the significance of both the materials and the activities with regard to independent community archives, means that all those engaged with archives, history and heritage should have an interest in providing solutions to the challenges that these independent endeavours face (notably in terms of achieving long-term sustainability and in accessing appropriate levels of assured funding as opposed to short-term project funds). Consideration of these issues of significance and threat also necessitates the examination of what these endeavours tell us about traditional archival thinking and practice. It is this that the rest of this chapter will try to address.

What is an archive?

Independent and community archives present a challenge to notions of what an archive is, or at least certainly what a public archive is, both in terms of the material held and the institution itself. As previously noted, the very existence of independent archives represents a public declaration of reproach to the formal heritage sector, including archives, drawing attention to whose stories they privilege and whose collections they hold

(Hopkins, 2008, 99). This is most clearly the case in those politically inspired activist archives, where the desire to correct biases, absences and mis-representations in mainstream collections and narratives ('the strongest reason for creating the archives was to end the silence of patriarchal history about us' [Nestle, 1990, 87]) is explicitly articulated. Writing about the establishment of the African and Asian Visual Artists' Archive, Stuart Hall (2001, 91–2) emphasized how the 'absence of any sustained attention' and 'a systematic marginalisation' meant that the artists felt compelled to act as archivists. For Hall (and these archival activists) 'the activity of "archiving" is thus always a critical one, always a historically located one, always a contestatory one'. For archives seeking to represent the endeavours of people of African, Asian and other heritages, or of gays and lesbians, or of women, or in an earlier period of the organized working classes, these endeavours exist as a challenge to mainstream archives and museums and to the professionals within them who make the decisions about what they collect and how they re-present those collections.

More than this, independent archives not only indicate the limitations of existing collections and conventional narratives, they seek also to rebalance and subvert these narratives by creating their own, providing a space for the discussion of diverse histories. In the context of lives which have been edited out of history ('the silenced voices, the love letters destroyed, the pronouns changed, the diaries carefully edited, the pictures never taken' [Nestle cited in Loeb, 1981, 2]), the archive is a conscious act at recovery and rewriting.

Even in the case of those community archives less explicitly aligned to a political agenda, there is often a strong sense that these initiatives preserve stories that might otherwise be lost, where occupations, localities, or other activities and interests are not covered by a local repository or not considered worthy or of sufficient interest to merit preservation. The Waltham Forest Oral History Project (www.wforalhistory.org.uk) emphasizes the impact that interviewees can have on the untold history of their part of London: 'By recording your story you will have contributed to the history of this corner of London, not just for now but forever. Your story will be part of tomorrow's history, and your place in it will be assured.'

As suggested earlier, these acts of preservation take on a particular sense of urgency when these localities or occupations are threatened with change or loss. On London's Isle of Dogs, the long-standing curator of the Island History Trust reported how a community faced with massive change brought about by de-industrialization and redevelopment 'were very proud of their own history, felt they knew their own history . . . they didn't want to be told their own history, they didn't mind telling it but they didn't want to be told it' (Hostettler, 2009).

Whilst the purpose and intentions of independent community archives pose questions of public archives about what they collect and from whom, the collections also encourage archivists and others interested in archives to consider what is given the status and aura of an 'archive'. A feature common to many independent community archives is the great variety of materials they collect and preserve. As one of the founding members of the Black Cultural Archives (BCA) in London, Len Garrison's personal collection is at the heart of the BCA's holdings. This collection, not untypically, includes 'handbills, flyers, posters, programmes for a wide range of events' and according to one commentator represents the 'only way of understanding whole movements and trends' within the experience of people of African descent in Britain (Phillips, 2003, 297). Similarly the Feminist Archive (South) (www.femarch.freeserve.co.uk) includes amongst its holdings 'diaries, calendars, conference papers, personal letters, photographs, stickers, postcards, drawings, posters, banners, badges, vinyl records, mini-disks, audio cassettes, video cassettes, a 16mm film, clothing, and various other ephemera' from the 1960s onwards and documents much that would otherwise be lost of second-wave feminism in the UK.

These collections, and many independent archives like them, are often the product of the collecting activities of one or two key individuals, and therefore in the eyes of some professionals 'constitute private and idiosyncratic collections developed *ex post facto* and thus are far from the contextually based organic bodies of evidence that comprise most of the [professional] archives' (Maher, 1998, 255). Such dismissive and defensive reactions to these non-professional collections fail to register their significance to those who collected them and perhaps to broader society as well. These materials are preserved, made use of, and cherished alongside more formal correspondence and other documentation of organizational and individual lives and activities. Within archival education and practice much time and erudition has been expended in trying to identify and fix precisely the details of what a record is, and what an archive is. Particularly in those traditions strongly influenced by Hilary Jenkinson's (1965, 11) writings (an archive being 'drawn up or used in the course of an administrative or executive transaction . . . and subsequently preserved for their own information by the person or persons responsible for that transaction . . . . Archives were not drawn up in the interest or for the information of Posterity'), professional characterization of archives and records have tended towards narrower, more functional and transactional definitions and have emphasized their impartiality, authenticity and objectivity as a form of evidence. However there are also more inclusive, less restrictive ways of thinking about archives and records which are more in tune with the practices of independent and community archives. In particular, more appropriate are those definitions which recognize the historical and cultural value of archives and the agency of the archivist and collector in subjectively assigning these values (Greene, 2002). There are three further points about what constitutes 'archival' value in the context of independent and community archives in particular (but by extension to broader conceptions of that value as well) which follow from this.

First, there is the issue of the surviving trace. As Verne Harris (2002, 65) has argued, instead of a discourse which views archives as the memory of society, or a mirror reflecting the complete reality of that society, it is more accurate to recognize that archive collections are only 'a sliver of a sliver of a sliver'. Furthermore, it is likely that those voices which are to be heard within these partial remains are overwhelmingly those of the powerful and the elites within any given group. In the case of those whose histories go largely unremarked and unrecognized, surviving traces (particularly those in which these marginalized persons speak with their own voice) are typically rare and fragmentary. Thus when seeking to record grassroots organization, the emergence of new, particular forms of 'underground' cultural expression, or just the realities of 'everyday' life, the only surviving material traces of these activities may be slight and ephemeral such as a leaflet announcing a meeting, a ticket to a performance, a brief diary entry or letter. In the digital world, the physical existence of such ephemeral traces may be even more short-lived. The fact that something may be isolated and not part of a larger surviving documentary accumulation, should not undermine its archival significance. Rather its archival context lies not only in the collection that it becomes a part of and the circumstances of its creation but also in the understandings which archivists and users bring to it. In such circumstances, these traces, in whatever form, acquire significance and value for those collecting them comparable to an information-rich source in more well documented contexts. By this measure it is the very rarity of the trace and the lack of conventional recognition given to the person, activity or organization to which it refers that gives such ephemera its archival and historical value.

Second, further to the idea of the archive as a trace or cherished fragment, some of the traditional archival identifiers such as uniqueness, originality and, to a lesser extent, authenticity, are accorded less absolute authority in the context of independent and community archives. When engaged in the recovery of hidden histories copies of original materials produced by the archivist or others, surviving remnants of once mass-produced series, and uncorroborated and uncertain testimony may all acquire a status not matched in more mainstream source-rich fields of collection and research. As Mark Greene writes when discussing an inclusive, 'chaotic and messy' archival paradigm:

> Because it throws its net wide in terms of identifying and preserving material that may usefully serve one or more of its many purposes and audiences, it does not comfortably wear strictures about what is or is not 'authentic', 'reliable', or 'complete' enough to be called a record or archival.
>
> (Greene, 2002, 45)

With broken chains of custody and uncertain provenance doubts about accuracy or authenticity may attach themselves to a particular item or source but its rarity and significance may tend to outweigh those concerns at least until further sources are located. Certainly a reasonable level of doubt is unlikely to prevent such a source being deemed of archival value under these circumstances.

Transformed notions of what might be properly deemed a record (and hence an archive), including orality, song, performance, indeed anything which transmits history, tradition and memory, clash with traditional Western and in particular Jenkinsonian definitions which rely on authenticity and evidential value (Greene, 2002, 46). The importance of oral testimony and visual materials to most independent and community

archives as a key way of revealing hidden histories challenge these
traditional archival notions in a similar way that these notions of the record
challenge and are challenged by the attitudes of indigenous and other
largely non-script cultures towards orality and recordkeeping. Discussing
the frequent doubts expressed in Australia about the 'veracity of oral
records coming from Aboriginal people', Glen Kelly observes:

> Underneath it all, however, is the fact that the type of information that is
> gathered in a native title case from witnesses isn't necessarily factual information
> such as events, times or dates but cultural information and understandings. So
> even if detail on days, times and the like becomes hazy through the oral record,
> the principles of Noongar law and custom don't.

> (Kelly, 2009, 60–1)

What is crucial, not only for indigenous archives and independent
community archives but also, and by extension, for a truly transformed, re-
imagined notion of conventional archives and archival practice, is the value
placed on these sources by their communities as bearers of
understandings, memories and traditions, either in the absence of, or
alongside, other more conventionally recognized written, evidential records
(Hopkins, 2008, 92; Galloway, 2009, 81).

Finally (and again the truth of this for independent community archives
only goes to suggest the same for the more formal and traditional archives
held within public repositories) is that the recognition that the significance,
the record-ness and the archival-ness of what is in the collection is assured
and denoted by those who create and keep the archive. Something
becomes an archive when it is put in an archive or is designated as an
archive. Just as the 'constitution' of the archive is an act of active creation
and choice, so the designation of an item as a part of an archive is an act
of conscious decision making, with the archivist or collector bestowing
an importance and significance (an 'archival value') through the subjective
act of declaring something to be an archive. That importance and
significance might be agreed (or acceded) to by only the individual
concerned, or by a wider group or community, or ultimately by wider
society itself, but the archival value is reliant on external and subjective
judgement. Ultimately this, so clear in the independent community archive,
is what always happens with archives. Except in perhaps a few iconic types

of records (treaties and constitutional or founding documents, for instance), the value of an archival document is not best understood as something innate to it, but by the significance invested in it by those who, including the archivist, have created, selected, shaped and used it as an archive. Ultimately an archive is an archive because someone decides that is what it is and then acts upon that decision in certain ways, not through some magic application of a purely objective and organic formula (Jimerson, 2009, 215–20).

Where is an archive kept?

In the past one of the defining characteristics of an independent or community archive was that it existed, in some fashion, outside of the walls of formal, professionally staffed, repositories. As we have seen, independence and autonomy, a place of one's own from where to speak without interference or control, were historically key concerns for a number of the more politically active archives (Small, 1997, 61; Loeb, 1981, 2). A geographical remoteness, a lack of contact with local heritage services and an independence of spirit could also explain the separateness of some less political, local community or occupational based archives (Mander, 2009, 30–1). For many independent archives in the early 21st century, such as the Black Cultural Archives and the George Padmore Institute and Archive, both in London, building and sustaining an independently owned and run physical institution which holds and makes their collections accessible remains a key objective, one that at times is only achieved at the cost of great personal effort and sacrifice. This aspiration arises out of a variety of perspectives including a critical engagement with the State and conventional heritage bodies, unease with notions of professionalism and concern that 'community' collections might be 'swallowed up' and made inaccessible, the promotion of group or community-owned institutions as a measure of empowerment, a means of asserting control over access and use of the materials, and as a powerful physical symbol of presence and collective identification.

Nevertheless many other independent community archives and archival initiatives are now less focused on having the independent physical building and transfer their materials into conventional, professionally staffed archives or exist in virtual spaces only, directing physical materials if they come their way to local heritage services. This stance may have evolved over time with once strongly independent archives transferring their collections into conventional (often university-based) archives because they are unable or unwilling to continue attempting to sustain direct management of the collections. Others such as Eastside Community Heritage and rukus! decided almost from the point of inception that their preference would be to ensure that their materials received the best possible professional care whilst they concentrated on the intellectual control and use of the materials, often in digital form (Ajamu X, Campbell and Stevens, 2009, 291; Garfield, 2009).

Ultimately there is not, and should not, be one single model of custody dictating where an archive collection should be held. Rather the custody models should be best suited to the community or group that has created or collected the archives, whether that be a shared custodial relationship with the collections being transferred into a conventional archive and being jointly managed by the community archive and the professional staff or an independent archive employing professional staff if resources and inclination allow and receiving, if required, postcustodial advice and guidance from a conventional heritage body, or indeed some completely different arrangement. What is most significant is not where an archive collection is held – there is not a convincing argument for believing that archival material can only be relied upon if it has been held in a conventional archive – but rather why it has been preserved and what value has been assigned to it and by whom. There may be good practical reasons for material being held in high-standard professional storage and care but there are also many good reasons for keeping it in the political and cultural context it was created. If the archival heritage is to include all those materials that are held outside formal and conventional public archives, including in independent, community and private archives as the ATF report implies that it must, then the question for professional archival thinking and practice is how these archives are going to be sustained and supported as 'responsible custodians' (Flinn, 2008).

Who looks after the archive?

According to this understanding, and this is also the case for personal and private collections, the question of who looks after an archive collection then becomes one of negotiation; at best a partnership based on equity and mutual respect for what each partner has to offer in terms of expertise and knowledge (Flinn, 2008; Stevens, Flinn and Shepherd, 2010, 72). If the archive is taken inside the conventional archival institution, then the creators should be involved (if they so desire) in the decision-making processes, contributing their expertise and perspective on appraisal, description and access decisions. Allowing depositors to retain legal custody and to specify certain requirements for use and access, is of course nothing new, but framing this as a sustained collaboration of shared custody and responsibility seems to be taking it a step further. If the archive remains outside of a formal repository and within the context of its creation, then professional archivists should be able to offer (if requested) postcustodial support and advice on how best to look after and preserve the collection.

In both these approaches there is significant potential for building sustained equitable relationships between conventional archive bodies and 'community' groups. Indeed there are already many good examples of such relationships between professional archivists and independent community archives, including the guidance materials developed by the CAHG, the publications available in Australia and New Zealand on how to set up and sustain a successful community archive, and the outreach strategies actively developed by local record offices in the UK like London Metropolitan Archives, Hampshire Archives and Local Studies (the Living Links project), Hertfordshire Archives and Local Studies (the Making Memories project) and many others to support and offer advice to independent and community archives in their areas. Certainly it is clear that there is great demand from many independent and community archives for advice, guidance and, if equitably delivered, partnerships, to ensure the best possible care of their collections (Stevens, 2010, 64–9; Flinn, 2008).

There is also a broader context into which these relationships, and community archives in particular, fit. In a number of fields of study and knowledge production activity, including historical and scientific research, archaeology and archives, there has been a growing recognition of the need to dissolve (or at least make more permeable) the barriers between users and practitioners, amateurs and professionals, the independent and the institutional to benefit from both sets of understanding and expertise, and from an extension and democratization of knowledge production (Finnegan, 2005). In terms of archives, this has taken the form of various experiments in engaging users and non-professionals in decisions about what to collect and what to keep, and by seeking to incorporate external knowledge into professional description (Flinn, 2010). In the past this process (including the recognition of the value of independent community archives) has been resisted as a threat to jobs and professional standing (Maher, 1998, 254–5). However, increasingly, as the above examples demonstrate, such attitudes are beginning to diminish with more professional archivists seeking to work with, support and help sustain independent and community archive collections inside and outside the walls of their own archival institutions. What is now crucial is for this type of outreach activity to be viewed as a core responsibility for professional archive services, and not therefore to be seen as an optional or simply box-ticking exercise subject to cuts and perhaps being sacrificed in times of recession and mounting financial difficulties.

Conclusion: choosing inclusion and diversity

In the end the question that this chapter poses is to what extent do independent and community archives challenge and transform the theory and practice of archivists? Does 'radical archiving' (even if it applied to all independent and community archives) represent a real radical departure from traditional thinking and practice? In the final analysis, for theory we might only respond with a guarded yes. Certainly these archives disturb and undermine (perhaps fatally) narrow and overly business-oriented definitions of what records and archives are, how something comes to be assigned the value of archive, and in what format a record or an archive might be recognized. Although some professionals have sought to reject IT definitions of 'archiving' (moving a digital object from an active context into a semi-structured environment for temporary storage for future reference or use), this actually sums up very neatly what archives are and what the process of archiving is. A document or object has archival status whenever someone (be it an individual, a community or an employee of a national archives) gives it that status on the basis of whatever value (evidential, informational, legal, cultural, personal) that individual, group or institution deems significant or valid. The wide variety of materials which are then considered to be bearing important 'cultural information and understandings' suggests that the distinctions between the materials held in museums, libraries and archives should be viewed as increasingly artificial and meaningless, particularly in the digital environment. The point is not that the criteria of value should be the same across all of these decision-making processes (the National Archives and other public archives will clearly have different conceptions of what government records should be considered archival to that which an individual dealing with their own records will have) but that each is deciding what is an archive on the basis of a set of externally applied criteria about what is significant within a particular context. Notions of permanency, uniqueness, recordness and chains of custody are ultimately less important than significance and context. In this, the challenge to archival theory posed by individual and community archives is neither unique nor particularly innovative. Rather it is part of a series of challenges (often, but not only, inspired by consideration of the digital or postmodern reflections) to narrow business and administrative-fixated archival thinking which seeks to close down the possibilities of broader, less defined and more inclusive archival heritages. In the end whether we are considering personal papers, a private business archive or an independent community archive, a person or groups' archives are whatever they say they are, and it seems rather pointless and self-defeating for anyone else, including archivists, to try to tell them otherwise.

With regard to notions of custodialism (and the significance of professional custody), this is again similarly challenged and not just in a digital environment by postcustodial or shared custodial thinking and approaches. Whether it be for reasons of particular local, cultural and political significance or because of technical appropriateness, the maintenance of certain archival materials (or materials designated by their holders as archives) by those who collected or created them should not, and increasingly do not, prevent their preservation, processing, description and accessibility being (where requested) guided and supported by a raft of professional services.

In general then it is not so much the theory as the practice that is challenged by independent community archives, although they do encourage us to adopt a competing strain of archival thinking which is active and interventionist and which rejects the chimeras of objectivity and neutrality in favour of more transparent interventions, an acknowledgement of subjectivity and an embracing of active engagement with the archives and their creators. Particularly for those working in public archives with a commitment to represent all sections of society, it is by encouraging us to choose (or reject) different notions of archival thinking, that consideration and engagement with community archives most fundamentally challenges professional practice.

References

Archives Task Force (2004) *Listening to the Past, Speaking to the future*, MLA.

Ajamu, X., Campbell, T. and Stevens, M. (2009) Love and Lubrication in the Archives, or rukus!: a black queer archive for the United Kingdom, *Archivaria,* **68**, 271–92.

Alleyne, B. (2002) An Idea of Community and its Discontents: towards a more reflexive sense of belonging in multicultural Britain, *Ethnic and Racial Studies,* **25** (4), 607–727.

Community Archives and Heritage Group (CAHG, 2009) Vision, www.communityarchives.org.uk/page_id__901.aspx.

Community Archives Development Group (CADG) (2007) *The Impact of Community Archives,* www.communityarchives.org.uk/page_id__575_path__ 0p6p63p61p.aspx.

Cox, R. (2009) Conclusion: the archivist and the community. In Bastian, J. and Alexander, B. (eds), *Community Archives: the shaping of memory,* Facet Publishing.

Drake, M. (2005) Inside-Out or Outside-In? The case of family and local history. In Finnegan, R. (ed.), *Participating in the Knowledge Society: researchers beyond the university walls,* Palgrave Macmillan.

Eales, K. (1998) Community archives: introduction, *South African Archives Journal,* **40**, http://jag85.com/classes/lis490/CommunityArchives%20Introduction.html.

Featherstone, M. (2006) Archive, *Theory, Culture & Society,* **23** (2–3), 591–96.

Finnegan, R. (2005) Introduction: looking beyond the walls. In Finnegan, R. (ed.), *Participating in the Knowledge Society: researchers beyond the university walls,* Palgrave Macmillan.

Flinn, A. (2007) Community Histories, community archives: some opportunities and challenges, *Journal of the Society of Archivists,* **28** (2), 151–76.

Flinn, A. (2008) Archives and their Communities: serving the people, *COMMA,* 157–68.

Flinn, A. (2010) 'An Attack on Professionalism and Scholarship'?: democratising archives and the production of knowledge, *Ariadne*, **62** www.ariadne.ac.uk.

Flinn, A., and Stevens, M. (2009) 'It is noh Mistri, wi Mekin Histri': telling our own story: independent and community archives in the United Kingdom, challenging and subverting the mainstream. In Bastian, J. and Alexander, B. (eds), *Community Archives: the shaping of memory*, Facet Publishing.

Flinn, A., Stevens, M. and Shepherd, E. (2009) Whose Memories, whose Archives? independent community archives, autonomy and the mainstream, *Archival Science*, **9** (3–4), 71–86.

Francis, H. (1976) Workers' Libraries: the origins of the South Wales miners' library, *History Workshop*, **2** (1), 183–93.

Fullwood, S. (2009) Always Queer, Always Here: creating the Black Gay and Lesbian Archive in the Schomburg Center for Research in Black Culture. In Bastian, J. and Alexander, B. (eds), *Community Archives: the shaping of memory*, Facet Publishing.

Galloway, P. (2009) Oral Tradition in Living Cultures: the role of archives in the presentation of memory. In Bastian, J. and Alexander, B. (eds), *Community Archives: the shaping of memory*, Facet Publishing.

Garfield, J. (2009) interview with author.

Garrison, L. (1994) The Black Historical Past in British Education. In Stone, P. G. and MacKenzie, R. (eds), *The Excluded Past: archaeology and education*, 2nd edn, Routledge, 231–44.

Greene, M. (2002) The Power of Meaning: the archival mission in the postmodern age, *The American Archivist*, **65** (2), 42–55.

Hall, S. (2001) Constituting an Archive, *Third Text*, **15** (54), 89–92.

Harris, V. (2002) The Archival Sliver: power, memory, and archives in South Africa, *Archival Science*, **2** (1–2), 63–86.

Hopkins, I. (2008) Places From Which to Speak, *Journal of the Society of Archivists*, **29** (1), 83–109.

Hostettler, E. (2009) interview with author.

Hunt, A. J. (2005) A Brief History of Field Archaeology in the UK: the academy, the profession and the amateur. In Finnegan, R. (ed.), *Participating in the Knowledge Society: researchers beyond the university walls*, Palgrave Macmillan.

Jenkins, D. (2009) interview with author.

Jenkinson, H. (1965[1937]) *Manual of Archive Administration*, 2nd edn, Percy Lund, Humphries and Co.

Jimerson, R. (2009) *Archives Power: memory, accountability and social justice*, Society of American Archivists.

Jordan, G. (2009) interview with author.

Jura Consultants (2009) *Community Archives and the Sustainable Communities Agenda*, MLA.

Kelly, G. (2009) The Single Noongar Claim: native title, archival records and aboriginal community in Western Australia. In Bastian, J. and Alexander, B. (eds), *Community Archives: the shaping of memory*, Facet Publishing.

Loeb, C. (1981) Radical Archiving: the lesbian herstory archives, *Feminist Collections*, **2** (4), 2–4.

Maher, W. J. (1998) Archives, Archivists, and Society, *American Archivist*, **61** (2), 252–65.

Mander, D. (2009) Special, Local and about Us: the development of community archives in Britain. In Bastian, J. and Alexander, B. (eds), *Community Archives: the shaping of memory*, Facet Publishing.

Martin, S. (2005) Inheriting Diversity: archiving the past. In Littler, J. and Naidoo, R. (eds), *The Politics of Heritage: the legacies of 'race'*, Routledge.

McKay, J. (2005) Community Historians and Their Work Around the Millennium. In Finnegan, R. (ed.), *Participating in the Knowledge Society: researchers beyond the university walls*, Palgrave Macmillan.

Nestle, J. (1990) The Will to Remember: the lesbian herstory archives of New York, *Feminist Review*, **34**, 86–94.

Phillips, M. (2003) Obituaries: Lenford (Kwesi) Garrison (1943–2003), *History Workshop* **56**, 295–97.

Shepherd, E. (2009) Culture and Evidence: or what good are the archives? Archives and archivists in 20th century England, *Archival Science*, **9** (3–4), 173–85.

Sivanandan, A. (2008) Race and Resistance: the IRR story, *Race and Class*, **50** (2), 1–30.

Small, S. (1997) Contextualizing the Black Presence in British Museums: representations, resources and response. In Hooper-Greenhill, E. (ed.), *Cultural diversity: developing museum audiences in Britain*, Leicester University Press.

Stevens, M., Flinn, A. and Shepherd, E. (2010) New Frameworks for Community Engagement in the Archive Sector: from handing over to handing on, *International Journal of Heritage Studies*, **16** (1–2), 59–76.

Swadhinata Trust, UCL project interview, 2009.

Waterton, E., and Smith, L. (2010) The Recognition and Misrecognition of Community Heritage, *International Journal of Heritage Studies*, **16** (1–2), 4–15.

Notes

1   This chapter is partially informed by a UK Arts and Humanities Research
    Council funded project (2008–9), 'Community archives and identities:
    documenting and sustaining community heritage'. The research team
    comprised Andrew Flinn, Elizabeth Shepherd and Mary Stevens. This research
    would not have been possible without the help and partnership provided by all
    our case studies (Future Histories, rukus! the Black Lesbian, Gay, Bisexual and
    Trans [LGBT] archive, Moroccan Memories, Eastside Community Heritage)
    and all the other participants and interviewees. For further details see
    www.ucl.ac.uk/infostudies/research/icarus/community-archives.

2   Examples would include the proceedings of a South African conference on
    community archiving in 1998 (*South African Archives Journal*, **40**), the fourth
    International Conference on the History of Records and Archives (ICHORA)
    Perth, 2008 entitled 'Minority Reports: indigenous and community voices in
    archives' (*Archival Science*, **9** (1–2), 2009), publications by the National Archives
    of Australia and Archives New Zealand offering guidance to those groups
    considering establishing community archives and the guide 'Information for
    Community Archives' produced by the Society of American Archivists'
    Lesbian and Gay Archives Roundtable.

3   This history and the various antecedents of contemporary independent
    community archives in the UK are examined at more length in Flinn (2007). I
    would suggest that although this pattern of development will have elements
    specific to the UK, many of the circumstances and pressures which have
    encouraged these developments will be recognizable in other countries as well.
    See, for instance, the account of similar concerns and initiatives in the USA
    (Jimerson, 2009, 267–77).

Part 4

Archives in the information age: is there still a role for the archivist?

9

The postcustodial archive

Adrian Cunningham

Introduction: F. Gerald Ham and the 'postcustodial era'

In a landmark address to the 1980 annual meeting of the Society of American Archivists, the State Archivist of Wisconsin F. Gerald Ham (1981) presented a set of archival strategies for what he called 'the postcustodial era'. He characterized archives in the custodial era as being passive and introspective and almost exclusively concerned with the custodial management of archival holdings. He argued lucidly that archives and archivists could not afford to persist with this narrow custodial mindset, especially if they were to both survive the challenges of, and take advantage of, the opportunities presented by automation and the growth of born digital information and online networks.

Ham characterized the postcustodial era as featuring a decentralized computer environment where every individual will become their own records manager. In such an environment, archivists would need to be much more active and interventionist if they were to have any hope of fulfilling their mission. He called for much greater levels of inter-institutional co-operation between archives programmes, the development of strategies for providing easy and centralized access to increasingly complex and decentralized archives, and for greater archival involvement in the process of information creation and management.

Importantly, Ham did not argue that archives should stop managing custodial holdings, but rather that archives needed to expand their repertoire of strategies in order to navigate the increasingly complex realities of the late 20th century. This expansion of archival strategies was not a renunciation of custody, but rather a recognition that custody on its own was insufficient to ensure archival success into the future. Ham was not recommending a 'non-custodial era', but a 'postcustodial era' where archival programmes and archivist self-image would not be defined by custody alone.

During the 1990s, in the midst of a fevered (sometimes almost panic-stricken) discourse on electronic records, Ham's postcustodial vision re-emerged as a divisive fault line in the archival discourse. That it took over a decade for Ham's challenge to be taken up in the discourse itself demonstrated just how prescient his 1980 address really was. Ham's paper proposed a radical new definition of archival methods, one that was probably guaranteed to meet with conservative resistance. Looking back on the debate from the comfort of 2011, however, there is little doubt that Ham was right and that what once was a radical new vision is now almost archival orthodoxy. Most larger archival programmes now allocate significant resources to inter-institutional co-operation, including the development of co-operative online access services for distributed holdings, and to 'front-end' engagement with records' creators (often through influencing the design and implementation of recordkeeping systems). Significantly, almost all archival programmes still favour taking custody of archival materials most of the time. They have not foresworn custodial strategies, even if distributed custody has become more common than hitherto. So, despite the fact that archival custody is still a central component of the strategies of most archival programmes, we are now living the postcustodial realities that Ham envisaged back in 1980.

What is the postcustodial archive and how has its advent been made possible? How does the vision of the postcustodial archive sit with resilient notions of archives as a place of secure deposit?

Archives as a place?

Throughout the ages one of the regularly recurring functions of archival institutions has been to provide a secure place for the safekeeping of valuable records to guarantee the ongoing legal authenticity of those records. This is especially common for archives that serve solely or primarily a legal/administrative role, where control and possession of the records is recognized as a source of power. Luciana Duranti (1996) has highlighted the importance of this function in archives stretching back to the days of the Justinian Code and the Tabularium in Ancient Rome, while Michel Duchein (1992, 15) has identified the same issue as being important to archives in Flanders and Hungary. One of Sir Hilary Jenkinson's (1922) more influential contributions to the archival discourse is the related notion of the need to guarantee an uninterrupted transmission of custody from records' creator to archival institution – the physical and moral defence of the record. Duranti (1996, 244) has argued that when records 'cross the archival threshold' they are attested to be authentic and henceforth guaranteed to be preserved as such by an archives that is independent from the records' creating office and for which the preservation of the authenticity of its holdings is its *raison d'être*.

While this is a common theme in the history of archival institutions, it is not a universal one. Duchein (1992, 15) has argued that there are many countries in which the notion has never existed, including France 'where the fact of its being preserved in a public archival repository does not give a document any guarantee of authenticity'. Similarly, while the preservation of authenticity is undoubtedly an objective of most collecting/historical archives programmes, it cannot be said to be their *raison d'être*. More recently, archivists who agree with Duranti and Jenkinson about the absolute importance of guaranteeing the authenticity of records, have disagreed with Duranti's argument that this can be achieved only by means of archival institutions taking physical custody of the records. To these critics adequate control of records in order to guarantee authenticity in the digital age can be achieved without the need for archives to provide a physical place of safekeeping. In the digital age the very physicality of records is superseded by a virtual concept or 'performance' where the idea of a record having a set physical location becomes meaningless. These critics also object to the notion of records crossing an 'archival threshold' at some point in time after their creation. They argue that the 'archival bond' (Duranti, 1997) and subsequent guarantees of authenticity should commence at the point of records creation which, by definition, cannot be physically in the archives. If the archival bond is achieved and guaranteed at the point of records creation the decision when or whether to perform a physical act of custodial transfer to an archives becomes a minor administrative consideration, not a matter of central significance (Cook, 1994; Hedstrom, 1991; Upward and McKemmish, 1994).

Another strand to this topic is the architectural use of archival buildings to make symbolic statements about the role and significance of archives in society. Many archival buildings throughout the ages have architectural features suggestive of solidity, impenetrability, durability and authority. Indeed, such featurism is so common as to be almost a cliché – something which itself speaks volumes about perceptions of archival institutions. Recent, more imaginative architectural representations of the form and function of archives, such as the Gatineau Preservation Centre in Canada, have attempted to convey an image of archives as 'the epitome of a liberal-humanist and objective-scientific activity', but perhaps unwittingly reflect instead the ultimately indeterminate and mutable nature of the archival pursuit (Koltun, 2002).

One feature of the 'archives as a place' debate has been the perhaps naïve assertion by the postcustodialists[1] that technological change has made it possible, indeed essential, for digital records to be archivally captured, described and controlled in such a way as to guarantee the long-term authenticity and integrity of the records from the instant of creation onwards. Perhaps the closest that archivists have thus far come to achieving this vision is with the 'VERS encapsulated objects' (or VEOs) of the Victorian Electronic Records Strategy (VERS).[2] The fact remains, however, that the assertion remains an unproved – although appealing – hypothesis. VEOs, which are versions of records captured into a standardized archival file format and locked with digital signature to guarantee authenticity, can live anywhere securely. The problem is, however, convincing creating agencies to capture all of their records as VEOs at the point of records creation, as only a small proportion of the total records of an agency will need to be retained for long-term archival purposes. The overheads for such a commitment are high and may often be viewed as a case of 'the archival tail wagging the business dog'.

Ultimately, different archives will make their own choices as to how important guarantees of authenticity are and, if they are considered vital, which strategies they feel will give them the best chance of achieving that objective. Certainly, the postcustodialists argue for a more proactive and virtual 'archives without walls' as an antidote to the traditional passive custodial view, although there is absolutely no reason why a custodial approach cannot also be combined with a more proactive role. Jeannette Bastian (2002) has argued that (distributed) custody and authenticity should not be ends in themselves, but rather means to a more important end – that of facilitating use of the archives by those who stand to benefit from such activity. As Frank Upward (1996, 282) has argued, 'the externalities of place are becoming less significant day-by-day . . . the location of the resources and services will be of no concern to those using them'.

In the online world the development of virtual archives is not only desirable, but also essential for continued relevance and survival. Many users will wish to be assured of authenticity, but will not care less about the existence of, or necessity for, places of custody. As archival institutions respond to new user expectations of 24-hour online virtual access and the opportunities offered by digitization programmes for transforming and democratizing archival access programmes, they are becoming increasingly flexible in their approaches to preserving records in both centralized and distributed custodial settings.[3]

David Bearman's 'indefensible bastion' and Australian skirmishes

During the 1990s electronic records debates, there was no figure more divisive than American David Bearman. Ten years after F. Gerald Ham, Bearman reshaped Ham's radical call to arms as a visceral polemic that reverberated for years to come. In his paper 'An Indefensible Bastion: archives as a repository in the electronic age' (1991) Bearman argued that, not only should archives adopt strategies based on distributed custody, but they should avoid (except as a last resort) taking any custody at all of electronic records. According to Bearman there were 'few imaginable advantages and considerable disadvantages to the archival custody of electronic records' (Bearman, 1991, 16). He argued that in a networked world 'if archives have intellectual control over the records that are deemed archival, it doesn't matter much where records or users are' (19). According to Bearman, archival strategies of the future should consist largely of being standards setters, auditors, regulators, training providers and metadata managers.

In a commentary published simultaneously with Bearman's polemic, Margaret Hedstrom (1991) demurred. While agreeing with Bearman's call for an expanded role for archival programmes and that there would be many circumstances where custody of records by archives would be 'unnecessary and even ill-advised' (28), she did not agree that custodianship was always going to be incompatible with these broader imperatives and strategies. Hedstrom presented some helpful criteria to help archives decide whether or not it was best to take custody of electronic records. There will be times, Hedstrom argued, when creating agencies will be much better prepared than any archives to take physical custody of archival records in electronic form, for example agencies whose primary mission is data collection and analysis. In any case, until archives develop the requisite technical capacity, the archival mission would in many cases be better served by temporarily leaving electronic records in the custody of the creating agency. To Hedstrom, such issues ultimately were trivial matters of implementation and timing. What was more important was for archival institutions to become sources of expertise in digital media, formats, management, preservation and dissemination.

Margaret Hedstrom's common sense rejoinder to Bearman's intentionally provocative paper should have been an end to the matter. Instead, however, Bearman's 'non-custodial' arguments gained some significant traction in Australia, traction that served largely as an unhelpful distraction in the context of the broader postcustodial discourse, in which certain Australians became prominent participants. In 1994 the then Australian Archives (now National Archives of Australia) announced a distributed custody policy for electronic records that was, for all intents and purposes, Bearman's indefensible bastion paper in the guise of official archival policy (Ellis and Stuckey, 1994). Interestingly (perhaps infuriatingly from the perspective of Australian Archives), Bearman himself (1995) responded to this development by disowning the policy as some kind of illegitimate offspring!

The custodial battle lines were drawn, with regular skirmishes fought throughout the mid-1990s in the pages of the Australian journal *Archives and Manuscripts,* on e-mail listservs and in conferences the length and breadth of the land. Leading the anti-Bearman charge was none other than Canada's Luciana Duranti (1996). The debate generated much heat but little light. Within seven years the National Archives of Australia (NAA) officially moved on from its policy of non-custody of electronic records when it established a digital preservation project and an accompanying custody policy which argued that archival value digital records should ideally be transferred to archival custody sooner rather than later. In retrospect the NAA was simply doing what Margaret Hedstrom had recommended in 1991, namely to leave electronic records in the custody of creating agencies until such time as the archives had the necessary technical capacity to receive and preserve digital records. Had the NAA said clearly in 1994 that 'distributed custody' was simply a stopgap measure few eyebrows would have been raised. Instead, however, its 1994 announcement was accompanied by elaborate and contentious justifications for a policy regime that had the appearance of being a long-term commitment. As such, 'postcustodial' became fatally confused with 'non-custodial' in the minds of many observers and participants in the discourse.

Moving beyond custody . . . to the records continuum

The irony was that, at the same time as the National Archives of Australia found itself embroiled in a largely sterile debate about custody, it and many other Australian archival programmes, educators and practitioners were exploring the exciting 'postcustodial' terrain first envisaged by Gerald Ham back in 1980. In essence, the core of the postcustodial discourse was all about inventing a new archival paradigm within which custodial strategies were, at most, a minor implementation consideration. The ur-text in this discourse, and arguably the most significant contribution to the discussion since Ham's seminal 1980 paper, was a 1994 review article by Monash University's Frank Upward and Sue McKemmish called 'Somewhere Beyond Custody' (1994). For some years Upward had been endeavouring to reconcile the emerging new paradigm with the age-old Jenkinsonian principles to which he cleaved. Jenkinson's requirements for unbroken chains of custody and the physical and moral defence of records had, according to Upward (1993), been honoured by the Australian Archives during the 1960s when it attempted to implement a universal system of documentation for all Australian Government records, 'without regard to location or the designation of permanency' (Upward, 1993, 45). The father of the Australian 'series system' for intellectual control and archival description, Peter Scott, together with his colleague and mentor Ian Maclean, were recognized as the first postcustodialists. Scott's groundbreaking 1966 article on the series system argued crucially that the archivist is essentially 'a preserver and interpreter of recordkeeping systems' and that 'series registration may be extended to cover series not yet in archival custody' (Scott, 1966, 500). According to Upward (1993, 44), 'Jenkinson's concept of custody is that of guardianship, not imprisonment, and can be readily extended out from the archival institution.' While the realities of limited resources meant that this brave experiment was only ever partially successful, it nevertheless pointed the way ahead towards a truly postcustodial recordkeeping paradigm.

At around the same time the University of Melbourne's Australian Science Archives Project (now the e-Scholarship Research Centre) was hitting its stride as a non-custodial documentation programme, the aim of which was to promote the preservation, awareness and use of Australia's distributed archival collections relating to science and technology (McCarthy, 1995).[4]

Validation of emerging Australian postcustodial thinking came from none other than leading Canadian writer and practitioner Terry Cook (1994) in a widely referenced paper 'Electronic records, paper minds', which was written following Cook's 1993 Australian speaking tour. According to Cook, archivists needed to 'stop being custodians of things and start being purveyors of concepts' (304) and to reorient themselves from 'records to the acts of recording' (305). Cook argued that the future of archives was as access hubs and 'virtual archives without walls' (314) – an assertion that in the 21st century seems wholly unremarkable, but which in 1994 caused some discomfort to traditionalists. Cook then proceeded to make the discourse even more interesting by intertwining postmodernism with postcustodialism, taking a few potshots along the way at the otherwise revered Sir Hilary Jenkinson for his unreflective positivism. In prefiguring the following decade's dominant archival discourse about the power relationships that are integral to all information systems and related social and organizational systems, Cook managed to simultaneously applaud Australian postcustodial thinking while at the same time question some of its neo-Jenkinsonian foundations.

Without jettisoning Jenkinson, Frank Upward (1996) further upped the conceptual ante by articulating the records continuum theoretical framework, henceforth the locus of postcustodial discourse – a subject for another time and another place.

Today's postcustodial realities in archival programmes

In 1996 in a commentary on the custody debate, the author optimistically (although perhaps a little naïvely) summed up the way forward in the following terms:

> Once good electronic recordkeeping practices become accepted and established (this is in fact our major challenge), then custody becomes a non issue. The real issues are archival control, the management of access and use, and the ongoing preservation of records of continuing value through migration and/or emulation. Archives can take such records into custody with ease and confidence, should that be deemed to be desirable. Equally, the records may be stored in a distributed environment with the archives exercising its control functions of physical and moral defence by technological means.
>
> (Cunningham, 1996, 318)

Thirteen years later, it is instructive to revisit these assertions in the light of the experiences of archival programmes around the world. To what extent have we realized the vision of postcustodial archives? What has been achieved and what are the remaining pressure points and areas of difficulty?

Unquestionably the functions of very many archival programmes have expanded greatly since Gerald Ham added the phrase 'postcustodial' to our professional lexicon. While traditional custodial functions have been retained, albeit often with proportionately fewer resources, such archives are now usually far more proactive and outwardly engaged – with records' creators, with other archives and documentation programmes, and with an expanding base of users in cyberspace. As evidenced by the proliferation of international and national standards in the archives and records field, we have become standards setters *par excellence*, even if all too often our track record on standards implementation (or achieving implementation by those who we seek to influence) has been patchy. Archival institutions world wide routinely provide records management training to records' creating agencies. In Australia it has become routine for public records institutions to partner with Auditor-General's offices to audit the state of recordkeeping in government agencies (Australian National Audit Office, various dates; Victorian Auditor-General's Office, 2008). Most Western developed countries have online archival networks of one kind or another that provide information about (and in some cases access to copies of) distributed archival holdings (Thibeaud, 2001).

Appraisal has been in a state of reinvention in many countries for a number of years. Functions-based appraisal is now commonplace. More fundamentally, appraisal is increasingly regarded as a process of proactively identifying needs for records, rather than retroactively deciding which records from a pre-existing body should be selected for archival preservation. Appraisal is now commonly a process combining functional analysis, work process analysis, risk analysis, historical analysis and stakeholder consultation to determine recordkeeping requirements. In other words the results of appraisal are as likely to be applied prospectively for records that do not yet exist as they are to be applied retrospectively to records that may already exist and may be brought into archival custody (Piggott, 2001; Reed, 2003).

Archives and archivists are far less introspective and holdings-focused than was the case a generation ago. For most archives user services, access and public outreach are at least as important as physical and moral defence of records. Digitization programmes abound and users vote with their fingers in cyberspace in far greater numbers than has ever been the case with users voting with their feet in visiting reading rooms. The National Archives of Australia, for instance, has digitized about 20 million pages of records, or about 2% of its total holdings. Usage figures for this 2% of holdings that are available in cyberspace outstrip usage figures for the 100% of holdings that are available in search rooms by orders of magnitude (Styles, 2008). The community expects its information sources to be available online and increasingly regards anything that is not online as being irrelevant. It is tempting therefore to conclude that it is just as irrelevant for collections managers to agonize over custodial arrangements.

Nevertheless, despite the explosion in online access to archives, physical custody of holdings remains the stated preference of the overwhelming majority of archival programmes, both for traditional format and for digital records. Why has a preference for old-fashioned archival custody proved to be so resilient when almost everything else in archives has been almost unrecognizably transformed? In the digital collections world, the notion of 'trusted digital repositories' (RLG-OCLC, 2002) has achieved widespread acceptance. This reflects a recognition of the fragility of digital information objects and the need for reliable infrastructure and professional curation skills to ensure the authenticity, integrity, accessibility and longevity of those objects. Indeed, digital curation (Cunningham,

2008, 531) is emerging as a specialist field in its own right, partly one suspects as a reaction against the notoriously short-term perspectives of the great majority of information and communication technologies (ICT) professionals. Trusted digital repositories usually store their 'archival masters' in standardized file formats, in deep and secure offline storage to protect against deliberate or accidental tampering, while outputting separate access copies for loading into online access repositories. Metadata management in such repositories is recognized as requiring high level ICT and archival skills – skill-sets that are not yet commonly found amongst graduates new or old. Experience has taught archivists that, except for a small minority of exceptional cases, creating agencies cannot be relied upon to manage born-digital archival value records over the long term. Agencies may keep legacy systems limping along for a certain period of time or may devise compromise solutions for exporting or migrating business critical data from such systems, but it is not their core business to ensure the long-term preservation of records that have broader societal or historical value but little or no ongoing legal/administrative value. That is the core business of archives – core business that is most effectively carried out by transferring archival value digital records into archival custody at the earliest possible convenience, when the archives in question has the technical capacity to preserve those records.

None of which means that archives should be disconnected from current recordkeeping in records-creating environments, or that archives should not maintain a strong interest in documenting and assisting the sound management of records that are in agency custody. Nor does it mean that archives should not support those agencies that have good business reasons for retaining and preserving digital records over the medium to long term when they can be relied upon to do so. The UK National Archives' Digital Continuity Project[5] is a fine example of postcustodial innovation, expert outreach and co-operation by an archival institution that nevertheless remains committed to taking archival value digital records into archival custody at the earliest possible opportunity.

Community archives: distributed custody at work

The final aspect of the archival endeavour that is consistent with the postcustodial mindset, and which indeed celebrates the concept of distributed custody, is the strength of community, regional and grassroots archival programmes. One of the great things about the archives is that they are all around us. They do not just exist in large, well funded national institutions in capital cities – they are in almost every school, church, community organization, family and interest group. The human urge to document one's achievements and activities is universal, manifesting itself in a multiplicity of archival and social memory endeavours. To be sure, some of these endeavours might not look like archives to Sir Hilary Jenkinson, were he still alive, but broadly speaking they are archives and will remain so for as long as groups and individuals are motivated to maintain and preserve them.

Using a Caribbean islands community to illustrate her case, Jeannette Bastian (2003, 3–6) has articulated the notion of 'communities of records', whereby archival collections help define and sustain the communities that should create, maintain and use those archives. To lose your archive is to risk losing your community identity. In Britain Andrew Flinn is leading an Arts and Humanities Research Council Project on 'Community archives and identities', which is examining community archive and heritage initiatives amongst black and minority ethnic groups. His research is revealing a vibrant and extensive network of grassroots archives that sustain themselves through community support in what is almost an alternative archival universe to that occupied by the mainstream government-funded institutions. These are archives for and of the people, where the communities have direct control/custody of their own archives and for whom notions of transferring their archives to the custody of some distant and unfamiliar centralized archive would, quite simply, be beyond their powers of understanding (Flinn, 2007, 2008). The National Archives of Australia (with support from the National Archives of Australia and others) has, for over 15 years, run a Community Heritage Grants scheme[6] which provides small monetary grants together with expert training and advice on managing and preserving documentary heritage collections to thousands of community level archives and historical societies. The growth and ongoing success of this programme demonstrates the levels of often voluntary commitment that communities are prepared to devote to their own archives. Neither the National Library of Australia nor the National Archives of Australia seek to obtain custody of the collections they support through this programme, yet their support is a visible sign of commitment to the wider archival endeavour and the distributed national collection. Such networks of mutual support are about as postcustodial as you can get.

Conclusion

There is no doubt that the archival paradigm shift into the postcustodial era envisaged by Gerald Ham a generation ago has indeed occurred. Archives are very different institutions nowadays and archivists, by and large, think and operate in very different ways. We have different priorities and different partnerships and we use very different tools and processes. Our conceptual framework is in many respects startlingly different and some of our core principles have been recast in ways that are far more open ended and much less absolute than hitherto. The central importance of provenance has been, if anything, strengthened and enriched – even if somewhat different definitions and understandings of the term now exist. Now, instead of talking about 'original order', a concept that is all but meaningless in the digital world, we are inclined to emphasize the importance of linking records to their business and societal context and ensuring that such linkages persist over time – which arguably is the real principle underlying the old principle of 'maintaining original order' and *respect des fonds*. Archivists are less beholden to sacred texts, such as those by Muller, Feith and Fruin, Jenkinson and Schellenberg, and are more open to different and often contested views of the archive. Archivists are less inclined to see themselves and their role as being passive and objective defenders of records created by other people and instead recognize the significance of their own role in shaping records that are 'always in a process of becoming' (McKemmish, 1994, 200; 2001, 335). In the words of Verne Harris (2007, 157), we are as much 'record makers' as we are 'record keepers'.

Tensions remain, and probably will always exist, between the legal and accountability role of archives and their social, cultural and historical roles. While there is no reason why these different roles should be incompatible, they usually reflect contingent circumstances and often entail differences in orientation, emphasis and language – differences that can lead to misunderstandings and competition for scarce resources. Either way, it is essential for archives to have a clear understanding of the higher purposes than their programmes and activities serve. While moral and physical defence of the record (through either custodial or postcustodial means) may be a means to an end (or a variety of ends), they are not useful ends in and of themselves. Ultimately, that is why being flexible, open-ended and postcustodial is by far a better orientation for archives than being rigid, narrow-minded and passively focused on custodial considerations and operations. Over the past 30 years archivists world wide have come to recognize this and have been busy putting the new outlooks and mindsets into operation. This is a never ending process. The postcustodial archive is always in a process of becoming! Nevertheless, the postcustodial archive is not only our present reality – it is a reality that is here to stay.

References

Australian National Audit Office (2002) *Recordkeeping: Audit Report No. 45 2001–02*, Australian National Audit Office, www.anao.gov.au/uploads/documents/2001-02_Audit_Report_45.pdf.

Australian National Audit Office (2003) *Recordkeeping in Large Commonwealth Organisations: Audit Report No. 7 2003–04*, Australian National Audit Office, www.anao.gov.au/uploads/documents/2003-04_Audit_Report_7. pdf.

Australian National Audit Office (2006) *Recordkeeping including the Management of Electronic Records: Audit Report No. 6 2006–07*, Australian National Audit Office, www.anao.gov.au/uploads/documents/2006-07_Audit_Report_61.pdf.

Bastian, J. (2002) Taking Custody, Giving Access: a postcustodial role for a new century, *Archivaria*, **53**, 76–93.

Bastian, J. (2003) *Owning Memory: how a Caribbean community lost its archives and found its memory*, Libraries Unlimited.

Bearman, D. (1991) An Indefensible Bastion: archives as a repository in the electronic age, *Archives and Museum Informatics Technical Report*, **13**, 14–24.

Bearman, D. (1995) Playing for Keeps, *Archives and Museum Informatics*, **9** (1), 43–54.

Cook, T. (1994) Electronic Records, Paper Minds: the revolution in information management and archives in the post-custodial and post-modernist era, *Archives and Manuscripts: Journal of the Australian Society of Archivists*, **22** (2), 300–28.

Cunningham, A. (1996) Journey to the End of the Night: custody and the dawning of a new era on the archival threshold, *Archives and Manuscripts: Journal of the Australian Society of Archivists*, **24** (2), 312–21.

Cunningham, A. (2008) Digital Curation/Digital Archiving: a view from the National Archives of Australia, *The American Archivist*, **71** (2), 530–43.

Duchein, M. (1992) The History of European Archives and the Development of the Archival Profession in Europe, *The American Archivist*, **55**, 14–25.

Duranti, L. (1996) Archives as a Place, *Archives and Manuscripts: Journal of the Australian Society of Archivists*, **24** (2), 242–55.

Duranti, L. (1997) The Archival Bond, *Archives and Museum Informatics*, **11** (3–4), 213–18.

Ellis, S. and Stuckey, S. (1994) Australian Archives' Approach to Preserving Long-Term Access to the Commonwealth's Electronic Records. In Yorke, S. (ed.), *Playing for Keeps: the proceedings of an electronic records management conference hosted by the Australian Archives, Canberra, Australia, 8–10 November 1994*. Australian Archives, 113–32.

Flinn, A. (2007) Community Histories, Community Archives: some opportunities and challenges, *Journal of the Society of Archivists,* **28** (2), 151–76.

Flinn, A. (2008) Other Ways of Thinking, Other Ways of Being: documenting the margins and the transitory: what to preserve, how to collect. In Craven, L. (ed.), *What are Archives? Cultural and theoretical perspectives,* Ashgate, 109–28.

Ham, F. G. (1981) Archival Strategies for the Postcustodial Era, *The American Archivist*, **44** (3), 207–16.

Harris, V. (2007) The Record, the Archive, and Electronic Technologies in South Africa. In Harris, V., *Archives and Justice: a South African perspective*, Society of American Archivists, 157–70.

Hedstrom, M. (1991) Archives: to be or not to be: a commentary, *Archives and Museum Informatics Technical Report*, **13**, 25–30.

Jenkinson, H. (1922) *A Manual for Archive Administration*, The Clarendon Press.

Koltun, L. (2002) The Architecture of Archives: whose form, what functions?, *Archival Science*, **2** (3–4), 239–61.

McCarthy, G. (1995) *Australian Science Archives Project: power, drugs and glamour in the nineties*, Paper presented at a meeting of the International Council of Archives Science Archives Group at the Center for History of Physics, American Institute of Physics, College Park, Maryland, USA, 29 August 1995, www.asap.unimelb.edu.au/pubs/articles/gjm/ica_seminar95.htm.

McKemmish, S. (1994) Are Records Ever Actual? In McKemmish, S. and Piggott, M. (eds), *The Records Continuum: Ian Maclean and Australian Archives First Fifty Years*, Ancora Press in association with Australian Archives.

McKemmish, S. (2001) Placing Records Continuum Theory and Practice, *Archival*

Science, **1** (4), 333–59.

Piggott, M. (2001) *Appraisal: the state of the art,* Paper delivered at a professional development workshop presented by the Australian Society of Archivists South Australia Branch, 26 March 2001, www.archivists.org.au/appraisal-state-art-26-march-2001.

Reed, B. (2003) Diverse Influence: an exploration of Australian appraisal practice, part one, *Archives and Manuscripts: Journal of the Australian Society of Archivists,* **31** (1), 63–82.

RLG-OCLC (2002) *Trusted Digital Repositories: attributes and responsibilities,* Research Libraries Group, www.oclc.org/programs/ourwork/past/trustedrep/repositories.pdf.

Scott, P. (1966) The Record Group Concept: a case for abandonment, *The American Archivist,* **29** (4), 493–504.

Styles, C. (2008) *Push for Pull: the circuit of findability, use and enrichment,* Paper presented at the Annual Conference of the Australian Society of Archivists, August 2008, www.naa.gov.au/Images/cath-styles-08_tcm2-13023.pdf.

Thibeaud, C. (2001) Access to Archives: England's contribution to the National Archive Network, *Ariadne,* **30**, www.ariadne.ac.uk/issue30/archives.

Upward, F. (1993) Institutionalizing the Archival Document – Some theoretical perspectives on Terry Eastwood's challenge. In McKemmish, S. and Upward, F. (eds), *Archival Documents: providing accountability through recordkeeping,* Ancora Press.

Upward, F. (1996) Structuring the Records Continuum Part One: Post-custodial principles and properties, *Archives and Manuscripts: Journal of the Australian Society of Archivists,* **24** (2), 268–85.

Upward, F. and McKemmish, S. (1994) Somewhere Beyond Custody, *Archives and Manuscripts: Journal of the Australian Society of Archivists,* **22** (1), 136–49.

Victorian Auditor-General's Office (2008) *Records Management in the Victorian Public Sector,* Victorian Government Printer, http://download.audit.vic.gov.au/files/Records_Report.pdf.

Notes

1   A good explanation of postcustodial archival thinking was provided by Terry Cook (1994, 308) when he said 'our traditional focus on caring for the physical things under our institutional custody will be replaced or (at the very least) enhanced by a focus on the context, purpose, intent, interrelationships,

functionality, and accountability of the record and especially its creator and its creation processes. All this goes well beyond simple custody, and thus has usefully been termed postcustodial.'

2   See the website of the Victorian Electronic Records Strategy at
www .prov.vic.gov.au/vers/vers/default.htm.

3   'Online archives unlock the past', *The Australian*, 6 November 2007,
www.australianit.news.com.au/story/0,24897,22707582-5013037,00.html.

4   www.esrc.unimelb.edu.au.

5   www.nationalarchives.gov.uk/electronicrecords/ digitalcontinuity/default.htm.

6   www.nla.gov.au/chg.

10

Information management, records management, knowledge management: the place of archives in a digital age

Nicole Convery

Introduction: Professional challenges in the digital era

The 'digital age' is upon us, the 'information society' flourishes undisturbed: with the advent of at least one personal computer in most offices and homes, information is now consumed and produced en masse and primarily electronically. The call for high-speed internet connection as a utility rather than just a commodity is only the latest sign of how far the internet has penetrated every sphere of public and private life (DCMS, 2009). Many are now online at all times, go shopping on eBay and Amazon, buy groceries via Ocado, meet friends on Facebook and talk to colleagues all over the world via Twitter – and most of all leave a trail of data in the digital world that goes widely unnoticed, unmanaged and unwanted. Lynne Brindley (2009), head of the British Library, calls it 'personal digital disorder' and claims that we are in danger of creating a 'black hole'. The idea of losing parts of our collective memory through technological obsolescence and inadequate digital preservation mechanisms has worried the archival profession as the traditional collectors and keepers of society's historical records for some time now (Forde, 2007; Waller and Sharpe, 2006) and the focus has shifted from long-term to mid-term preservation requirements due to rapid technological change (Smith, 2007, 129). In a recent consultation draft for the archives of the 21st century The National Archives (2009a, 1) acknowledge 'that people have come to expect information to be accessible online, at all times, and their approach to archives is no different. It is essential that the archives sector is able to respond to this challenge and continues to increase the proportion of records that are accessible online.'

This statement demonstrates that digital preservation and access are no longer just a technical issue but also a cultural one. Archivists need to take into account changes in the way that information is consumed in a digital age because cultural use influences how information is being valued by a society that now lives in an age of information overload. Social media tools like Facebook, Twitter, Flickr and Zoho – to name but a few – enable information exchange, consumption and alteration on a much larger and faster scale than ever before, and these tools have an immense impact on how information is being created, stored and evaluated – and selected and preserved for permanent retention. The pervasiveness of information and communication technologies (ICT) and of access to the internet has so dramatically altered the way that people live and work, that 'digital cultures have had, or are having, a transformational effect on cultural values' (Tredennick, 2008, 3). Individualization, active engagement and participation in online social and cultural practices are now the main forces behind information consumption (Tapscott, 2009; Leadbeater, 2008, 210–13). Information, rather than being a precious resource managed by specialists, is becoming a daily commodity used and re-used by everyone for everything depending on individual contexts. This rather postmodern multiplicity of information contexts generated through a search for individualism and identity challenges the defining archival practices of appraisal, preservation and access.

Moving away from the image of the user as passive consumer of information offered in the static Web 1.0 world, the social web now consists of hugely successful sites such as YouTube, Flickr and Wikipedia which not only actively encourage individual contributions but are often wholly dependent on the user. These users now expect to be able to contribute (Myburgh, 2005, 97), have their say (BBC, 2009) and improve what information is offered. The National Archives' 'Your Archives' wiki is just one example of how archives attempt to engage the user in archival research and make use of widespread knowledge resources that have so far been unattainable. Many archivists and archival institutions have also risen to the challenge and now actively connect with users in the digital social space by writing blogs (http:// specialcollectionsbradford.wordpress.com) and posting photos on Flickr for sharing and commenting (www.flickr.com/photos/ nationallibrarynz) but many others (TNA, 2008) are still trying to come to grips with having to secure government information from Flickr, YouTube or Twitter to keep for posterity (see, for example, www.number10.gov.uk). The problem here is less how archivists can appropriate new technologies for their purposes than how the outputs of these technologies can conceivably be managed and preserved. Recordkeeping methodologies and practices are no longer 'just' challenged by the format of records but much more by the way that information is used, accessed and consumed both by the individual and by society as a whole. All information professionals need to closely re-examine their existing approaches to managing information and need to respond to the change in cultural practices in innovative ways. Handing over control and enabling users to take over large parts of information management responsibilities themselves appears to be the way forward because, as Helen Tibbo (2006, 19) states, 'a document's author is now assuming a more important role in its long-term future than has been true in the past'.

Traditional approaches to information management are based on the idea of control over information in a physical environment and the user at the receiving end of expert services (Megill, 2005, 8). In a digital, networked society control over information through custody is no longer a valid concept. Access to e-books, e-journals, online newspapers and the unimaginable richness of information online from any computer and now even any mobile phone calls the idea of libraries and archives as physical spaces of information provision and authentication of what is deemed to be valuable information into question (Deegan and Tanner, 2002, 211–23). Tredinnick (2008, 70) argues that authenticity in a digital age is no longer rooted in the material cultural artefact, and thus in physicality, but in the way it is used and contextualized. Information professionals have too long focused on information as object and now need to revisit information as cultural practice in a collaborative environment. Digital information management depends as much on user input and responsibility as on professional expertise and guidance. The postcustodiality of the digital object affects all information professions because it led to widespread disintermediation between the user and the information. In the library sector, 'the ability to create value in information provision is changing from service providers to users' (Cullen, 2008, 255) and librarians need to expand their roles to catalyze innovation and knowledge sharing. Records managers have long tried to battle the onslaught of e-mails and instant messages as new types of corporate records and more recently of company information literally disappearing into the 'cloud'. Similarly, knowledge managers who not so long ago experienced a surge of interest in the exploitation of employees' individual knowledge for an information-based, innovative corporate culture are now in danger of being sidelined by the easy access to collaboration and social tools that enable knowledge-sharing across ever wider platforms without the need for formal knowledge systems. Archivists, who have dwelt in the wonderful world of paper (not to mention parchment) for centuries, are seeing their treasures replaced by a stream of data that, if it ever actually reaches them, is often non-contextual and technologically unstable. Due to the widening availability of traditional archival sources through online catalogues and digitization projects, the physical place of archives is disappearing into the ether and archives might well soon lose their traditional mandate as keepers of society's memory to the accidental permanence of a widely accessible world wide web.

Achieving organizational goals

The information professions have long maintained that their work and expertise ultimately improve an organization's business processes and thereby its competitive advantage (McLeod and Hare, 2006, 3–10; Megill, 2005, 56). Some professions (knowledge management (KM), records management (RM)) more than others (archivists, librarians) see themselves as closely linked to the business as it happens and seek a strategic position which will enable them to influence and support executive decision making (Cullen, 2008). In reality, however, the information professions are often marginalized into support functions with little regard for their competitive potential. Information has been declared the fourth resource but its management is widely regarded as a laborious, unglamorous, if necessary, evil. It is often overlooked that the exploitation of information in order to achieve operational efficiency and competitive advantage in a service-based society is based on management processes developed and implemented by information professionals. Information professionals support businesses in knowledge creation, compliance and risk management, if they are integrated into the overall business process management and strategic decision making that affects information assets (ARMA, 2009). Whereas some professions such as knowledge and records management have recently received more attention in the corporate environment, others like archivists and librarians seem to be increasingly marginalized from the actual business of the business and are often seen as an optional extra. A common fate of records and knowledge managers versus that of archivists and librarians seems to emerge as a pattern reflecting Schellenbergian ideas of information value (Schellenberg, 1956). Whereas records and knowledge managers can be linked closely to the primary, business-driven evidential value of information, archivists and librarians are oriented towards secondary, cultural value, which in a materialist business environment can easily appear to be of less importance. It is interesting that the debate about archivists' position within the organization seems to have intensified ever since the rise of records management as a perceivably separate discipline due to the demands of modern bureaucracies on the management of ever growing mountains of information. The focus of managing records as a business solution rather than to facilitate the survival of historically important information can be closely linked with new demands on the modern organization for accountability, auditability and transparency (Harries, 2009, 16).

In the external environment, organizations face increasing demands for transparency and accountability in all areas of their business dealings. The resulting focus of managing corporate information for compliance and risk agendas placed the records manager firmly in the minds of company executives (Stephens, 2005, 99). Internally, ever more flexible work processes such as cross-functional team working and agile development are needed to achieve vital advantages in research and development (R&D) and productivity in the online market in which most companies now compete (Mohamed, Stankosky and Murray, 2004, 130). Project-based team structures in modern organizations require instant access to high quality, reliable information sources provided, managed and made available by information professionals. Personalized skills and cross-disciplinary knowledge of the information worker are now seen as attractive sources for tapping into in order to gain competitive advantage (Holsapple and Wu, 2008, 31). In a Web 2.0 environment crowdsourcing has transcended company borders, and organizations such as InnoCentive (www. innocentive.com) use websites to match independent scientists and amateur researchers with their clients' R&D projects (Anderson, 2007, 16).

Consistently applied knowledge management methodologies will foster the merging of individual expertise with diverse skill sets across the organization and even across the world. The advance of more collaborative working environments in our widely knowledge-based economy, led to the rise of the knowledge management profession and with it of the professions that manage the information on which knowledge production is essentially based. 'The fundamental issue in managing knowledge in an organisational context is to identify features of context and enable processes that can facilitate the flow of knowledge of individuals in organisations for a particular purpose' (Gao, Li and Clarke, 2008, 5). Exchange 'knowledge' for 'information' in the previous statement about the essence of knowledge management and we have a characterization of the work of information professionals in general. Indeed, knowledge management seems to apply an additional layer to what information and records managers try to achieve – it adds individual expertise and understanding to information contexts which then lead to the development of research and product improvement. This layering of expertise in the information management area provides a glimpse of the interdependence between distinct professional specialisms.

The contextualization of data and information is an important mechanism for translating thought into action. According to organizational theorist Drucker (cited in Gao, Li and Clarke, 2008, 5), knowledge is information that 'changes something or somebody either by becoming grounds for action, or by making an individual or an institution capable of different and more effective action'. Records managers need to concentrate more on this essential translation of information into action to become strategically important in the organizational context rather than playing the well established compliance card or practicing their profession as *l'art pour l'art*. Especially in times of economic uncertainty, organizations look for a return on investment for all corporate activities. Information professionals, who historically have had a hard time to provide quantifiable benefits of their activities, will soon be scrutinized for their contributions to organizations' balance sheets (Cullen, 2008, 256). One area in which benefits of information work are somewhat measurable in terms of cost and time savings has been business process review. Choksy (2006, 48, 53–5) supports the claim that records managers are essentially business analysts preoccupied with requirements gathering, and that any definition of records management processes must arise directly from business requirements. In the same line of argument, she continues to separate records from archive management as the latter is perceived as not being involved in managing the living environment that created historical record. Here again, the close alignment of the archival profession with what is often perceived as the secondary quality of records in a difficult economic climate can have hazardous consequences. In a recent draft business archives strategy concerned with finding ways to promote the value of archives for business use, proclaimed benefits (TNA, 2009b, 3) seem to focus on the historic record being used for marketing, public relations (PR) and the creation of a 'retro' line. This perspective might provide an indication as to why only about a quarter of FTSE 100 (Financial Times and the London Stock Exchange) companies employ professional archivists: none of these 'historicist' activities link archives to the strategic agenda of the organization which would be needed to demonstrate more than just an ideological return on investment. When the value of records for legal compliance and evidence is stressed, it is ironically stated that 'archivists have a dual qualification in modern records management so will ensure that record keeping across a business is both compliant and efficient' (TNA, 2009b, 4).

Against the recent unifying trend propagated by continuum thinking, archivists' perceived separation from the organization's dynamic processes and their sister profession records management has not only implications on their position as a profitable activity within the organization but also on the kind of corporate or societal memory that will in future reach their shores. The real threat to the archival profession and the value of its archives comes from an ever-expanding need for stringent records management programmes. In the aftermath of corporate scandals such as Arthur Anderson and Enron in 2001 and the resulting tightening of governance legislation (e.g. Sarbanes-Oxley Act 2002 and Basel II), the focus for most organizations is to better control potentially discoverable evidence in case of external audits or litigation (Mat-Iza, 2006, 76–81). Records management processes can provide the amount of control over corporate information that is needed to both ensure compliance and to avoid risk (Myler, 2008, 58–63). Moss (2005, 105) rightly argues that with the increasing convergence of regulatory regimes retention is determined by organizational risk management. A risk-based retention regime will inevitably lead to the destruction of information as soon as legal and business requirements allow and little regard will be paid to archival concerns. The retention schedule will in future determine what little information is being kept for permanent preservation – usually a risk-free, sanitized version of organizational history. This view reinforces the Jenkinsonian view of archivists as passive custodians of dead records (Jenkinson, 1937, 144–6). To counter their vanishing influence in the selection of records for permanent preservation, archivists must become active within the organization by fostering understanding of the value of an inclusive corporate memory as an active knowledge resource. Organizations too often lose sight of the value of a corporate knowledge-base which includes the archive and which can only be established through consistent recordkeeping regimes applied from the point of information creation to its permanent retention. More than just concentrating on archives' value for PR and marketing strategies, putting the focus on this knowledge resource enables learning from the past, avoiding re-inventing the wheel and generating new knowledge based on previous experience. In the light of corporate governance regimes, it appears that archivists and records managers no longer work as two sides of the same coin but could conceivably end up working against each other: the one morphing into risk managers with the organizations' interest their main focus and purging information of its dangers, while the other, in longstanding tradition, trying to disclose and document these dangers for posterity thereby being 'all things to all Archives, his [*sic*] interests identified with theirs, his period and his point of view theirs' (Jenkinson, 1937, 124).

Whereas risk and governance are often regarded as the pre-occupation of the private sector, the public sector has come under similar pressure to be accountable for its actions. Access legislation such as the Freedom of Information Act 2000 and the Data Protection Act 1998 are seen as a milestone to furthering citizens' rights and to holding the government accountable. 'Indeed, they [the public sector] are accountable to the members of the public, and therefore a balance between risk and the types of records to keep is crucial' (Mat-Isa, 2006, 69). In 2008, the Cabinet Office (2008) published a report titled 'Excellence and fairness: achieving world class public services' detailing how it intends to improve public services over the next few years. It promises to empower citizens through local accountability and transparency of performance by radically improving the quality and availability of information on the performance of services. Effective empowerment then rests on reliable and trustworthy information about government business – information that needs to be managed, classified, appraised and preserved by information professionals (Willis, 2005, 90–2). Whereas greater public insight into authorities' actions has been part of every democracy since Aristotle, the recent accountability drive somewhat contrarily leads to an audit society that tends to keep only what is safe and opportune to disclose, which could essentially undermine public trust in what is presented as official history (Currall and Moss, 2008, 70). Governments have a long history of 'historical engineering', often through the destruction of documents that could inform history otherwise, and European history is ripe with examples that demonstrate 'that in forging of the collective memory, the role of governments has always been greater than that of historians' (Wilson, 1996, 2). Nowadays the obstacle is less one of attaining access to closed government archives than getting 'sensitive' material past a premature destruction decision and into the actual archive in the first place. It is here that archivists can act to elicit the hidden realities of political discourse from a variety of sources. Archivists have always collected more than the official narrative and preserved the loose ends – the unofficial, unorthodox and sometimes uncomfortable. Greater engagement with all sectors of society such as activists groups and non-governmental organizations (NGOs) can help ensure that 'collections more fully represent all within society . . . and not just dominant and institutional elements' (Flinn, 2008, 110). Appraisal as a core function of archive management can be re-enforced by extending collection policies and by employing methods that reflect the way that information is being created and used in a digital culture. Then archives can become treasures of hidden histories and re-address the flawed relationships between archives, history and objectivity (Johnson, 2007, 133).

. . . in a user-centred world

Engagement with the user is probably the most prevalent paradigm shift in the digital world. Huvila (2008, 16) noted in a recent study on the participatory archive that, unlike in libraries and museums, 'user and use perspectives have received little attention in archives and records management operations' and that the role of the user is seen as limited to making use of resources as they are. As discussed above, this passive view of the user, and indeed the passive archive and archivist, is no longer tenable in a Web 2.0 environment. Information creation is no longer the exclusive reserve of a select few in a structured environment but a widespread preoccupation of the masses in the virtual sphere – there were 82.5 million user-generated content creators in 2008 in the US alone (Verna, 2009). In an electronic environment, not only who created information and the amount of information created has changed dramatically but also how information is created and where. First the internet and now a variety of widely available, free social software changes the landscape of information production. Blogging, twittering, and having an active virtual presence on Second Life is now often encouraged by private sector organizations in a bid to attract attention from a new kind of consumer. Many universities and businesses (IBM, Reuters, Mazda, Toyota, etc.) use Second Life as meeting places and as e-learning tools (Shepherd, 2007); others (O'Reilly, Skittles, LOVEFiLM and even President Obama) use Twitter to get in contact with customers, and most public and private organizations now have a Facebook page (BBC, Guardian, Accenture, IBM, Procter & Gamble) used for marketing and recruitment. While social media can add value and provide new marketing outlets, it also results in a blurring of the traditional division between private interest and work-related issues as users blog from everywhere about everything at all times. Blogs, just like e-mail, instant messaging and even LinkedIn activities, raise questions of ownership, function and management and have been the subject of recent court actions (The Register, 2008). Web 2.0 applications and services now invade the business world and some organizations already work with what can be called Office 2.0 – a collaborative working environment using often externally hosted services and applications. Many private sector organizations and universities weighed security concerns against better service provisions and stability and are increasingly outsourcing e-mail clients and office applications (Cook, 2008, 33–43). The move from in-house server systems that hold and protect all information and applications behind a firewall to access through the web has strong implications on information access, security, management and preservation. Technology has shifted the power away from the organization (and the information professional) towards the individual user, and the information professions need to find a way of dealing with this power shift.

Harnessing the network effect through social networking, collaboration and sharing can facilitate knowledge creation and innovation. Knowledge managers will need to be instrumental in the selection and dissemination of new knowledge environments which will increasingly be customized to suit individual needs and preferences (Marfleet, 2008, 153). The interest of many large organizations in Web 2.0 applications is based as much on its 'cool' status as it is on affordability and low risk implementation, but is also to do with the potential of Web 2.0 applications to exploit social information (Cunningham and Wilkins, 2009, 23). It is archivists, records and knowledge managers who provide the expertise and the methodologies to exploit the knowledge of the masses in a structured and productive way for organizations. Records managers face the daunting task of regaining some form of control over various types of information that can now be stored outside the organization's firewall in a multitude of not centrally accessible software applications. The use of diverse office support applications, business systems and cloud computing in a rising number of organizations have rendered traditional Electronic Discovery Reference Model (EDRM) systems somewhat obsolete in their current configuration and business use (Harries, 2009). Not only have mechanisms of creation and storage changed dramatically, new ways to classify and search for information have emerged. Folksonomies and tagging are replacing painstakingly built corporate taxonomies and classification systems because they are easy and quick to use, instinctive and user-focused and therefore more successful than often highly conceptual, alien classification schemes (Reed, 2008, 8–9). The creation of tools to allow users to locate the items they seek has been described as the 'essence of librarianship' (Deegan and Tanner, 2002, 111) and is to some extent what drives records and archives management but what these tools look like will change dramatically in the age of digitization. From a business perspective it can be cheaper and more efficient to allow users to tag documents and to invest in one of the range of full-text desktop search tools than to invest in the resource intensive development of classification schemes. Records managers need to learn how to capitalize on the users' willingness to attach tags and keywords to documents – using the power of the masses to deduce how useful a document is in real terms for the organization rather than according to a retention schedule (Bailey, 2008, 73). Traditional retention management as part of an organization's compliance and risk agenda is most under pressure in a distributed environment. Records managers must find a way to formalize the access and structure of these external applications in order to apply retention rules and ensure access to corporate information in terms of e-discovery. Much has been written about the security implications of distributed information storage ranging from data protection issues, and e-discovery to the protection of valuable information from the wider public or competitors (Cunningham and Wilkins, 2008, 28–30). Less has been suggested on how 'efficient and systematic control of the creation, receipt, maintenance, use and disposition of records (ISO 15489)' can be achieved in this context. Steve Bailey (2008, 117) rightly demands a re-adjustment of existing methodologies to result in a professional practice that moves away from the centrality of the records manager to end-user responsibility. Rather than being in control, information professionals need to let go of the custodial imperative and entrust responsibility to the actual records' creator and user – and this really is the paradigm shift that was so much anticipated.

Access to a wealth of online information led to a decline in the demand for intermediation from information specialists (Cullen, 2008; Marfleet, 2008). Archivists and librarians can no longer be seen as the gatekeepers to knowledge and information bases in times when every internet user can find more information online than can be held by the predominantly physical spaces of libraries and archives. Although the provision of access, especially to information in physical form, appears in decline, intermediation in the sense of quality control is very much in demand. Not only do users often need expert help to sift through the long list of search results, make sense of a variety of portals, databases and open access publications and to evaluate exactly which information to trust and use, archivists and librarians should have a lead role in authenticating new, valuable information resources created by users for users such as Wikipedia and YouTube. Archivists and librarians can play an important part in a training and advisory role by enabling research rather than conducting it, and by providing guidelines on content sharing and information security (Marfleet, 2008, 155). The librarian of the future is seen as a knowledge mediator and information architect with a stronger focus on technical and managerial skills (Deegan and Tanner, 2002,

218–20). Similarly, the shift from custody to facilitation is probably the biggest challenge for archivists who have frequently prided themselves on safeguarding society's treasures. In a digital age, those treasures will now often become digitized and be available for everyone from everywhere. Archivists not only possess expert skills uncovering very specialized information but also the expert knowledge to provide the user with contextual information that is often lost in the digital environment. Johnson (2008, 153) found in her recent research into digital archive users, that 'it is a lack of archival intelligence, as opposed to technical skill, that leads users to seek mediation'. In order to guide users through a valuable research experience, all information professions need to acquire technical skills that have long been the domain of the IT professional. Understanding content management platforms, information portals and their underlying database structure as well as technical details of new social software are now essential prerequisites and can open up new career paths. The demand for training in more technical skills for archivists and records managers has been noted throughout the profession and in particular by traditional training providers, but so far technical training is missing from any serious curriculum (Tibbo, 2006, 30).

Digital preservation is one area in which technical skills are in greater demand than ever previously and which in an electronic environment can no longer be separated from access and appraisal. 'In the digital age, the future of the past is under threat' (Tredennick, 2008, 151) – and there is already much electronic information lost in the digital dark ages. The proliferation of electronic information in both the public and private sphere has challenged traditional processes in order to ensure long-term accessibility in many different ways. One dilemma of digital preservation arises from the status of information in society. When information is available so easily and in such vast quantities, much of it is regarded as ephemeral. On the whole the internet culture is directed towards the here and now with little concern for documenting what has gone past. Information is being used and re-used, altered, enhanced and transformed or, as McKemmish (2001, 334), a continuum researcher, put it, 'in a constant state of becoming'. The non-custodial nature of digital information and a breakdown of traditional transfer mechanisms of information to archives render traditional selection criteria futile. Although as mentioned earlier, stringent records management programmes will ironically ease the burden of appraising terabytes of information, electronic records management still has a long way to go to catch up with the technological development within organizations. There also seems to be a misguided ambition to preserve the whole of the digital sphere. Projects such as the Internet Archive (www.archive.org/index.php), which aims to offer permanent access for researchers, historians and scholars to historical collections that exist in digital format, seem to suggest, however laudable, that all digital information is of permanent value. Just because there is now more information than ever before does not mean we also have to preserve more information than ever before. In a postmodern world in which multiple narratives are seen to form a valid approximation to truth and memory, no collection of archival or information material can be seen as all-encompassing and complete (Johnson, 2007, 134–6). Selection criteria for the preservation of our digital heritage then need to be open, flexible and accommodating to the unlikely and unexpected. Archivists will have to accept that selection and appraisal 'by their very nature privilege some information over others' (Currall, Moss and Stuart, 2006, 99) and that most criteria are socially constructed.

The information management continuum

Until ten years ago the main role of archives was often described as selection, preservation and access but these roles have changed dramatically over time (Ceeney, 2008, 58). Selection or appraisal of records with archival value which has traditionally taken place at the end of a record's life has become virtually impossible when faced with terabytes of electronic information and now needs to be applied at creation stage. Selection more and more becomes part of recordkeeping regimes carried out by records managers through comprehensive retention and destruction regimes. Even though this process is influenced by archival concerns, risk management agendas are likely to have the prerogative over long-term historical visions in the future. Archivists are beginning to look at new ways of selecting and collecting the loose ends to support multiple societal narratives (Moss, 2005, 109) and of creating a W*underkammer* in which archival objects are continuously re-contextualized (Moss, 2008, 83) and thereby kept alive. Similarly, the preservation of society's now largely digital memory will need to be a distributed, cross-disciplinary effort that relies to a great degree on user involvement to be effective. Openness and flexibility are needed to engage with wider, more diverse user communities but also with other professions such as IT, KM, and RM to ensure the survival of our digital past for future generations. Access to information in the archival paradigm is a double-edged sword. With access legislation and the currently debated reduction of the 30-year rule to 15 years (30 Year Rule Review, 2009, 30), there is now more information than ever available to the public but less and less of it is held in archival custody. Information is no longer authenticated through preservation in official custody (Jenkinson, 1937, 12) and is used, re-used and re-contextualized without the need for interference from the traditional source keeper.

But all is not lost as archivists face immense opportunities to gain renewed validity in the online world by no longer providing access physically but through contextualization. As the traditional role of the archive as a place will become somewhat obsolete, archivists should perhaps reverse their duties as defined by Jenkinson (1937, 15) and make as their primary task the provision for the needs of historians by contextualizing collections. Rather than focusing on selection and appraisal strategies, archivists could concentrate their efforts and expertise on making sense of the increasing amount of disconnected digital information through the provision of sub-texts and linking narratives. Authenticity and reliability of records depend on context more than anything else and it is here that archivists can exercise their expertise and help legitimize dispersed collections of records by situating them in their wider societal context. Huvila (2008, 25) argues that the participatory archive will need to focus on a radical user orientation which includes their actual participation in the archival process and on contextualizing both the records and the archival process itself. The community archive movement is just one example amongst many in which archivists work alongside individuals with shared areas of interest helping them to create their particular account of local realities (www.communityarchives.org.uk). Communities of people now form everywhere in the collaborative Web 2.0 environment, helping people to link forces to promote their political, religious or ethical beliefs or even just to share the same preference for music, literature and film (Shirky, 2008, Chapter 6). These specialized networks symbolize a new way of looking for and establishing identity because 'the groups that individuals belong to define who they think they are' (Rheingold, 2002, 25). This new individuality is no longer limited to space or time but can be formed interactively in the digital sphere or space–time (Upward, 2000, 120). Archivists have a role to play in ensuring that these new identities are documented for posterity and sometimes the search for who we are can lead back from specialized social networks to the traditional and formalized archives thereby fostering new relationships and developing new means of engagement with a new user community. In the light of this drive to establish identity and redefine communities, it is not surprising that a document on proposed national records legislation in 2003 states that 70% of archive users are researching their family history (TNA, 2003, 3). These examples demonstrate how crucial archivists are in providing not only societal but also personal context from the vast information resources now available to every researcher and every accidental visitor. At the risk of sounding paradoxical, re-specialization of archivists in the historical and research area could actually lead to a closing of the gap between them and other information professionals. If archivists, librarians, knowledge and records managers all look to define their particular area of influence over information under a common theoretical framework, then we can close the gap by specializing, by establishing clear boundaries and firm connections.

A shift of focus towards the societal dimension of recordkeeping based on the idea of identity and memory will seemingly place archivists at the end of the traditional life cycle of information and will appear to further a professional separation between archives and records management that has recently been fiercely disputed (Ghetu, 2004; Flynn, 2001). The Australian continuum approach to recordkeeping (Upward, 2000; Upward and McKemmish, 1994) has been perceived as a methodology that attempts to overcome such a demarcation by pushing archivists back into the business context and by focusing on all possible recordkeeping contexts, from operational, strategic to societal, that apply to records continuously. However, archivists seem to stand apart from other information professions such as knowledge and records management not only because of an essentially different intellectual outlook on records but also often by a very apparent physical separation. Based on Upward's conceptual model of the records continuum (Upward, 2000, 123), it can be argued that archivists and records/knowledge managers are placed in opposite spheres of the continuum. On the one hand, knowledge and records managers, and to an extent librarians, share a strong focus on the organization's day-to-day business processes; they therefore look forward at how to build on existing knowledge in order to move to the next product or service and at the same time look inward towards what the business needs, leaving societal concerns as secondary. Archivists, on the other hand, appear to have an opposing focus on past organizational practice; they are looking backwards into how information use shaped corporate identity, documenting past actions while always focusing outwards to future, societal uses for information gathered in the course of past business activities. However, archivists' perceived separation from other information professions can be seen as just an expression of specialism within the continuum of the wider framework of information management within which all professions work together by approaching the management of information from their various expert positions. Building a metatheory for a metacommunity 'means designing a new idiosyncratic interdisciplinary speciality of information management' (Myburgh, 2005, 146) and could be *the* approach to unite the fractured information professions. Natalie Ceeney (2008, 66) recently concluded that archivists 'need to engage in the whole information arena within our area in the UK' and it is part of the National Archives' vision to lead and transform information management. This inclusive view of the realm of archivists as only a part of the wider information management arena has long been buried under a struggle for professionalization of its component disciplines. It is the very essence of the archival profession's orientation towards the past and with it its expertise in providing context that has an important role to play in bringing information and knowledge together into a collaborative environment in which information can be shared and re-used while at the same time maintaining its contextual linkages.

Records and knowledge managers as well as archivists and librarians all essentially manage information in its various guises based on very similar methodologies. The definition of and distinction between such concepts as 'information', 'records' and 'publication' has always been somewhat incoherent and from a user's perspective there is little difference between them. The Office of Government Commerce (2009; see also JISC, 2008) is not alone in defining information management as 'the means by which an organisation efficiently plans, collects, creates, organises, uses, controls, disseminates and disposes of its information, both structured records and unstructured information'. This definition does not distinguish between the information professions explicitly but unites activities of librarians, records managers and archivists under one area of responsibility for both structured and unstructured information and even subsumes knowledge management 'as a key aspect of information management' (OGC, 2009). Although archival activities can be assumed to take place under 'disposal', they are not further elaborated in the remaining explanations in contrast to paragraphs on library and records management information. It is here that archivists have some work to do to impress their objectives firmer on to the information management agenda and thereby close the gap to establish a continuum of care for information throughout its continuing use in many different contexts. A wider, more united and more inclusive definition of the objects that all professions are concerned with could be a first step to a more structured definition of professional specialism within an information management framework. The FOI Act (Freedom of Information) and tougher corporate accountability laws led records managers to focus their attention on the whole information environment of an organization and not just the 20% of corporate information that have somewhat arbitrarily been classified as records (Bailey, 2008, 63). Here too, contextualization determines what constitutes evidence of business activity, and what makes a record reliable or authentic depends on a particular organization's business requirements and its approach to risk management (Choksy, 2006, 67). Similarly, archives have long accessioned not only records but all documents and information that have provided collections with context and that often reflect the non-official aspect of an organization's work. In a digital environment, professional separation along the such vague conceptual lines as 'records', 'information' and 'archives' is not just impractical, it can lead to a digital dark age in which vast amounts of digital information end up unmanaged, inaccessible and de-contextualized. Emerging conceptual models such as continuum thinking in Australia have rejected the idea of professional demarcation and promoted ideas of inclusive recordkeeping regimes (Upward and McKemmish, 1994, 1). The records continuum with its focus on inclusivity of all societal, organizational and operational aspects of recordkeeping can be seen as a meta-theory that is capable of uniting all information professions under the umbrella of 'information management' in its widest sense within which specializations can work hand in hand. In reverse to

Upward (2000, 120), it can be argued that rather than blurring the boundaries between specializations, a more distinct positioning can lead to a space–time world view in which all information professionals 'are keen to assist in the process of reorganising their own knowledge and to contribute to the development of new rules for a new game'. This new game needs to be a more user-focused, user-enabled approach to managing all information resources not as objects but on a conceptual level to provide a flexible and collaborative service to the business so that it is perceived as adding value and providing return on investment both financially and intellectually.

References

30 Year Rule Review (2009) *Review of the 30 Year Rule*, www2.nationalarchives.gov.uk/30yrr/30-year-rule-report.pdf.

Anderson, P. (2007) What is Web 2.0? Ideas, technologies and implications for education, *JISC Technology and Standards Watch*, www.jisc.ac.uk/media/documents/techwatch/tsw0701b.pdf.

ARMA (2009) *Generally Accepted Recordkeeping Principles*, www.arma.org/GARP/.

Bailey, S. (2008) *Managing the Crowd: rethinking records management in the Web 2.0 world*, Facet Publishing.

Brindley, L. (2009) We're in Danger of Losing our Memories, *Observer*, 25 January, www.guardian.co.uk/technology/2009/jan/25/internet-heritage.

British Broadcasting Corporation (2009) *Have Your Say*, http://news.bbc.co.uk/1/hi/talking_point/default.stm.

Cabinet Office (2008) *Excellence and Fairness: achieving world class public services*, www.cabinetoffice.gov.uk/strategy/publications/excellence_and_fairness/report/html.aspx.

Ceeney, N. (2008) The role of a 21st-century National Archive – the relevance of the Jenkinsonian tradition, and a redefinition for the information society, *Journal of the Society of Archivists*, **29** (1), 57–71.

Choksy, E.B.C. (2006) *Domesticating Information: managing information inside your organization*, Scarecrow.

Cook, N. (2008) *Enterprise 2.0: how social software will change the future of work*, Gower.

Cullen, J. (2008) Catalyzing Innovation and Knowledge Sharing, *Business Information Review*, **25** (4), 253–8.

Cunningham, P. and Wilkins, J. (2009) A Walk in the Cloud, *Information Management*

Journal, **43** (1), 22–30.

Currall, J. and Moss, M. (2008) We are Archivists, but are we OK?, *Records Management Journal*, **18** (1), 69–91.

Deegan, M. and Tanner, S. (2002) *Digital Futures: strategies for the information age*, Library Association Publishing.

Department for Culture, Media and Sport (2009) *Digital Britain: interim report*, www.culture.gov.uk/images/publications/digital_britain_ interimreportjan09.pdf.

Flinn, A. (2008) Other Ways of Thinking, Other Ways of Being: documenting the margins and the transitory: what to preserve, how to collect. In Craven, L. (ed.) *What are Archives? Cultural and Theoretical Perspectives: a reader*, Ashgate.

Flynn, S. J. A. (2001) The Records Continuum Model in Context and its Implications for Archival Practice, *Journal of the Society of Archivists*, **22** (1), 79–93.

Forde, H. (2007) *Preserving Archives*, Facet Publishing.

Gao, F., Li, M. and Clarke, S. (2008) Knowledge, Management, and Knowledge Management in Business Operations, *Journal of Knowledge Management*, **12** (2), 3–17.

Ghetu, M. (2004) Two Professions, One Goal, *Information Management Journal*, **38** (3), 62–6.

Harries, S. (2009) Managing Records, Making Knowledge and Good Governance, *Records Management Journal*, **19** (1), 16–25.

Holsapple, C. W. and Wu, J. (2008) In Search of the Missing Link, *Knowledge Management Research and Practice*, **6**, 31–40.

Huvila, I. (2008) Participatory Archive: towards decentralised curation, radical user orientation, and broader contextualization of records management, *Archival Science*, **8**, 15–36.

ISO 15489-2:2001 *Information and Documentation – Records Management – Part 1*, International Standards Organization.

Jenkinson, H. (1937) *A Manual of Archive Administration*, Percy Lund, Humphries & Co Ltd.

JISC (2008) Infokits: Information Management, www.jiscinfonet.ac.uk/information-management.

Johnson, A. (2008) Users, Use and Context: supporting interaction between users and digital archives. In Craven, L. (ed.), *What are Archives?: cultural and theoretical perspectives: a reader*, Ashgate.

Johnson, V. (2007) Creating history? Confronting the myth of objectivity in the archive, *Archives: The Journal of the British Records Association*, **117**, 128–43.

Leadbeater, C. (2008) *We-Think*, Profile Books.

Marfleet, J. (2008) Enterprise 2.0 – What's your game plan? *Business Information Review*, **25** (3), 152–7.

Mat-Isa, A. (2006) Risk Management and Managing Records. In Tough, A. and Moss, M. (eds) *Record Keeping in a Hybrid Environment: managing the creation, use, preservation and disposal of unpublished information objects in context*, Chandos Publishing.

McKemmish, S. (2001) Placing Records Continuum Theory and Practice, *Archival Science*, **1** (4), 333–59.

McLeod, J. and Hare, C. (2006) *How to Manage Records in the E-environment*, Routledge.

Megill, K.A. (2005) *Corporate Memory: records and information management in the knowledge age*, K.G. Saur.

Mohamed, M., Stankosky, M. and Murray, A. (2004) Applying Knowledge Management Principles to Enhance Cross-functional Team Performance, *Journal of Knowledge Management*, **8** (3), 127–42.

Moss, M. (2005) Archivist: friend or foe? *Records Management Journal*, **15** (2), 104–14.

Moss, M. (2008) What is an Archive in the Digital Environment? In Craven, L. (ed.), *What are archives?: cultural and theoretical perspectives: a reader*, Ashgate.

Myburgh, S. (2005) *The New Information Professional: how to thrive in the information age doing what you love*, Chandos Publishing.

Myler, E. (2008) Minimising Risks Through a Corporate Information Compliance Initiative, *Information Management Journal*, **42** (1), 58–63.

The National Archives (2009a) *Archives for the 21st century, Consultation Draft*, www.nationalarchives.gov.uk/documents/archivesconsultation/archives-for-the-21st-century-england.pdf.

The National Archives (2009b) *National Strategy for Business Archives*, Draft, www.businessarchivescouncil.org.uk/materials/draftbusinessstrategy.pdf.

Office of Government Commerce (2009) *Information Management*, www.ogc.gov.uk/delivery_life cycle_information_management.asp.

Reed, B. (2008) Service-oriented Architectures and Recordkeeping, *Records Management Journal*, **18** (1), 7–20.

The Register (2008) *Man Accused of Using LinkedIn to Steal Clients*, 9 June, www.theregister.co.uk/2008/06/09/linkedin_hays_ions.

Rheingold, H. (2002) *Smart Mobs: the next social revolution*, Basic Books.

Schellenberg, T. R. (1956) The Appraisal of Modern Public Records, *National*

Archives Bulletin, **8**, www.archives.gov/research/alic/reference/archives-resources/appraisal-foreword.html.

Shepherd, J. (2007) It's a World of Possibilities, *The Guardian*, 8 May, www.guardian.co.uk/education/2007/may/08/students.elearning.

Shirky, C. (2008) *Here Comes Everybody*, Allen Lane.

Smith. K. (2007) *Planning and Implementing Electronic Records Management: a practical guide*, Facet Publishing.

Stephens, D.O. (2005) The Sarbanes-Oxley Act: records management implications, *Records Management Journal*, **15** (2), 98–103.

Tapscott, D. (2009) *Grown Up Digital: how the net generation is changing your world*, McGraw-Hill.

Tibbo, H. (2006) Creating, Managing, and Archiving Records: changing roles and realities in the digital era. In Bütikofer, N., Hofman, H. and Ross, S. (eds) *Managing and Archiving Records in the Digital Era: changing professional orientations*, hier+jetzt.

Tredennick, L. (2008) *Digital Information Culture: the individual and society in the digital age*, Chandos Publishing.

Upward, F. (2000) Modelling the Continuum as Paradigm Shift in Recordkeeping and Archiving Processes, and Beyond – a personal reflection, *Records Management Journal*, **10** (3), 115–39.

Upward, F. and McKemmish, S. (1994) Somewhere Beyond Custody, *Archives and Manuscripts,* **22** (1), 136–49.

Verna, P. (2009) A Spotlight on UGC Participants, *eMarketer*, 19 February, www.emarketer.com/Article.aspx?id=1006914.

Waller, M. and Sharpe, S. (2006) *Mind the Gap: assessing digital preservation needs in the UK*, www.dpconline.org/docs/reports/uknamindthegap.pdf.

Willis, A. (2005) Corporate Governance and Management of Information and Records, *Records Management Journal*, **15** (2), 86–97.

Wilson, K. (ed.) (1996) *Forging the Collective Memory: government and international historians through two world wars*, Berghahn Books.

11

Appraisal and the future of archives in the digital era

Richard J. Cox

Introduction

It is risky to predict the future, especially in the volatile information professions, but it is always fun to try. Some make wild predictions with the assurance that they won't be around to be held accountable for them. David Friedman (2008, 4) states that the 'future is radically uncertain', basing this on what is presently happening with intellectual property, personal privacy, transparency and its mixed blessings, e-business, open space and scholarship, computer crime, biotechnology and virtual reality – all issues with implications for what archivists do, especially the critical aspect of their work as appraisers and documenters. Archival appraisal is also the task that might seem to be completely contrary to where we are heading in the digital era, as some predict that a hallmark of our future may be a new ability to save everything (ending any need for selection).

This chapter examines three key areas. First, it characterizes how information technologies are transforming our world. Second, a brief case is made for why appraisal is the central and most important archival function. Third, it relates the new digital technologies to archival appraisal (and vice versa), making a case for how more rigorous archival appraisal must become, and speculating about the archivist of the future.

The world flashes by

The world of the archivist has changed substantially in the past generation. The world of archives has changed significantly in the last 40 years when there were no computers, queries were answered by telephone and postal mail, reference services were provided during certain hours on specific days, finding aids were only available in printed form, and archivists dealt mostly with paper-based materials. Today, the typical archivist stares at a computer screen most of the day, provides answers to queries via e-mail, answers reference questions on an almost 24/7 basis, distributes finding aids on the world wide web, and works with an increasing array of digitally born documentary materials. The archival universe is populated with Blackberries, iPods, cell phones, GPS (global positioning system) navigation systems, Flickr, blogs, MySpace, wikis, flash mobs, open source software, digital cameras, GPS trackers, YouTube, and Facebook (just for starters).

Emerging information technologies suggest major issues for archivists. Researchers, relying on online sources, may cease visiting physical spaces or even the use of traditional documentary materials housed in physical repositories (unless major digitalization efforts are undertaken [see Howard, 2008] or there are renewed efforts to teach information literacy skills [see Rein, 2007; Snelson, 2007]). The persistent archival paradigm has been the archives as a place to be visited in person based on the collecting of documentary artefacts, but this looks uncertain in the future, leading some to defend real library and archives spaces as necessary places for contemplation (Levy, 2006). Anyone who has done research in an archives will tell you that it is a contemplative process, where you work carefully through masses of letters, diary entries, and/or accounting ledgers, listening for the voices from the past. Reflection is the order of the day, a process that is different from web searching where speed and efficiency is often the primary objective.

New forms of digital scholarship are emerging, requiring new and different kinds of digital repositories like we have never envisioned before, with a greater commitment to open access (Borgman, 2007). In effect, archivists, and other professionals, need to socialize these information technologies, as Donald Norman (2007, 172–3) argues, in order to make the machines 'truly useful'. What will be the role of the archivist in accomplishing this? How will archivists cross boundaries that they have been reluctant to cross in the past, building new kinds of mental landscapes (see Gardner, 2006, identifying five cognitive abilities that we need to develop and nurture).

Cautionary voices, advocating the need for both traditional and digital archives and libraries, are often lost in the crush of the many voices championing the virtual rather than physical spaces (see, for example, Darnton, 2008). While archivists might be tracking the impact of digital natives (individuals who have grown up with the internet) whose ideas of archives are only what they can access online, universities are developing new forms of information competency programmes, with some professors taking online systems into their classrooms (Guess, 2008a). The new information technologies suggest ways for people to work together in groups and organizations to manage differently, all built around concepts such as 'knowledge commons' (Hess and Ostrom, 2007; Shirky, 2008). Archivists can utilize these new technologies in innovative ways to reach their research communities and the public, assuming archivists themselves have gained a sufficient understanding of the digital technologies.

There are many issues generated from the digital information technologies. The growing reliance on digital technologies, now some in their own right becoming older sources, requires careful maintenance of hardware, software, digital content – all posing technical standards perhaps requiring a nearly constant appraisal (see, for example, Guess, 2008b, commenting on a 2006 report from Britain's Digital Preservation Coalition). Librarians and archivists alike are reconsidering their own digitization efforts in light of large-scale commercial efforts by companies such as Google and Microsoft, especially as some abandon or scale back their efforts or become more proprietary about content (Guess, 2008c). Nicholas Carr (2008) wonders if our immersion in networked communications isn't transforming the way that we read or even what we read, hindering our ability to read longer texts and certain kinds of documents. If humanity's connection to text is altered, surely the manner in which it uses historical sources will change as well.

There are temptations for archivists in the digital era, especially the claim that every document, book, article, work of art, and piece of ephemera will be digitized and placed on the web (continuation of a historic quest to build a universal library or archive). Google, aiming to digitize all of the world's books, has drawn considerable commentary, most of it, at least by the public and the media, quite positive. Ian Wilson, the head of Canada's National Archives and Library, writes in an introduction to Jean-Noël Jeanneney's book on Google, that Google's offer is 'seductive to chronically underfunded libraries and archives, the custodians of our societies' (Jeanneney, 2007, viii) cumulative documentary heritage. Jeanneney, president of France's National Library, contrasts the long-term cultural mission of librarians and archivists with the short-term business aims of Google, arguing that there is a need for a renewed commitment to the work of librarians (and by implication, archivists) to be not merely caretakers but to 'stand beside professors and schoolteachers as essential intermediaries of knowledge' (Wilson in Jeanneney, 2007, 23).

Not long ago digitization was seen as opposed to preservation, but this has since shifted dramatically, partly because of digitization's usefulness for enhancing access to our documentary heritage and partly because of progress in making digitization a more reliable approach for administering documents. Archivists and their tasks are being redefined. David Holdsworth (cited in Deegan and Tanner, 2006, 57) for example, questions the need for selection, noting, 'If it costs very little to keep digital data, we might resist the temptation to discard those items of little interest to us, but which later researchers might find valuable.' Some who believe in the possibility of saving everything are also advocates for 'lifelogging', recording everything they do and say (and suggesting something about the future of public and personal archives) (Carlson, 2007).

There also are opportunities for archivists posed by the new information technologies. If Wikipedia has managed to take hold, there is reason to believe that other Web 2.0 technologies and social computing will have an impact on what archives do and how archivists operate (Wilson, 2008). The many charges levelled against Wikipedia, concerning its effort to give everyone a voice at the expense of its reliability, suggests caution with how archivists use social computing, perhaps with archivists teaching their researchers how to evaluate the quality of online resources (see, for example, Clifford, 2007). Archivists should make available draft appraisal reports and seek public input into these decisions. This will require archivists to be much more coherent in their appraisal practices, enriching society's knowledge of the archival mission and its significance.

The digital era also claims (or hopes) that amateurs will replace professional gatekeepers, although some have questioned the wisdom of this (Keen, 2007). Others have embraced the notion of professional convergence, a:

state in which collaboration around a specific function or idea has become so extensive, engrained and assumed that it is no longer recognized by others as a collaborative undertaking. Instead, it has matured to the level of infrastructure and becomes, like our water or transportation networks, a critical system that we rely upon without considering the collaborative efforts and compromises that made it possible.

(Zorich, Waibel, and Erway, 2008, 12)

The report provides a model for considering how convergence can occur, such as in co-ordinated searching and users being able to add knowledge via 'social tagging or community annotation' (Zorich, Waibel, and Erway , 2008, 14). It is a brave new world, one where authors manage 'open book' blogs, inviting commentary by other experts and the public. Perhaps archivists can write drafts of both theoretical and practical volumes in blogs and wikis to generate a lot more openness about their foundational knowledge. Some of my writing in the past few years has derived from my writing in a blog, but very few archivists participate by providing comments (in fact, I get more comments from those interested in archives from outside of the field). Are archivists ready yet for the digital era?

Archivists and the challenge of the digital era

The greatest challenge for archivists may be generational issues. Many archivists working today did not grow up with a rich array of information technologies, but now they are working with the first generation of digital natives (Palfrey and Gasser, 2008). We need to be cautious not to get ahead of ourselves. Peter Shillingsburg (2006, 4) reminds us that we are 'but 15–20 years into an era whose counterpart introduced a 500-year reign'. Alistair Tough and Michael Moss (2006, ix) believe recordkeeping to be a 'relatively new field of study', with 'boundaries . . . poorly defined and porous', typical of 'emerging disciplines'. Seamus Ross (cited in Tough and Moss, 2006) thinks that we have overstated the fragility of the digital materials, when the more serious problem is the lack of collaboration among records professionals, IT workers, and managers. Archivists are not working in a static world and relying on static principles. A lot of archival angst generated by the digital era relates more to professional status and authority than the basic nature of archival work, challenging old comfort zones. There may be new careers out there, incorporating archival functions, such as in 'digital data management' or 'data curation' (National Science Foundation, 2007, 38).

Digitizing documentary sources prompts questions about the appraisal function. Selection is hindered by the fact that we can never fully anticipate the use of anything in the future. Does this mean that archivists should be conservative or cautious in their approaches to using digitization (or in evaluating digitally born materials)? As Deegan and Tanner (2006, 10) suggest, archivists must understand the alternatives, the possibility of losing important stuff if no surrogates are created. If archivists don't embrace digitization fully, will they see their holdings neglected (as researchers and scholars go elsewhere, namely online, to find sources in more convenient ways)? Probably.

The potential loss of our digital documentary heritage draws more public attention (and sometimes major national funding, such as in the National Digital Information Infrastructure and Preservation Program) than the possibility that the new technologies allow us to save everything. Estimates about the growth of information and data may be difficult to make, but they are always impressive and capture our attention. Alex Wright (2007, 6) reminds us that we now write 'more than five exabytes worth of recorded information per year . . . more than 50, 000 times the number of words stored in the Library of Congress, or more than the total number of words ever spoken by human beings'. This speed of growth today is impressive. Wright (2007, 229) writes, 'Twenty years after Johannes Gutenberg invented his printing press, a bare handful of people in Germany and France had ever seen a printed book. Less than 20 years after its invention, the World Wide Web has touched billions.' Surely, the world that archivists worked in during the past few generations is disappearing (or, maybe is gone already).

The challenges to archival appraisal in the digital era seem well defined. We may see a decline in personal visits and the rise of a new kind of cyber-researcher, the loss of reflection or contemplation in archival research rooms, social computing approaches requiring the archivist to be more engaged with their real and potential researchers than ever before, the fashioning of new varieties of information literacy, different interactions with texts affecting why and how people use archival sources, new pressures generated from commercial enterprises in the digitization of the world's documentary sources, access trumping preservation in the question of digitization, demands for archivists to be more coherent and publicly open about how they conduct appraisal, archivists clarifying their claims as experts, archival discussions about their knowledge and practice on the web, the coming of age of digital natives with very different expectations of archives (and museums and libraries), and the emerging of new disciplines (maybe digital curators?). These are all tantalizing issues to consider. And all of them suggest moving appraisal to the forefront of archival activities, because appraisal is a distinctive archival task.

Appraisal as the core archival activity

Appraisal is easily defined as the 'process of evaluating actual or potential acquisitions to determine if they have sufficient long-term research value to warrant the expense of preservation by an archival repository' (Ham, 1992, 2). Archivists have long understood that managing both their programmes and their share of the documentary universe implies setting appraisal and acquisition objectives, measuring success in meeting those objectives, and revising objectives as progress is attained (Bearman, 1995). Such basic definitions are widely accepted, but in the digital era it also generates questions. Given the scale of the documentary universe, and its rapid expansion, can archivists really apply appraisal processes to it? Given the nature of the digital documentation, can archives acquire such sources as they have other materials in the past?

While appraisal may be essential, the contentious issue of the re-appraisal of documentary sources suggests that archivists have not resolved everything (Haas, 1984; Powell, 1991–2; Greene, 1994; Daniels-Howell, 1998). Archivists have lamented that they lack a coherent approach to appraisal, or that it is more art than science (Sink, 1990; Rapport, 1981). Starting about a quarter of a century ago or more, archivists began to reveal how complicated appraisal is (Cook, 1992) and how messy the notion of the archive can be (Ketelaar, 2002; Foote, 1990; Bradley, 1999; Schwartz and Cook, 2002). Recent writings about archival appraisal have been influenced by postmodernism, playing with the elusive nature of truth and evidence (Cook, 2001; MacNeil, 2001; Nesmith, 2002). Postmodernism perhaps possesses its greatest significance for understanding the symbolic role of archives in society, and, by extension, better understanding of the appraisal function because this perspective shows appraisal to be an endlessly complex activity.

Such challenges have led a number of archivists to articulate better the role and process of appraisal (such as Schaeffer, 1992; Brown, 1991–2). The complexity of archival appraisal suggests the need for a great deal more analysis – by archivists, by those who use archival materials, and by those studying the creation of documentary and information systems and the evolution of cultural organizations. Is there a single model or scheme guiding archival appraisal? How does preservation fit into appraisal? Does the continuing shift to digital records and information systems change the nature of the appraisal application? Is appraisal as much about saving artefacts as anything else? Is there an inherent societal impulse to do the opposite of the archival appraisal approach, that is, destroy the recorded past? How do non-traditional sources fit into the appraisal scheme? How does archival appraisal relate to the records management approaches? Are archivists doing well in documenting themselves and the appraisal function? Is re-appraisal a legitimate archival activity? Can appraisal only be carried out in a co-operative fashion? And has the emergence of new personalized information technologies made obsolete the appraisal responsibility? Given the centrality of appraisal to all things archival, it is surprising that we still possess so many questions and issues, although this is both an attribute of the complexity of archival appraisal as a task and the ever-changing features of recordkeeping systems in our organizations and society. It is what makes archival work so intellectually engaging (whether one wants to be so engaged or not).

To understand how the emerging digital era has affected the archival community and its mission, it is critical to consider the impact on appraisal. When the modern archival profession took root, the focus seemed to be on acquiring everything and anything, something that is still prevalent among some practitioners (where the emphasis has been more on keeping than selecting). Thirty years ago, David Gracy (1975, 22) likened it to a 'vacuum cleaner' and termed it 'unrealistic'. Given some of the renewed claims that everything can be saved, maybe this is not the case for twenty-first century materials. In the not so distant past, archivists worried about how they competed with each other (Ericson, 2000), but today that competition might not be among archives but between archives and non-archival websites featuring documentary sources. Archivists, just like every other human being, like to accumulate possessions, and not always in a fashion that can be described rationally. Eventually, methodologies, such as the archival documentation strategy, were developed to encourage co-operation, recognizing the documentary universe is complex and becoming more complex (Samuels, 1986).

Archivists have been looking for better strategies in the appraisal and acquisition function for generations, understanding that the technologies of recordkeeping are not static, but evolving. Traditional ideas about the evidential and informational values of records may have contributed to the need for clearer methodology and more precise criteria; the older models of values are not only subjective, but they suggest the possibility that almost everything ought to be preserved (because nearly any documentary scrap has potential value). What examining appraisal approaches usually tells us is that this is a responsibility that is always messier than one might imagine, if, for no other reason, because, in appraising records reflect all the problems and challenges of complex organizations and individual lives, even before considering the greater challenges of the digital era.

If grand appraisal schemes are worth pursuing, how should they be evaluated and, when necessary, re-evaluated? Often, archivists have tried to track trends in historical research, so that, when historians shift themes then archivists try to provide relevant documentation. In the digital era archivists could switch to gathering data in much greater detail than ever before about what researchers are doing (assuming, of course, that archivists have built the kinds of websites that allow such analysis). Many archives and archivists remain mostly reactive rather than proactive, seeing proposals for planned and analytical approaches to appraisal as too much for busy archivists (Abraham, 1995). Even with the massive quantity of records, in all media forms, the fear that some will be lost can lead to strange and poor appraisal decisions, often the result of lacking resources and strategies.

Archivists face many issues when they examine the documentary universe, due to its complexity and scale. Some of these challenges have been met, such as the development of sampling techniques (although it is difficult to gain a sense of just how well or often they are employed) (Kolish, 1994). Not everyone has been happy about the experimentation with new appraisal methodologies and models. However, whatever problems may result from archivists' efforts to be more pro-active in appraisal, to do otherwise creates a situation where the archivist is little more than a passive custodian (Booms, 1987). Archivists must have schemes when they approach the documentary universe, so it should be no surprise that some archivists also adopt the concept of saving everything, no matter how impractical this might be in reality.

Digital preservation and appraisal

Preservation is an old archival aim, and it has been seen as part of appraisal criteria. Earlier ideas associated copying, as in documentary editing, and accessioning, as in the movement of records to archival facilities, with preservation. When preservation is connected with a process of simply moving records into a facility, regardless of the condition of the facility, it is difficult to see a connection between preservation and appraisal. However, when preservation is focused on activities such as conservation treatment or digitization for enhanced access and reduction of wear on original sources, it is clearer that preservation is a selection function akin to appraisal.

Even though preservation and conservation approaches are a form of reappraisal, by means of reselecting records for additional and more costly treatment or protection after their initial appraisal, it is difficult to discover much explicit writing about preservation as a criterion in appraisal theory or practice. Preservation, in archival appraisal, has always been an assumption, and writings about preservation have made few references to archival appraisal (Conway, 1990, 1992; Boles and Young, 1985). How does any of this relate to the digital documentary universe and the archival mission?

Whether digitization will ever be universally accepted as a preservation mechanism or not, the point is that it is a necessary function. Most people and institutions have avoided the debate about this by focusing on matters such as using digitization to lessen the use of fragile originals. Many discussions occur as if everything can and will be digitized, but the greater likelihood is that there will always need to be some strategic criteria that can be easily understood, readily defended, and comfortably justified. Librarians and archivists alike have tried to develop reliable and verifiable selection criteria for preservation in general and digitization more specifically (Astle and Muir, 2002; Childs, 1990; Gertz, 2000; Hazen,

Horrell, and Merrill-Oldham, 1998; de Stefano, 2000; Vogt-O'Connor, 2000). Embracing digitization, even while realizing its limitations, can be understood as just another stage in the effort both to preserve our documentary heritage and enhance meaningful access to it (Smith, 1999). Selection needs to be applied in experimental and testable ways in digitization projects, although it has been shoved aside by the attractive access enhancement aspects of placing digital materials on the web.

There has been no resolution about digitization as preservation or access tool, but there have been a lot of interesting debates and cogent arguments. Although access seems to have been, thus far, the clear winner with digitization, librarians and archivists alike have sounded alarms about the implications of how they select items and collections for digitizing, usually with a focus on 'commonly used materials' (Anderson, 1999, 76). Some have argued for risk management, considering the potential harm to, or loss of, archival and other valuable resources if some remedial action, such as digitization, is not taken. As digitization is increasingly applied, there is both a greater need to resolve the debates about what its purpose is, as well as to continue to test out technical solutions for its utility as a preservation mechanism.

While there has been tremendous discussion about appraisal, it was mostly a side issue to the concerns about whether archivists could preserve the digital documentary heritage. Archivists have been wringing their hands about how to identify, preserve and administer electronic records for decades, contending both with the constantly changing technology and the explosion of records. Terry Cook (1991a, Section 4.21) recognizes the challenge of contending with the 'billions of bytes' of scientific data with permanent value, while understanding that 'no archives is equipped to acquire them directly'. Archivists and records managers alike have speculated about how digital systems change the work, knowledge, and identity of records professionals (Stephens, 1998, 5). Archivists need to co-operate with information disciplines, from librarians to knowledge workers, while wrestling with new concepts, such as the records continuum, since records don't easily divide along specific phases of a life cycle because of their technological dependency (Cook, 1991a, Section 4.7; Upward and McKemmish, 1994).

At the heart of the challenge of the electronic documentary universe is the acknowledgement, grudgingly accorded, that the transformation from paper to digital has forced a rethinking of basic approaches and assumptions about the record or professional mission. In developing new approaches for selecting and managing the archival documentary universe, however, others have worried that the new approaches have excluded certain kinds of recordkeeping, such as personal archives (Cunningham, 1996). The search for practical archival approaches, with the understanding that many new recording technologies challenge the premises of these approaches, has stimulated a rethinking of the nature of records and the evidence and information in these records. Sue McKemmish (1996, 36) suggests that we need a 'better understanding' of how documents operate, while Verne Harris (2001, 12) worries that her concept of 'recordkeeping functionality' excludes what personal papers exist for and the purposes that they serve. What complicates all this is that individuals are increasingly creating personal archives directly in digital form.

The challenge posed by new information technologies may be defined, but the appraisal of digital records continues to be an area needing more experimentation, research and success. As nearly every basic recording system we know about makes the transition into digital forms, archivists need to sort out the various appraisal implications. The idea that the digital systems will enable everything to be saved and ultimately retrieved has never been confirmed – and it is unlikely that it will be. As records professionals mull over the appraisal of correspondence, memoranda, financial records, maps, architectural drawings, sound, and moving images, they must also contemplate the implications of appraising these record forms in their newer and often still emerging digital versions. The pundits proclaiming the wonders of the digital era, when considering matters such as archival appraisal, just sweep it aside, declaring that there is no need for selection any longer. This seems foolhardy, as can be seen by examining a variety of other issues that archivists and their repositories and community face in our modern culture. Despite the challenges of appraising the digital documentary universe, there is an immense array of documentary forms with physical attributes to be accounted for. We have long understood, for example, the limitations of copying (Tanselle, 1998, 23).

All through the 1980s archivists addressed these (and other) questions, offering guidelines on percentages of records saved, the attributes for determining intrinsic value, and procedures for selecting records to be preserved. Most of these questions re-emerged in the digital age, virtually unchanged, except for greater attention by non-archivists and non-librarians. Thomas Tanselle (1998), Sven Birkerts (1994), Nicholson Baker (2001), and others questioned the loss of evidence from the destruction of the physical attributes of books and manuscripts via reformatting approaches (see also my response, Cox, 2002). Scholars, from a variety of disciplines, also argued for the need to use documentary materials in their original form, even while hoping that new digital technologies enhance access to such materials (Franklin, 1993). Continuing debate led to uncertainty about decision-making schematics allowing the disposal of original materials that have been reformatted, and by the mid-1990s one microfilming manual indicated that it could make no such recommendations because it was 'clear that the issue is unsettled across the archival profession' (Elkington, 1994, 3–4). These critics rejected outright the concept of appraisal because they resisted anyone assigning value. Terry Cook, nearly two decades ago, reflected:

> Even if archivists could keep everything, they should not do so. The role of archivists is to preserve the clearest image possible of contemporary society and of its records creators by choosing the best records, not to add indiscriminately to the chaos of the information explosion by keeping too much or by keeping that which distorts or duplicates the image of the past.
>
> (Cook, 1991b, 33)

Archivists, along with nearly every cultural resources management and information science discipline, have a lot of work to do about when and when not to preserve the original textual document in its physical form. The idea of saving everything digitally complicates, rather than resolves, this matter.

Archivists face a variety of new challenges to their mission. While the substance of archives may change, from artefacts to virtual, the archival mission and its importance to society will remain, functioning as community memory or cultural heritage (Owens, 2003, 31). Obviously, the destruction of archives could be a way of striking at the memory and identity of a people, community and nation, and there is an immense difference between malicious destruction and the careful, planned appraisal (allowing destruction) carried out by archivists. There is evidence that archivists don't always do appraisal as well as they should, and that many records disappear through neglect or lack of attention. We have accidental incidents of destruction (such as fire or flood), but often such accidents occur because documentary materials have not been identified, acquired, and accorded the necessary precautions. From country to country, place to place, we see neglect lead to unfortunate destruction, even when everyone recognizes the importance of archival records (see, for example, Locke, 1993). In the digital world, the chance of such destruction increases exponentially, as individuals and institutions can remove documents as quickly as they place them on the web.

Getting a grip on the digital documentary heritage is critical, especially since many non-textual documentary sources, such as moving images and sound, also generally ignored in the development of appraisal criteria and selection methodologies, are becoming digital. From the very beginning of the origins of modern archival theory and practice, moving images were neglected. This lacuna is particularly seen when considering the recent work of one pioneering moving image archivist, Sam Kula, who, when he addresses the topic of appraisal, provides a partial view of appraisal approaches. The breakdown in extending appraisal approaches to such non-traditional sources can be seen when we consider ephemeral moving images such as home movies, documentaries, educational and corporate training films – the kinds of moving images collecting dust in repositories such as historical societies, archives and museums, when and if they make it to these institutions. Everyone becomes an archivist.

Looking ahead

We need to be sceptical about the hype surrounding digital information technologies and their applications. Historians, taking the long view, remind us that every era harnessed information via innovations. Ian F. McNeely and Lisa Wolverton (2008, 271) remind us that 'Promoters of the vaunted "information age" often forget that knowledge has always been about connecting people, not collecting information.' David Edgerton (2007, 68) argues that a 'futurology of the past' affects how we understand these technologies. We focus on 'invention and innovation' and lose sight of how older technologies persist, take on new roles, and continue to be important in our society. We confuse descriptions of technology, usually written with an eye on what's ahead, with the realities of the impact, past and continuing, of the technologies themselves. David Nye (2006) neatly lays out how our decisions to adopt or adapt certain technologies bring with them all kinds of implications for us, from the hearth to the workplace. This is a process that suggests constantly re-evaluating archival practice, tinkering with the accepted archival best practices, and negotiating with the public and those who fund and employ archivists. Archivists have a long way to go in seeing such efforts applied to a function such as archival appraisal.

Archivists need to become more proficient technically, but they also have to enhance other knowledge and skill areas. Legal issues, especially copyright, are the probable starting point now, daunting because of the often-mixed nature and origins of the documents, donor restrictions, sensitivity to family and personal privacy, and often unreliable information about ownership. Digitizing only documents with clarity of institutional ownership and rights can result in ignoring vast amounts of important archival evidence, while digitizing documents of questionable ownership can result in legal quagmires for archival programmes, even as archivists are able to compile greater amounts of information about their users, follow new opportunities for teaching by providing archival documents online, and open up more powerfully archival collections for use by both scholars and the public.

The nature of archival work, the defining of archival positions, and some ancient archival principles and practices might be transformed. Long ago, Hugh Taylor (2003, 186) advocated shucking off old textual approaches, arguing that archivists 'must resist reading the "new" media in a literal, textual manner and begin to learn unfamiliar grammar, syntax, and semiotics, and then teach our users to do the same'. Others have expressed similar sentiments since then (Koltun, 1999). The best archivists might do in appraisal is document what they do, something they have long espoused the benefits of in pioneering appraisal manuals (Haas, Samuels and Simmons, 1985). More than ever before, archivists are being asked to justify the decisions they have made to their employers, constituents and the public. Checklists, descriptions of procedures and general mission statements will no longer suffice. As Terry Cook (1991b, 39–41) describes 'exemplary selection', archivists must be able to explain – in order to be accountable – just what they are doing in their appraisal work.

Archivists need to admit their fallibilities, mistakes and problems in conducting appraisal, as well as acknowledging that the public really does not understand how archives are formed (nor, for that matter, do many of the researchers using archives). One of the challenges may be due to the lack of standardized appraisal approaches and efforts to analyze appraisal results and implications, as Jennifer Marshall (2002) determined in her study on the collection policies of academic archives. Marshall also has made a major contribution to our understanding of appraisal documentation for accountability purposes in her comparative analysis of the national archives of Australia, Canada and the United States, discovering that while all three institutions produce a range of documentation regarding this important archival function, there is still much to be done regarding making the appraisal process transparent (Marshall, 2006).

Appraisal documentation is necessary since the nature of the new digital documentary universe requires re-thinking appraisal as a continuous rather than one-time process (as it has often been thought of). Archivists have long known that many of the larger collections or *fonds* they bring into their repositories create challenges with their bulk versus their quality of evidence, as Leonard Rapport (1981) reminds us. While there has been a modest amount of research done into how archivists use re-appraisal, the evidence seems to be that it is viewed by most as conceptually acceptable but impractical in actual application (too many other pressing tasks and insufficient time).

Archival appraisal may be the core function, but it is under-developed and needs to be re-focused on the fluid digital documentary universe. We are living in a land that may seem foreign to many of us. Most of us grew up in an analogue and textual world, and our interests in archives were shaped by the prospects of working with old documents, printed ephemera, and other old stuff. It may surprise some to know that the majority of individuals attracted to graduate archival education programmes still come with romantic notions of what archivists do and what they work with. While some get energized with deep challenges posed by the digital documentary universe, others complain and sometimes drop out. If one is looking for fascinating challenges, these are good times indeed.

We have more predictions about the transformation of society by the digital technologies than careful study and reflection about the actual impacts. Ones with particular implications for archivists and appraisal in the digital era include the convergence of disciplines, the rise of new professions and the end of old ones, and the empowerment of ordinary citizens to become their own experts.

Convergence runs the risk of eliminating the distinctive sense of the archivist and the possibility of weakening the archival mission by embracing trendier notions (digital curators rather than archivists, cyberspecialists rather than librarians, and interdisciplinarity at the expense of a focused mission). However, the risk might be worth it. Within universities new research centres are regularly created, intended to bring together faculty and graduate students from a variety of departments and even individuals from outside of the university (such as in corporations), opening up the possibility of supporting the creation and sustenance of a new kind of digital archivist who could apply old approaches, such as appraisal, to the digital universe. I sometimes tell my students that there may not be a profession known as archives in the future, meaning that what we are called may one day change and the primary nature of our work (although all this may make communicating our mission much easier as the public engages more deeply in digital personal archives and online work). Armed with a modestly priced laptop the average person can create virtual archives, publish books, and access more information, consolidating all of the roles from information consumer to information creator, from reader to publisher, from archival researcher to archival custodian.

Some of what we are seeing happen is due to what has been labelled Web 2.0, the use of the web to allow and promote social networking through approaches such as wikis, blogs, and so forth. Add to this Web 3.0 with a stronger stress on eliminating gatekeepers, and we see even different roles for archivists and their allies in the future. Obviously, archivists ought to be involved in such activities, enhancing how they work with the users of archival sources in an online environment. Whether researchers cease to come to physical spaces known as archives (or libraries or museums) may not be the issue; the issue is that the way in which researchers interact with archival sources will be more varied and complex than anything we have experienced before. The continued evolution, and growing power, of the web will have dramatic impacts on how archivists and librarians function and what their future will be. It will certainly transform how archivists rethink appraisal.

Conclusion

One of the primary issues archivists need to deal with in the digital era is the notion that everything can be saved, directly challenging the idea of archival appraisal. The belief in this is pervasive, from individuals developing software, such as MyLifeBits, to record everything, to leaders (and many followers) in the library, information and computer sciences fields who regularly state such a belief. The idea that everything can be saved may be the mantra of the digital true believer. Not only does this idea and its supporters ignore the other technical issues of retrieval, the ability to retrieve and retain important contextual meaning, and the costs of maintenance, the reason for or logic behind saving everything is usually avoided.

The archival community can make a contribution here, if it wills itself to look beyond the false promises of saving everything. Challenged about this at a conference and confronted with the idea that technicians tell us that this can be done, my response was that archivists are *not* technicians, but play other roles (such as selectors). While archival appraisal practice has been weaker than it should be, the theoretical and methodological literature is quite interesting and useful for such tasks in the digital universe. Over the course of more than a half-century, archivists have articulated appraisal schemes using values of records, more precise definitions of records, macro approaches considering the reasons for recordkeeping, functional analysis, sampling models, intrinsic values of records (or, records as artefacts or the symbolic value of documents), documentation strategies, and reappraisal methodologies. Archivists (at least those engaged in this function) have accumulated a high level of expertise about the means of identifying the evidence and information found in documents of all sorts, even if their application in the digital realm has been limited and their efforts to work with other fields (such as preservation administrators) have been just as limited. What archivists need now to do is to develop new versions of the appraisal approaches to be applied effectively to the digital documentary universe and, just as importantly, evaluate some of the approaches for dealing with this universe, such as the Internet Archive (really a sampling method).

Appraisal is the core, critical function of archival work. For more than a hundred years, individuals in the modern archival community have discussed the challenges posed by the immense scope of the documentary universe (see, for example, Cox, 2004). Yet archivists agree that the scope of the present documentary universe is far more complex and larger than anything we have considered before (or ever could have imagined). And, when we consider such shifting identities, different missions or greatly re-engineered methodologies, it is when we wonder just how much chaos we can really handle or how much confusion we might bring upon ourselves.

Technology is not the major challenge facing archivists in their work. The main challenge instead can be seen as being an expansion of the archival mission from just a cultural role to one encompassing ethics and accountability matters, issues that have been exaggerated in significance partly because of the increasing powerful applications of the digital information technologies. Records and recordkeeping systems, especially as they move deeper into the digital realm, pose greater problems with intellectual property, preservation and privacy. The cultural mandate remains (and always will be the main attraction for many), but it is also the case that corporate, government and academic archives will generate more and more instances where archivists are called upon both to help records' creators and users guarantee access to documents and to assist the organizations in defending themselves (sometimes in unethical or illegal ways, resulting in individual archivists needing to consider their own ethical and moral foundations) (Cox and Wallace, 2002; Cox, 2006).

What we need to focus on is the preparation of a new generation of archivists, professionals who have the knowledge of the history of recordkeeping systems, traditional archival principles (traditional in the sense that they are based on older recordkeeping systems and forms), and new and emerging digital information systems (including a solid working understanding of new digital document forms). Archivists will be more documentary shapers than documentary custodians, more digital forensic experts than documentary describers, and more archival activists than passive reference gatekeepers. How do we prepare this new generation of archivists? Our graduate archival education programmes are, at best, a mixed bag. Are they able to offer a comprehensive enough curriculum for digital era archivists? Graduate archives programmes have nearly all shifted to Library and Information Studies schools and, while there, some of these schools have made a shift to Information Schools (I-Schools). It is in these programmes, however, that we have the best chance to inspire new perspectives, build new leadership, and develop new principles for what looms ahead in both our profession and our broader culture. These opportunities have been enhanced in the rebirth of LIS schools as I-Schools, now addressing concerns such as the curation and preservation of primary and secondary sources that are born-digital, the life cycle/continuum concept of records, the preservation imperative, cultural and humanistic perspectives, public and institutional memory, the evolving notion of records in the digital era, and the implications of new portable digital technologies on issues such as the creation, maintenance and use of records and information sources deemed to possess long-term archival value.

Archivists have a lot of opportunities and challenges ahead of them. Patricia Zimmerman's contribution to a recent volume of essays on home movies describes how 'home movies constitute an imaginary archives that is never completed, always fragmentary, vast, infinite' (Ishizuka and Zimmerman, 2008, 18). She also adds that:

> In the popular imagination, archives often are framed as the depositories of old, dead cultural artifacts. But archives are never inert, as they are always in the process of addition of new arenas and unknown objects. The archive, then, is not simply a depository, which implies stasis, but is, rather, a retrieval machine defined by its revision, expansion, addition, and change.
>
> (Ishizuka and Zimmerman, 2008, 20)

Such concerns upset some, but these reflect the new reality we are dealing with, and, more importantly, suggest some wonderful new opportunities. As we reflect on functions such as appraisal, we need to be prepared to evolve in our approaches, perhaps at a rate much faster than archivists have been accustomed to doing.

References

Abraham, T. (1995) *Documentation Strategies: a decade (or more) later*, Paper presented at the Society of American Archivists, Washington D.C., www.uidaho.edu/special-collections/papers/docstr10.htm.

Anderson, B. (1999) What's Worth Digitizing?, *Behavioral & Social Sciences Librarian*, **18** (1), 75–7.

Astle, P. J. and Muir, A. (2002) Digitization and Preservation in Public Libraries and Archives, *Journal of Librarianship and Information Science*, **34** (2), 67–79.

Baker, N. (2001) *Double Fold: libraries and the assault on paper*, Random House.

Barksdale, J. and Berman, F. (2007) Saving Our Digital Heritage, *Washington Post*, 16 May, A15.

Bearman, D. (1995) Archival Strategies, *American Archivist*, **58** (Fall), 381–413.

Birkerts, S. (1994) *Gutenberg Elegies: the fate of reading in the electronic age*, Faber and Faber.

Boles, F. and Marks Young, J. (1985) Exploring the Black Box: the appraisal of university administrative records, *American Archivist*, **48** (Spring), 121–40.

Booms, H. (1987) Society and the Formation of a Documentary Heritage: issues in the appraisal of archival sources, *Archivaria*, **24**, 69–107.

Borgman, C.L. (2007) *Scholarship in the Digital Age: information, infrastructure, and the internet*, MIT Press.

Bradley, H. (1999) The Seductions of the Archive: voices lost and found, *History of the Human Sciences*, **12** (2), 107–22.

Brown, R. (1991–2) Records Acquisition Strategy and its Theoretical Foundation: the case for concept of archival hermeneutics, *Archivaria*, **33** (Winter), 34–56.

Carlson, S. (2007) On The Record, All the Time: researchers digitally capture the daily flow of life. Should they?, *Chronicle of Higher Education*, **53**, A30.

Carr, N. (2008) Is Google Making Us Stupid?, *Atlantic*, **302** (July/August), 56–8, 60, 62–3.

Childs, M. S. (1990) Selection for Microfilming, *American Archivist*, **53** (Spring), 250–55.

Clifford, T. (2007) Is Wikipedia Part of a New 'Global Brain'?, *Spiked*, www.spiked-online.com/index.php?/site/article/2852.

Conway, P. (1990) Archival Preservation Practice in a Nationwide Context, *American Archivist*, **53** (Spring), 204–22.

Conway, P. (1992) Preserving History's Future: developing a nationwide strategy for archival preservation. In Higginbotham, B.B. and Jackson, M.E. (eds), *Advances in Preservation and Access*, vol. 1, Meckler.

Cook, T. (1991a) *The Archival Appraisal of Records Containing Personal Information: a RAMP study with guidelines*, UNESCO.

Cook, T. (1991b) Many are Called but Few are Chosen: appraisal guidelines for sampling and selecting case files, *Archivaria*, **32** (Summer), 25–50.

Cook, T. (1992) Mind Over Matter: towards a new theory of archival appraisal. In Craig, B.L. (ed.), *The Archival Imagination: essays in honour of Hugh A. Taylor*, Association of Canadian Archivists.

Cook, T. (2001) Fashionable Nonsense or Professional Rebirth: postmodernism and the practice of archives, *Archivaria,* **51** (Spring), 14–35.

Cox, R.J. (2002) *Vandals in the Stacks? A response to Nicholson Baker's Assault on Libraries,* Greenwood Press.

Cox, R.J. (2004) *No Innocent Deposits: forming archives by rethinking appraisal,* Scarecrow Press.

Cox, R.J. (2006) *Ethics, Accountability and Recordkeeping in a Dangerous World,* Facet Publishing.

Cox, R.J. and Wallace, D. (eds) (2002) *Archives and the Public Good: accountability and records in modern society,* Quorum Books.

Cunningham, A. (1996) Beyond the Pale? The 'flinty' relationship between archivists who collect the private records of individuals and the rest of the archival profession, *Archives and Manuscripts,* **24** (May), 20–7.

Daniels-Howell, T. (1998) Reappraisal of Congressional Records at the Minnesota Historical Society: a case study, *Archival Issues,* **23** (1), 35–40.

Darnton, R. (2008) The Library in Your Future, *New York Review of Books,* 12 June, 55, 72–3, 76, 78–80.

Deegan, M. and Tanner, S. (eds) (2006) *Digital Preservation,* Facet Publishing.

de Stefano, P. (2000) Selection for Digital Conversion. In Kenney, A.R. and Rieger, O.Y. (eds), *Moving Theory into Practice: digital imaging for libraries and archives,* Research Libraries Group.

Edgerton, D. (2007) *The Shock of the Old: technology and global history since 1900,* Oxford University Press.

Elkington, N.E. (ed.) (1994) *RLG Archives Microfilming Manual,* Research Libraries Group.

Ericson, T. (2000) At the Rim of Creative Dissatisfaction: archivists and acquisition development. In Jimerson, R.C. (ed.), *American Archival Studies: readings in theory and practice,* Society of American Archivists.

Foote, K.E. (1990) To Remember and Forget: archives, memory, and culture, *American Archivist,* **53** (Summer), 378–92.

Franklin, P. (1993) Scholars, Librarians and the Future of Primary Records, *College and Research Libraries,* 54 (September), 397–406.

Friedman, D.D. (2008) *Future Imperfect: technology and freedom in an uncertain world,* Cambridge University Press.

Gardner, H. (2006) *Five Minds for the Future,* Harvard Business School Press.

Gertz, J. (2000) Selection for Preservation in the Digital Age, *Library Resources and Technical Services* **44** (2), 97–104.

Gracy, D.B. (1975) Peanut Butter and Spilt Milk: a new look at collecting, *Georgia*

Archive, **3** (Winter), 20–9.

Greene, M.A. (1994) Appraisal of Congressional Records at the Minnesota Historical Society: a case study, *Archival Issues,* **19** (1), 31–43.

Guess, A. (2008a) Research Methods 'Beyond Google', *Inside Higher Education,* http://insidehighered.com/news/2008/06/17/institute.

Guess, A. (2008b) At Libraries, Taking the (Really) Long View, *Inside Higher Education,* http://insidehighered.com/news/2008/07/23/preservation.

Guess, A. (2008c) Post-Microsoft, Libraries Mull Digitization, *Inside Higher Education,* http://insidehighered.com/news/2008/05/30/microsoft.

Haas, J.K., Samuels, H.W. and Simmons, B.T. (1985) *Appraising the Records of Modern Science and Technology: a guide,* MIT Press.

Haas, R.L. (1984) Collection Reappraisal: the experience at the University of Cincinnati, *American Archivist,* **47** (1), 51–4.

Ham, F.G. (1992) *Selecting and Appraising Archives and Manuscripts,* Society of American Archivists.

Harris, V. (2001) On the Back of the Tiger: deconstructive possibilities in 'evidence of me', *Archives and Manuscripts,* **29** (May), 8–21.

Hazen, D., Horrell, J. and Merrill-Oldham, J. (1998) Selecting Research Collections for Digitization, *Microfilm and Imaging Review,* **27** (3), 82–93.

Hess, C. and Ostrom, E. (2007) *Understanding Knowledge as a Commons: from theory to practice,* MIT Press.

Howard, J. (2008) Scholars' View of Libraries as Portals Shows Marked Decline, *Chronicle of Higher Education,* http://chronicle.com/daily/2008/08/4351n.htm.

Ishizuka, K.L. and Zimmerman, P.R. (eds) (2008) *Mining the Home Movie: excavations in histories and memories,* University of California Press.

Jeanneney, J-N. (2007) *Google and the Myth of Universal Knowledge: a view from Europe,* (trans. Fagan, T. L.), University of Chicago Press.

Keen, A. (2007) *The Cult of the Amateur: how today's internet is killing our culture,* Doubleday/Currency.

Ketelaar, E. (2002) Archival Temples, Archival Prisons: modes of power and protection, *Archival Science,* **2** (3–4), 221–38.

Kolish, E. (1994) Sampling Methodology and its Application: an illustration of the tension between theory and practice, *Archivaria,* **38**, 61–73.

Koltun, L. (1999) The Promise and Threat of Digital Options in an Archival Age, *Archivaria,* **47** (Spring), 114–35.

Levy, D.M. (2006) More, Faster, Better: governance in an age of overload, busyness, and speed, *First Monday,* special issue number **7** (September), http://firstmonday.org/issues/special11_9/levy/index.html.

Locke, I.F. (1993) Archive Destruction and Dispersal in the UK – an elementary overview, *Journal of the Society of Archivists*, **14** (1), 7–13.

MacNeil, H. (2001) Trusting Records in a Postmodern World, *Archivaria*, **51** (Spring), 36–47.

Marshall, J.A. (2002) Toward Common Content: an analysis of online college and university collecting policies, *American Archivist*, **65** (2), 231–56.

Marshall, J.A. (2006) Accounting for Disposition: a comparative case study of appraisal at the National Archives and Records Administration in the United States, Library and Archives Canada, and the National Archives of Australia, unpublished PhD dissertation, University of Pittsburgh.

McKemmish, S. (1996) 'Evidence of Me...' *Archives and Manuscripts* **24** (May), 27–45.

McNeely, I.F. with Wolverton, L. (2008) *Reinventing Knowledge: from Alexandria to the internet*, W. W. Norton & Co.

National Science Foundation (2007) *Cyberinfrastructure Vision for 21st Century Discovery*, (March).

Nesmith, T. (2002) Seeing the Archives: postmodernism and the changing intellectual place of archives, *American Archivist*, **65** (Spring/Summer), 24–41.

Norman, D. (2007) *The Design of Future Things*, Basic Books.

Nye, D.E. (2006) *Technology Matters: questions to live with*, MIT Press.

Owens, B.M. (2003) The Safeguarding of Memory: the divine function of the librarian and archivist, *Library and Archival Security*, **18** (1), 9–41.

Palfrey, J. and Urs, G. (2008) *Born Digital: understanding the first generation of digital natives*, Basic Books.

Powell, S. (1991–2). Archival Reappraisal: the immigration case files, *Archivaria*, **33** (Winter), 104–16.

Rapport, L. (1981) No Grandfather Clause: reappraising accessioned records, *American Archivist*, **44** (Spring), 143–50.

Rein, L. (2007) The Changing 'Place' of the Library, *Inside Higher Education*, http://insidehighered.com/views/2007/01/05/rein.

Samuels, H.W. (1986) Who Controls the Past?, *American Archivist*, **49** (Spring), 109–24.

Schaeffer, R.C. (1992) Transcendent Concepts: power, appraisal, and the archivists as 'social outcast', *American Archivist*, **55** (Fall), 608–19.

Schwartz, J.M. and Cook, T. (2002) Archives, Records, and Power: the making of modern memory, *Archival Science*, **2** (1–2), 1–19.

Shillingsburg, P.L. (2006) *From Gutenberg to Google: electronic representations of literary texts*, Cambridge University Press.

Shirky, C. (2008) *Here Comes Everybody: the power of organizing without organizations*, Penguin Press.

Sink, R. (1990) Appraisal: the process of choice, *American Archivist*, **53** (3), 452–8.

Smith, A. (1999) *Why Digitize?*, Council on Library and Information Resources.

Snelson, P. (2007) Libraries at the Cutting Edge, *Inside Higher Education*, http://insidehighered.com/views/2007/03/29/snelson.

Stephens, D.O. (1998) Megatrends in Records Management, *Records Management Quarterly*, **32** (January), 3–9.

Upward, F. and McKemmish, S. (1994) Somewhere Beyond Custody, *Archives and Manuscripts*, **22** (1), 136–49.

Tanselle, T. (1998) *Literature and Artifacts*, The Bibliographic Society of the University of Virginia.

Taylor, H. A. (Cook. T. and Dobbs, G. (eds))(2003) *Imagining Archives: essays and reflections*, Scarecrow Press for the Society of American Archivists.

Tough, A. and Moss, M. (eds) (2006) *Record Keeping in a Hybrid Environment: managing the creation, use, preservation and disposal of unpublished information objects in context*, Chandos Publishing.

Vogt-O'Connor, D. (2000) Selection of Materials for Scanning. In Sitts, M.K. (ed.), *Handbook for Digital Projects: a management tool for preservation and access*, Northeast Document Conservation Center, www.nedcc.org/digital/dman.pdf.

Wilson, M.A. (2008) Professors Should Embrace Wikipedia, *Inside Higher Education*, http://insidehighered.com/views/2008/04/01/wilson.

Wright, A. (2007) *Glut: mastering information through the ages*, Joseph Henry Press.

Zorich, D.M., Waibel, G., and Erway, R. (2008) *Beyond the Silos of the LAMs: collaboration among libraries, archives and museums*, OCLC: Online Computer Library Center.

Index

access 25, 43, 52, 103–4, 106, 127, 134–6, 163, 177, 182, 192, 202

ACCIS *see* United Nations Advisory Committee for the Co-ordination of Information Systems

activist 39, 104, 105, 147, 153, 154, 156, 199, 231

Alabama Department of Archives and History 132–3

Amsterdam City Archives 138

anarchontic 111–12

Ancestry 136

appraisal 42, 65–88, 89, 93, 182, 199, 203–4, 218–38
   see especially 218–26, 228, 230

archival
   bond 78, 81, 175
      see also archives, and context
   education 5, 39, 90, 157–8, 228, 231–3
   threshold 16–17, 44, 175
   traces 44, 49, 105, 110, 158–9
   turn 37–62, 94–5, 109, 149

archive buildings 175–6

archive economy 91

Archive Fever 8–9
   see also Derrida, J.

archives
   and authenticity 71, 77–83, 159, 174–5, 176–7, 182, 193, 205

and context 11–12, 13, 14, 16, 25–6, 27, 29, 32–3, 43, 47, 53–4, 65–8, 69–70, 78–9, 93, 108–9 137, 158–9, 185, 193, 203, 204–5, 208

democratization of 104, 125–6, 134–42, 163–4

and flexibility 136–8

and history 38–40, 45–7, 49–52

and identity 25, 43, 154, 184, 205–6

impact of technology on 15–17, 123–44, 200–1, 213–37
   see especially 217–19

and interactivity 135–6, 200

nature of 147, 155–61, 164–5

and objectivity 6, 11, 24, 39, 138, 140, 158, 165–6, 199

as place 174–7, 194, 205, 214, 229

and politics 110–17

in popular culture 23–8

and positivism 4–5, 9–11, 180

and postmodernism 5–9, 11, 12, 13, 15, 50–1, 180, 219

and power 104–10

and subjectivity 51, 166

and transparency 138–41, 198

and truth 4, 6, 7–9, 12–13, 27, 38–9, 40–2, 50, 204

value of 15–16, 66–8, 79, 83, 158–61, 164–5, 183, 195, 197, 221, 225, 230

Archives 2.0 134–42

Archives Task Force 145, 154

archives without walls 16–17, 176–7, 180

see also archives as place, postcustodialism, museums without walls
archivist, role of 24, 30–3, 140, 162–4, 194–5, 197, 198–9, 202–3, 204–9, 214, 216, 217–18, 229–31
archivization 9, 12
archons 103
archontic 111–12
arkheion 103
ARPANET 123
Arthur Anderson 197
Ash, T. G. 26–7, 111
aura of the archive 15–17, 157
  see also Benjamin, W.
Australian Archives *see* National Archives of Australia

Bancroft Library 132
Barthes, R. 8, 28–9, 53–4
Basel II 197
Baudrillard, J. 8
Bearman, D. 13, 177–8
Benjamin, W. 10, 15, 41, 45, 48
Berners-Lee, T. 123
Black Cultural Archives 152, 157, 161
Bloch, M. 45–6
blogs *see* Web 2.0
Boltanski, C. 33–4, 42
Booms, H. 66
Bowker, G. 107–8
Braudel, F. 46
Brooks, P. 67–8

CAHG *see* Community Archives Heritage Group
Canadian archives *see* Library and Archives Canada
catablogs 138
catalogues *see* finding aids
cataloguing 11, 24, 135
  see also description
Clanchy 17
classification 42–3, 107–8, 201
Chomsky, N. 108
circumcision, as act of record making 116
Coca-Cola Archives 132
College of William and Mary 133

colophons 139–40
Comma 152
Commentaries on Sources 70
community, definition of 146–7
community archives 145–70, 183–5, 205
  and custodialism 161–2, 165, 184–5
  definitions of 146–9
  development of 151
  first professional acknowledgment of importance 145
  types of collections 147, 148, 149–51
Community Archives Development Group 154
Community Archives Heritage Group 146, 149, 163
continuum *see* records continuum
Cook, T. 13 180, 223
corporate memory 198
  see also memory
Craig, B. 69
Craven, L. 25–6
Cunningham, A. 180–1
custodialism 173–7, 203
  see also archives as place, community archives

Darnton, R. 46, 51, 53, 54
data protection 40, 202
  Data Protection Act 1998 198
Davis, N. Z. 46
Dean, T. 47
death of the author 8, 28
  see also Barthes, R.
Delmas, B. 89
Derrida, J. 8–9, 29–30, 37, 44, 55, 104, 108–10, 111–12
description 11, 26, 79, 89, 91, 93, 138–40, 163
  see also cataloguing
Dickinson College Archives 128
digital curation 182–3
digital divide 141
digital records 72, 73–88
  characteristics of 6, 17–18, 73–4, 77–80
  and postcustodialism 174, 176–83
  preservation of 179, 192–3, 203
digital repositories 183, 214
digitization 182–3, 216, 218, 222–3, 227
diplomatics 70
  definition and methodology of 71

and digital records 71–86
Duke University 135
Duranti, L. 16–17, 69, 94, 174–5
Dust 52
   see also Steedman, C.
Dutch *Manual* 90

Eastside Community Heritage 153, 162
electronic records *see* digital records
Enron 197
Erway, R. 217
e-Scholarship Research Centre 180
ethics 117–18, 231

Facebook *see* Web 2.0
family archives 115–16
family history 24–6, 33, 136, 206
Featherstone, M. 154
Feeney, K. 125
Feith, J. A. 90, 91–3, 95
Feminist Archive (South) 157
file, as site of record making 112–13
The File: a personal history 26–7
finding aids 29, 123–4, 125–6, 128, 137–9,
   140–1, 195
flexibility of Web 2.0 tools 137–8
Flickr *see* Web 2.0
Flinn, A. 184
folksonomies 201
Footnote 136
Foster, H. 33, 48–9,
Foucault, M. 16, 43–4, 49, 55, 108–9
freedom of information 40, 103
   Freedom of Information Act 2000 198, 208
Fruin, R. 90, 91–3, 95
functional analysis 66, 68–71

Garrison, L. 157
Gatineau Preservation Centre 176
Gay and Lesbian Archives of South Africa 150
genealogy *see* family history
Geographic Information Systems 76
George Padmore Institute and Archives 152,
   161
GIS *see* Geographic Information Systems
Ginzburg, C. 53
Google 125–6, 215–16

Green, M. 159
Greenblat, S. 38, 47
Groot, J. de 24–5

Hall, S. 156
Ham, F. G. 173–4
Hampshire Archives and Local Studies 163
Hedstrom, M. 177–9
Hertfordshire Archives and Local Studies 163
Historical Notes from OSHU blog 128
Historical Society of Pennsylvania 128
Holocaust 42–3, 44, 47–8
Horsman, P. 92
Huvila, I. 199–200, 205
Hyry, T. 139–40

information management 193
information management continuum 204–9
interactivity of Web 2.0 tools 135–6
interdisciplinarity 38–40, 55
Internet Archive 204, 230
InterPARES 72, 76, 84–5
intertextuality 29
iPhone 134
Ishizuka, K. L. 217
Island History Project, Isle of Dogs 157

Jeanneney, J. N. 215–16
Jencks, C. 7, 20
Jenkins, K. 49–50
Jenkinson, H. 3–7, 38, 77, 91, 92, 96, 158, 159,
   175, 179–80, 198
Jimerson, R. 139
Jura Consultants 149, 154
justice 112

Kaplan, E. 4–5
Kelly, G. 160
Ketelaar, E. 92
knowledge management 196
knowledge managers 194–5, 201, 206–7
Kristeva, J. 29

Landis, W. 123–4, 142
Landow, G. P 32
Langlois, C. V. 38, 91
Latour, B. 105–108

Lesbian Herstory Archive 150
librarians 194–5, 202–3, 206–7, 215
Library and Archives Canada 9, 41, 215
Library of Congress 127, 130–1
life cycle, 13–14
Light, M. 139–40
LinkedIn *see* Web 2.0
Living Links Project, Hampshire Archives and
    Local Studies 163
London Metropolitan Archives 163
Los Alamos Historical Society 130, 135
Lyotard, J. F. 8

MacLean, I. 179
Making Memories Project, Hertfordshire
    Archives and Local Studies 163
Malraux, A. 15, 17
Manual for the Arrangement and Description of
    Archives 90, 91–3
Marshall, J. 228
Massachusetts Historical Society 180
McKemmish, S. 179
MediaWiki 133
memory 26–7, 109–10, 191, 194, 197, 198, 199,
    204
metadata 80–2, 183
metanarratives 8, 111
microblogs 129
    see also Twitter
microhistory 46, 49, 51
MLA *see* Museums Libraries and Archives
    Council
Mosaic 123
Muller, S. 90, 91–3, 95
museum without walls 15–17
    see also archives without walls, Malraux
Museums Libraries and Archives Council 145,
    149
MySpace *see* Web 2.0

NARAtions 135
National Archives, The (UK) 127, 130, 131–2,
    133, 135
    Digital Continuity Project 183
    Your Archives 133, 135, 192

National Archives and Records Administration
    (NARA) *see* US National Archives and
    Records Administration
National Archives of Australia 138, 178–9,
    182, 184
National Archives of Canada *see* Library and
    Archives Canada
National Archives of the Netherlands 129
National Digital Information Infrastructure
    and Preservation Program 218
National Library of Scotland 132
Nesmith, T. 95
new historicism 46–9
Ning *see* Web 2.0
Nova Scotia Archives 129, 135

Office of Government Commerce, The 207–8
Olalquiaga, C. 31–2
oppression 41, 106–7, 111
oral history 17–19, 39, 114–15, 149, 156,
    159–60
Oregon Health and Science University 128–9
O'Reilly Media 126
original order 4, 13, 43, 92, 93, 185
Orlow, U. 47–8

PBWorks 133
Piasecki, S. 128–9
podcasting *see* Web 2.0
postcustodialism 16, 193–4, 203, 205
Postmodern Condition, The 8
preservation 222–3
    see also digital records, preservation of
provenance 4, 12, 13, 43, 65, 67–8, 92, 93, 94,
    159, 185
psychotherapy, as site of record making
    116–17
punctum 53–4
Purdue University Archives 131

Ranke, L. von 38
reader response theory 28–9
reception theory 28–9
recordkeeping 193, 206, 208
    ancient ideas of 103, 104–5
    and organizational goals 194–9
    systems 85–6, 231

records continuum 13–14, 17, 44, 197, 206–7, 208–9
  see also information management continuum
records management 44–5, 197
records managers 194–5, 196–7, 198, 201, 206–7
reflexive turn 51
researchers *see* users
respect des fonds 13, 185
Ridner, J. 95–6
rukus! 162

Sarbanes-Oxley Act 197
scan on demand 138
Schellenberg, T. R. 38–9, 68, 90, 92–3, 96
Schwartz, J. M. 13
Scott, P. 179
Scott's Last Expedition 128
Seignobos, C. 38
Shovlin, J. 41–2
Sigmond, P. 70
sites of record making 112–17
social networking sites 132–4
  see also Web 2.0
Society of American Archivists 90, 93
South Africa History Archives 150
Star, S. 107–8
State Archives of Florida 130
State Records Office for New South Wales 132
Steedman, C. 30, 45
Stoler, A. 109
structural analysis 65–8, 70–1
studium 53
Swadhinata Trust 155

tagging 201
textuality 28–30, 42, 215
Thomassen, T. 92
Tibbo, H. 124–5
transparency 138–41
truth commissions 113–14
Twitter *see* Web 2.0

UMarmot blog 128, 138
United Nations Advisory Committee for the Co-ordination of Information Systems 70–2

University of Manitoba Archives 132
University of Massachusetts, Amherst 128, 133
University of Melbourne Australian Science Archives Project *see* e-Scholarship Research Centre
University of Pittsburgh Archival Service Centre 133
Upward, F. 179–80
  see also records continuum
US National Archives and Records Administration 135
users 24–5, 30–4, 124–6, 163–4,
  and postcustodialism 177, 182, 214, 218–19, 229
  and Web 2.0 25–6, 126–9, 140–2, 192–3, 201–3, 217, 229

VEOS *see* Victorian Electronic Records Strategy
Victorian Electronic Records Strategy 176

Waibel, G. 217
Wallace, D. 123–4
Waltham Forest Oral History Project 156
Web 2.0 123–43, 192–3, 195, 200–2, 205, 216
  blogs 127–9, 133, 135, 136, 140
  Facebook 132–3, 135, 137
  flexibility 137–8
  Flickr 130–1, 132, 133, 134, 135, 137, 152
  impact on archives 134–42
  interactivity 135–6
  LinkedIn 133
  MySpace 132, 133
  Ning 132
  podcasting 129–30, 134
  preservation of 141
  Second Life 133
  social networking 132–3
  tools 126–34
  transparency 138–41
  Twitter 128, 132, 133, 135, 136, 137
  users, impact on 141–2
  Wikipedia 137, 216
  wikis 132–3
  YouTube 131–2, 134, 137
Weinberger, D. 138–9
WetPaint 133

Who Do You Think You Are? 25, 26
wikis *see* Web 2.0
Wikipedia *see* Web 2.0
Wilson, I. 215–16
Working Class Movement Library 152
world wide web 123–43
Wright, A. 218

Wright, P. 54

Your Archives 133, 135, 192
YouTube *see* Web 2.0

Zimmermann, P. 232
Zorich, D. M. 217

Community archives
The shaping of memory
edited by Jeannette A. Bastian and Ben Alexander

How do archives and other cultural institutions such as museums determine the boundaries of a particular community, and of their own institutional reach, in constructing effective strategies and methodologies for selecting and maintaining appropriate material evidence? This book offers guidance for archivists, record managers and museums professionals faced with such issues in their daily work.

This edited collection explores the relationships between communities and the records they create at both practical and scholarly levels. It focuses on the ways in which records reflect community identity and collective memory, and the implications of capturing, appraising and documenting these core societal elements – with particular focus on the ways in which recent advances in technology can overcome traditional obstacles, as well as how technologies themselves offer possibilities of creating new virtual communities.

It is divided into five themes:

- a community archives model
- communities and non-traditional record keeping
- records loss, destruction and recovery
- online communities: how technology brings communities and their records together
- building a community archive.

This book will appeal to practitioners, researchers, and academics in the archives and records community as well as to historians and other scholars concerned with community building and social issues.

Jeannette A. Bastian is Associate Professor and Director of the Archives Program Graduate School of Library and Information Science, Simmons College, Boston.
Ben Alexander is Assistant Professor, Queens College Graduate School of Library and Information Studies, The City University of New York.

2009; 320pp; hardback; 978-1-85604-639-8; £49.95

Principles and Practice in Records Management and Archives
Series editor: Geoffrey Yeo

Archives
Principles and practices
Laura A. Millar

Whether an institution has a collections orientation or whether it is primarily responsible for managing institutional archives in conjunction with an organizational records management programme, those responsible for its archives and records management need specialist advice and practical guidance in the successful establishment and operation of an archival facility built on sound principles.

This authoritative handbook, written by an archival professional with over 25 years' experience, offers just that. Addressing the contextual, strategic and operational issues associated with archives, the text covers everything the archivist needs to know: establishing principles, policies and procedures; managing day-to-day operations; caring for different types of archival materials; enhancing outreach and public access; and ensuring the growth and sustainability of the institution and its services.

The key chapters are:

- What are archives?
- Archival institutions: creatures of history and culture
- Archival service: a matter of trust
- Protecting archives
- Provenance, original order and *respect des fonds*
- Appraising and acquiring archives
- Arranging and describing archives
- Making archives available
- The challenge of digital archives.

The final section of the book offers a glossary of terms and a wide range of specialist information including comprehensive lists of recommended further reading, national institutions, professional bodies and other sources of advice.

Dr Laura A. Millar is an independent consultant in the fields of archival and information management, publishing and education. She has taught archives and information management, publishing, editing and writing in universities and colleges in Canada and internationally and has written and edited a large number of books and articles on these subjects.

2010; 304pp; paperback; 978-1-85604-673-2; £44.95

Principles and Practice in Records Management and Archives
Series editor: Geoffrey Yeo

More titles of interest

Helen Forde & Jonathan Rhys-Lewis
Preserving archives 2nd edn

About the first edition:

'This book is highly recommended as a reference for anyone tasked with the presentation of physical materials. It is comprehensive in its coverage and yet highly readable – the clarity of writing is such that it could be useful as a resource by both trained archivists and non-specialists, including volunteers.'

THE AUSTRALIAN LIBRARY JOURNAL

978-1-85604-823-1; 336 pp; paperback £49.95

G. E. Gorman and Sydney J. Shep, editors
Preservation management for libraries, museums and archives

'It is a well-designed volume and an enjoyable read. If you know little about preservation management, I would recommend this to you.'

LIBRARY & INFORMATION UPDATE

'...extremely well-designed, with a neat and clear layout...I highly recommend this book...'

LIBRARY MANAGEMENT

2006; 224pp; hardback; 978-1-85604-574-2; £54.95

Ordering these and other Facet Publishing books is simple. You can phone, fax or e-mail our distributors, Bookpoint Ltd on:

(01235 827702   ℮ 01235 827703
⌨ facet@bookpoint.co.uk

or order online at:
www.facetpublishing.co.uk